The Financial Post

TURNING IT AROUND

How ten Canadian organizations changed their fortunes

The Financial Post

TURNING IT AROUND

How ten Canadian organizations changed their fortunes

Eva Innes and Lesley Southwick-Trask

Random House
Toronto

Published in Canada in 1989 by Random House of Canada Limited, Toronto.

Canadian Cataloguing in Publication Data

Innes, Eva
The Financial Post turning it around

ISBN 0-394-22130-3

1. Industrial management – Canada. 2. Success in business – Canada. 3. Organizational change – Canada. 4. Business failures – Canada. I. Southwick-Trask, Lesley. II. Title. III. Title: Turning it around.

HD70.C3I66 1989   658'.00971   C89-094462-8

JACKET DESIGN: Andrew Smith
JACKET ILLUSTRATION: Brian Deines

Printed and bound in Canada by
T. H. Best Printing Company Limited

To my family.

E.I.

To my husband Greg, and to our children for their great patience and undaunting support.

L.S.T.

And to *The Financial Post* for encouraging and supporting this project.

Contents

Introduction

How do you manage an organization in transition? What techniques does a chief executive officer have to use to turn a loser into a winner? What skills does he or she pick up in the process? And how do you measure the success of such a company during the reorganization? These are just a few of the questions raised during a business turnaround. The ten turnarounds described in this book provide some useful insights into the turnaround concept. The lessons learned by these diverse organizations provide useful guidelines for anyone trying to understand the changing face of business in Canada today.

The process involves more than an overnight transformation. In order to achieve long-term health, the company has to weather successive storms while strengthening itself in the process. Some organizations recognize the early warning signs of ill health, diagnose the disease, and apply medication before the infection rages unchecked. Some problems need bandages; others require major surgery. It is the organizations with foresight that avoid real trauma.

Other organizations appear less equipped to read the danger signs. The economic downturn of the early 1980s forced these less prescient companies into the intensive care unit. An instant transfusion was essential to ensure survival. These cases were so serious that only a specialized expert, brought in at the last minute, could save them. But unlike the medical example, in the case of corporate turnarounds it sometimes takes as long as three or four years before recovery is assured. At any stage, a relapse is all too likely.

The organizations profiled here started as victims of inattention and inadequate management techniques. With two exceptions, Royal Trust and Manufacturers Life Insurance Co., these were companies on the brink, in need of drastic measures to restore them to health.

The examples include both large and small firms, drawn from manufacturing, the resource and service industries, the financial sector, and from the non-profit world. What they have in common is a dramatic turn for the better. In every case, an individual or team of new managers was brought in to transform the faltering organization. And although not all of the turnarounds are outstanding success stories, in each case, a marked improvement can be measured.

Turnarounds involve recognizing that the patient is ill, identifying the nature of the disease, and prescribing the correct treatment. The illnesses that affected the organizations in this book were potentially fatal, but some, at least, were diagnosed at early stages of disease.

Royal Trust, for example, was by no means in danger of collapse; however, all the downward trends were visible – a stagnant organization with a reduced marketshare, lower profits, and a disinterested work force. They were prime candidates for a takeover. In this case, achieving a turnaround meant reversing the trends and regaining momentum. A gentleman's country club was transformed into a high-stakes global business.

Another company showing a distinct decline in marketshare was the Manufacturers Life Insurance Co. Although successful on an international scale, its Canadian operation was shrinking, threatening the ability of the corporation to maintain its operational base in Canada. Its risky turnaround strategy created change on a massive scale, resulting in chaos.

At the other end of the spectrum were the organizations on the brink of disaster, where immediate action was required. Turbo Resources came closest to bankruptcy with its $1-billion accumulated debt. In one sense, Turbo's story is the most dramatic of them all, because of the distance it and its backers had to travel to achieve their turnaround. By divesting itself of unprofitable subsidiaries, Turbo concentrated on its core business, enabling lifesaving financial restructuring to take place.

While the Turbo story is symptomatic of the woes affecting Canada's oil patch, National Sea reflects the crisis faced by the East Coast fishery. Its fight for survival was also a fight to stave off nationalization and remain a private organization. By broadening its focus, it changed from a Canadian fishing company to an international fish broker and processor.

Small organizations can also suffer the pangs of corporate illness, and, in fact, are often more severely affected by the volatility of economic conditions. Canadian Pizza Crust is one example of a small company that survived two major downturns. Having lost sight of its market, it had to quickly redefine the nature of its business. This forced the firm into capital expansion at a time when its financial stability was at risk. As a result, the company's long-term success is still not assured.

Fruehauf's story relates the importance of hands-on management. A management buyout of a deteriorating U.S.-owned business was the first stage of a laborious rebuilding process. Two years of disciplined attention to detail enabled it to become successful enough to buy out its largest competitor.

Federal Industries demonstrates the impact that one person, armed with a clear vision, can have in transforming a failing business. In a major restructuring, unprofitable operations were closed or sold off, allowing financial reorganization to take place.

The assumptions that guide a turnaround stay the same, even if they're not motivated by profit alone.

At Toronto's Hospital for Sick Children, an enormous budget deficit forced the hospital to apply hard-nosed business techniques to an organization that had always been run on traditional health care lines. This, coupled with a top to bottom cultural change, caused major upheaval throughout the whole organization.

The resurrection of Symphony Nova Scotia proves that the lessons learned in business can be directly applied to an arts organization. A dedicated group of high-powered volunteers, together with a gifted artistic director, co-ordinated its revival.

Other companies manage to come out of a decline, and keep climbing, as is the case with Niagara Helicopters. This classic turnaround success story demonstrates that it is possible to take a failing business and turn it into a high-performance organization using the most basic of steps.

Whether the strategy was simple or complex, each turnaround involved difficult decisions, risk-taking, and a step into the unknown. Taking a leap of faith into uncertainty brings with it tension and ambiguity. All too often there are no precedents to follow. Stress and anxiety ride hand-in-hand on the turnaround roller coaster, where there are no right answers, only a range of possible solutions.

Although they don't offer any ready-made formulas, the stories of these turnarounds create food for thought. They highlight the pace at which change is accelerating in the business arena, and the very real need to adapt. Learning how to cope with change is the first step to business survival. Anticipating and planning for the future has replaced mere coping as the key to success.

In some cases, the final outcome of the turnaround is far from clear. Many of these stories have no fixed starting point or clearly defined end—in fact, their drama is still unfolding.

Niagara Helicopters:

Doing It the Swiss Way

This is a simple success story, to lighten the hearts of all entrepreneurs embarking on the daunting prospect of trying to achieve a turnaround. Yes, it is possible, and no, not all turnarounds are fraught with drama, tears, and tightrope walking.

Some turnarounds can be achieved through straightforward adherence to basic business values: understand your business, set realistic strategic goals, work hard to achieve those goals, and use quality throughout. Niagara Helicopters is the story of a man who pursued a dream, found two partners willing to share his vision, and made it successful by applying those commonsense business values.

Juerg Sommer can't remember a time when he didn't love planes and just about anything to do with flying. As a small boy, he used to accompany his father on Swissair jaunts around Europe. His father, Hermann Sommer, had been one of the first employees of Swissair in the early 1930s, and eventually became managing director. "He opened up the door for me," recalls Sommer. That was the beginning of his love affair with the air.

Later, when he joined the Swiss air force, he trained as a pilot. Although he completed his compulsory military service serving as flight security officer for two squadrons of British Hawker Hunters and French Mirages, he was always pestering one of his friends, who was a helicopter pilot, to take him for flights into the mountains. At that time, air force helicopters were involved primarily in mountain rescue operations, but they also often gave free rides at local fund-raising events. That's when Sommer first realized the great business potential helicopters offered: "I saw how really excited people could get when they got a helicopter ride."

Years later, when Sommer was vice president of international lending at the Swiss Bank Corp., he and a helicopter pilot chum formed a company and bought a helicopter. They did a brisk business flying bank VIPs into the Alps for sightseeing excursions. Soon they were under contract to the Basel police to do traffic control on weekends. And they were also called in to comb the mountains for West German industrialist, Hanns-Martin Schleyer, during the massive 1977 manhunt for the kidnappers and their victim.

"That experience [the sightseeing excursions] convinced me that tourism, combined with helicopters, could become a good business," he said. Sommer knew that one day he would make a success out of a helicopter business, but the only question was where? In 1982 the Swiss Bank Corp. transferred Sommer to Canada, putting him in charge of commercial lending.

On his first weekend in Canada, Sommer went sightseeing to Niagara Falls. Impressed by the tourist attraction of the cascading falls, Sommer was intrigued to discover there was a helicopter flying overhead. Determined to find out more about the helicopter, Sommer inquired about the company. The tourist booth didn't know anything about it, nor did it have a brochure on hand. After two hours, Sommer finally tracked down the elusive helicopter company. Pan Air was located on the site of the former town dump, just off the Niagara Parkway, on the edge of town.

And it was a dump in more ways than one. A dingy and

ramshackle helipad, surrounded by dilapidated buildings, greeted the unwary tourist. Not recommended for the weak-hearted. "I couldn't believe what I saw – because it was so run-down, and yet Niagara Falls is one of the biggest tourist attractions in the world," recalls Sommer. But he was intrigued in spite of the disheartening outward appearances. Convinced that helicopters had a great future in the tourist trade, he understood the potential offered by the location. Somehow, someday, he was going to buy that company.

Sommer kept the idea in the back of his mind, and it just wouldn't go away. One day he mentioned it casually to Peter Egger, the Swiss consul general in Toronto. And this is where coincidence played a part in the story. In late 1984, Egger attended a party and met another Swiss, Ruedi Hafen. In an unusual turn of fate, Hafen was a helicopter pilot, employed by Niagara Helicopters. He had been trying, unsuccessfully, for the past 18 months to find a backer to help him buy Niagara Helicopters. Egger quickly put Sommer in touch with Hafen. Although the two men had never met before, they both came from the same area of Switzerland, Hafen from Aargau, half-way beween Basel and Zurich, while Sommer had divided his time between the two cities.

Although formally trained as an architect, Hafen had fallen under the spell of the helicopter. In one of those strange quirks of fate, his first helicopter ride actually took place with Niagara Helicopters in 1971. At that time Hafen was 17 and had been sent on a tour of North America as part of his architectural training. On one leg of the tour, he took a helicopter ride over the falls. "When I look back on it now," Hafen says, "it didn't really leave a big impression on me." It was only later, after completing his training, that Hafen decided he didn't want to spend his life behind a desk and abandoned architecture for helicopter flying. Once he'd acquired a license, his goal was to become a pilot for Swissair Mountain Rescue Service. But first he needed to rack up 1000 hours of flying time. "Go to Canada," he was advised, "and get your flying hours there." Hafen got his first job flying for Niagara Helicopters, which at that time was called Pan Air.

When they met in late 1984, Sommer and Hafen quickly

realized that together they might succeed in buying the company they'd both been eyeing for some time. Owned by Ottawa-based Pan Air, and run in a hands-off manner, the company was on the sales block. However, there was an element missing from the partnership. Although Sommer could provide business knowhow and financial backing, and Hafen was an experienced helicopter pilot and knowledgeable about maintenance as well, the two knew very little about local business, and next to nothing about marketing. Ev McTaggart seemed ideal to fill the gap. The Newfoundland native with a marketing background was sales manager for a local newspaper, *What's Up, Niagara?*, and well tuned into the local business scene.

McTaggart and Hafen had met just a few months earlier, and she had impressed him with her ambition and gutsy, down-to-earth professionalism. Hafen quickly introduced her to Sommer as a potential partner in their fledgling venture. McTaggart was clearly eager to break into the big-time business world, a quality that appealed to the two enterprising Swiss. "I can remember saying, when I was about 14 years old, that my ambition in life was to become a millionaire," muses McTaggart.

Early in 1985, the new triumvirate spent many hours sitting around McTaggart's dining room table poring over cost projections, as well as business and marketing plans. McTaggart's first marketing plan was put together before she knew any real details about the operation. Her first-year goals were straightforward:

- Increase sales by 100%
- Gain greater percentage of tour sales through active promotion
- Get commitments from minimum of 20 tour bus operators
- Increase the company profile in the local business community

"As far as I was concerned, the number one question we had to consider was marketing," says Sommer. "You can have the best pilot and the best financing, but it doesn't matter if you don't get the people coming in to try your operation."

Sommer's dream, hatched three years earlier when he first viewed the site, became a reality in March 1985. The three partners and shareholders finally bought the struggling enterprise, after Sommer had obtained the necessary financing through the Swiss Bank Corp. Hafen was installed as president, operations manager and chief pilot, while McTaggart was named director of marketing. Their first move was to change the name back to Niagara Helicopters Ltd.

And what had these three entrepreneurs actually managed to buy? The company's assets consisted of a short-term lease on a 12 hectare parcel of land, situated 8 kilometers from the falls. There were two decrepit hangars, a ticket booth, and a sleazy snack bar, plus the rights to fly over the falls. The company's two helicopters were leased, not owned. They even had to buy their own helicopter license. They also inherited two employees. In 1984, in a seasonal operation that ran from mid-May to Thanksgiving, Pan Air had had revenues of $230 000, flying some 8000 passengers over the falls.

"Everything about it was falling down, including their reputation," is McTaggart's recollection of the company they bought.

The catchphrase, "We're all in marketing," could have been invented expressly for the new owners. The first thing McTaggart did was to conduct a market survey to determine how tourists viewed the helicopter service. The former owners had treated the operation as a transportation service offering helicopter flights. To her surprise, McTaggart's survey revealed that most tourists looked on Niagara's helicopters as a "ride," rather than a flight. That simple distinction put Niagara Helicopters on the right marketing track. As a result, their new promotional brochure offers "the longest and highest ride over the falls." Niagara's direct competitors are other "rides" — the *Maid of the Mist* boat that takes tourists for a close look at the falls and the Spanish Aero Car, an elevated cable car that whisks tourists over the Niagara gorge and the Whirlpool, a fast-flowing eddy of water, which changes direction depending upon the volume of water coming over the falls.

Although at $40 a ride, it's not cheap, Niagara's flight offers real value for the money. Even the jaded tourist who has seen the falls from the ground, or even from the close proximity offered by the *Maid of the Mist*, can't help but be impressed by the breathtaking panoramic view from one of the company's helicopters. The highly professional eight-minute ride whisks you up to a height of 490 meters for two complete circuits of both the American and the more spectacular Canadian Horseshoe Falls. Headsets provide a detailed commentary of the sights, in both English and French. Repeat customers provide some insights into the thrills offered by the ride. Niagara's market research indicates that the single element clients like most is "banking over the falls." And, paradoxically, "banking over the falls" is also the element that customers like least.

Joining the Niagara Falls, Canada, Visitor and Convention Bureau was another important step in promoting the new company. Not only would the company brochure be displayed in the information booth's pamphlet rack, but Niagara Helicopters would also become involved with the planning of promotional programs for the Niagara region as a whole. "The company had a bad reputation," explains McTaggart. "We had to mend the public relations fences, as well as the fences around the property."

Persuading the local community that things had changed for the better at Niagara Helicopters involved more than just doing a good public relations job. The group really had to start the whole operation again from scratch. After obtaining their own helicopter license from the Ministry of Transportation in Ottawa, their first priority was to buy their own machine. They purchased a four-seater Bell Jet Ranger in March, and by June of 1985, as soon as the volume of business justified the decision, they bought a second one as well. A full-time mechanic was also quickly hired.

Sprucing up the physical site was the next project. New fences were built, the helipad was reconstructed, while landscaping made the area around the helipad more attractive. Both the ticket booth and snack bar were rebuilt and modernized to create an attractive environment for the incoming tourist.

McTaggart and Hafen were putting in 14- to 16-hour days,

six days a week, getting the business off the ground. Their efforts soon began to pay off as traffic increased steadily. By the end of 1985, they had achieved the first goal of their marketing strategy by doubling their sales volume. A total of 76 bus tours came through in that first year, compared with just over 20 under the previous owners. Unlike Pan Air, which closed down after Thanksgiving, Niagara Helicopters stayed open throughout the winter season, continuing to draw tourists, as well as some charter business.

McTaggart conducted customer surveys by telephone to determine the nature of the market. She also followed both federal and provincial tourism forecasts closely to help plan her marketing strategy. Although the company does very little direct advertising, the majority of its customers now come from the tour bus business. McTaggart attends a number of travel trade shows to promote the operation, including a number of European events. An increasing proportion of the tour operators come from England, France, and other overseas markets.

By the spring of 1986, business prospects looked so promising that the group decided to purchase another machine—this time a six-seater Bell LongRanger. Instead of awarding themselves a performance bonus, the trio ploughed the profits back into the company, in the form of a down payment for the new whirlybird. The addition of the LongRanger to the fleet meant they were able to deal more effectively with the larger number of bus tour groups that were quickly becoming the mainstay of the business. And if one of the three helicopters was down for maintenance, then there were now two others to take up the slack.

Helicopter prices are so hefty, particularly for new machines, that Niagara usually looked for well maintained but used Bell helicopters, with a long component life. (The effective lifespan of a helicopter is gauged by its component life, since every component has to be replaced after a certain number of flying hours, regardless of whether it's still functioning well or not.) At 1989 prices for completely new machines, a four-seater costs around $750 000, a six-seater a cool $1 million, while a twin-engined 14-seater can put you back a whopping $5 million.

Niagara is committed to using Bell helicopters, made both in Canada and the U.S., because of their high reliability and excellent technical support.

The spring of 1988 stands out as a landmark period in the development of this young company. It was the point at which the group suddenly realized that they had arrived. Sommer says, "I always knew the company was going to be a success, but I never dreamed we would do so well, so soon." The business had grown so quickly that projections for the 1988 season anticipated 1200 bus groups.

Once again the company had to expand by purchasing another machine. This time, investing in the future, and taking a much bigger risk than ever before, they opted for the twin-engined 14-seater Bell 412. The purchase meant they could immediately take half a bus load on each trip. This machine is the only civilian-owned twin-engined helicopter in Canada, and much in demand for charter flights. In fact, it was hired to fly Prince Philip around Ottawa during his brief Canadian trip in the spring of 1989.

By the end of 1988, the company had exceeded projections, ending the year serving a total of 1449 coach tours. And 1989 looks like a banner year as well. Projections call for 100 000 satisfied customers and sales of approximately $2.5 million. Niagara Helicopters has managed to increase sales by a factor of 12 since they took over the company.

How did they manage to achieve this dramatic and steady increase? Sommer says he believes in running the business "the Swiss way. Switzerland is successful as a country because the few things they do, they do right. It's not important to make a lot of money in the first few years, but to have top quality— that's important in this industry and in every business." Sommer believes that attention to detail and high quality create the right kind of image for the company. "This has to run like Swissair, which is one of the safest airlines in the world." This attention to safety means that Sommer and Hafen can be justifiably proud of their flawless safety record.

Another key element in the group's success is involving the right people and making sure that they are shareholders. As chief executive officer, Hafen is the majority shareholder, with

McTaggart and Sommer retaining equal but smaller shares of the private company. "If the key people are not shareholders, they won't work longer than eight hours a day. Ev and Ruedi work much longer hours than that," explains Sommer.

All three are committed to making the organization a success. And although Sommer is not involved in day-to-day operations, his role as business adviser and financial backer is critical to their success. Sommer negotiated the loan to buy the 14-seater helicopter through a personal guarantee. He claims, however, that the trio have never taken on a needless financial risk and have always maintained a low debt-load. Ploughing all profits back into the business is another way the group has maintained a steady growth curve. "The company has not declared a dividend yet, although I believe that we will do so for the first time at the end of 1989," explains Sommer.

Expansion plans include buying more multiple-seat helicopters, but the group is getting close to maximum capacity in flights over the falls, so other business opportunities are being explored. One possibility includes establishing regular helicopter flights from Toronto to Niagara Falls, to allow busy business people to take in a whirlwind tour of the falls in just an hour.

Niagara Helicopters is an example of a real entrepreneurial success story. It's an elemental tale of how three people took a good idea, pooled their savings in the venture, and worked long hours to achieve a remarkable turnaround. Tenacity, risk-taking, and sheer hard work are part of the success formula. Smart marketing and attention to quality round out the picture. It can be done.

Snapshot of Niagara Helicopters

Crisis (March 1985):

Three entrepreneurs buy failing helicopter firm with annual sales of $230 000, based on 8000 paying customers.

Turnaround Strategy:

- Improve capitalization
- Buy own helicopter
- Conduct market survey
- Implement new marketing strategy
- Upgrade site and buildings
- Buy more helicopters
- Hard work and attention to detail

Result: Today Niagara Helicopters serves more than 100 000 customers a year and has sales of $2.5 million and growing.

Federal Industries:

The House That Jack Built

In 1978 a relatively unknown middle-aged Canadian business-man called Jack Fraser took over running a relatively unknown mid-sized Winnipeg-based management company called Federal Industries. The story didn't even rate a mention in the newspapers.

At first glance, Federal Industries appeared to be a solid, established company. Started in 1929 as Federal Grain, by the mid-1960s it had sensibly seen the advantages of diversification, got out of the unprofitable grain trade, and now operated a variety of businesses, from bulk transport terminals to kitchen cabinets, all in western and northern Canada. Primarily family-owned and -run, the company also had begun to be aware of its limitations, and realized the need to inject some professional management in order to survive and indeed expand. The company had $40 million in assets and a reliable profit track record. But in 1977 Federal lost money for the first time in its history, and the board began to express concern about the losses and an increasingly onerous debt-load.

Jack Fraser seemed perfect to take on the challenge. He was an entrepreneurial Westerner with a reputation for hard work, and more important, for turning flagging operations around. Not only that, he had worked in a variety of enterprises, including transportation and trucking, two of Federal's main businesses.

After graduation with a commerce degree, the Saskatchewan native sold soap for a year for Procter & Gamble. He quickly realized that working for a foreign-based multinational was not his style, so he relaunched his business career the way he intended to continue—from an entrepreneurial, equity-based position. Entering into a joint venture with two university chums, he found himself president of a failing Saskatoon petroleum-hauling trucking operation at the age of 22. Holding a 33% equity position in the company, Fraser set out to salvage the operation.

The now well-groomed and superbly dressed Fraser recalls his early style with down-to-earth humor: "I was a real punker. Why I still had zits then."

Eight years of hard work later, having moved out of petroleum and into general freight, Empire Freightways Ltd. was one of Saskatchewan's leading trucking companies. In 1960, in recognition of their success, Fraser and his partners were bought out by the Canadian National Railway. "It was more money than we thought had existed in the whole world," reminisces Fraser. "We were just kids from Saskatoon—I'd never had more than $300 at one time in my entire life—and now we split $700 000 between the three of us. That was my first turnaround."

Armed with an established capital base, Fraser moved into men's clothing. He devoted the middle years in the 1960s to turning around and then expanding Hanford-Drewitt Ltd., a high-quality Winnipeg men's clothing emporium. In the late 1960s, a bigger challenge came his way—this time in the mobile home industry. Selling his chain of prosperous clothing stores, Fraser negotiated a 25% interest in the new business. Over the next ten years, he built up a $35- to 40-million business at Norcom Homes Ltd. (it was called NorthWest Design and Fabrication Ltd. when he started). Riding a roller coaster of economic swings, he moved the business from Winnipeg, to Lethbridge, to St. Bruno, Quebec, and then to Mississauga, building and selling recreational vehicles, travel trailers, and mobile homes. In 1978, despite his efforts, the whole mobile home industry started to decline, and Fraser was just contemplating moving the business into a new area when the chance to join Federal Industries came up.

"When the board approached me, I said to my wife, 'My goodness, it's almost as if I had been spending my whole business life training for this job.' It was a natural for me," Fraser explains. "I had done turnarounds before. I knew there were wonderful opportunities in turnarounds: high risks but also high payoffs. Here was a company that was still big enough that it was challenging, and it also was in trouble, in a number of industries that I was quite reasonably knowledgeable about."

Whether by luck or good planning, Federal had certainly found its savior. But Fraser had underestimated the challenge the job represented.

In 1978, Federal Industries consisted of five main business groups: Standard Aero Engine Ltd., an aircraft engine overhaul operation; two bulk handling operations, Thunder Bay Terminals Ltd. and Neptune Bulk Terminals; Citation Cabinets Ltd., a kitchen and bathroom cabinet manufacturer; and the White Pass and Yukon Corp. Ltd., an integrated northern transportation system, which included rail, shipping, and trucking facilities as well as petroleum distribution.

The financial statements for 1978 showed net losses of $2.5 million on sales of $123 million. Standard Aero, the jewel in the crown, actually made a substantial profit; Neptune was scraping by; while Thunder Bay Terminals had not come into full operation yet, and so was still a drain on capital. Federal had to absorb significant losses from Citation's 20% drop in sales, and White Pass's operations went into the red that year due to the loss of a major contract.

"I thought I knew enough about the company. I had studied ten years' worth of annual reports, and had discussions with the directors," says Fraser. "But in hindsight, that was not enough.

"The company had a net worth of around $40 million, and I had come from running smaller companies and thought, '$40 million! Wow, imagine what I can do with that!' And boy, was that a lesson to me. The thing I didn't know, and learned my second day there, was that the company was out of cash. And when you're out of cash, you're out of business!"

That rude jolt was delivered by John Pelton, Federal's chief financial officer. The company was in a debt stranglehold. When the grain business had been sold ten years earlier, the company had been in a healthy cash-rich situation. But the cash quickly disappeared as a number of diversified companies were bought, all requiring cash support. Federal began borrowing money to support its new ventures. By the time Jack Fraser arrived on the scene, it had reached its $50-million credit limit, in addition to suffering losses.

"Can you believe it?" exclaims Fraser. "They were still paying dividends and borrowing at prime to pay them—in effect liquidating the company at prime."

As if the cash crisis wasn't a bad enough surprise for Fraser's inauguration, another emergency greeted him on his first day. The stacker reclaimer fell down. This sophisticated bit of machinery, a 37-meter-long bucketwheel for stacking coal, was the most vital part of the Neptune Terminal's equipment. Without it, the terminal couldn't continue to operate. The collapse of this essential piece of equipment cost the company more than $7 million before the reclaimer was repaired and back in operation.

A superstitious man might have called the whole thing off right then and there. But adversity seemed to fire Fraser's determination even higher. His horror at discovering the gravity of the financial situation sent him flying to Toronto for an urgent meeting with Hart MacDougall, at the time executive vice president of corporate banking at the Bank of Montreal, Federal's chief banker.

"I'll never forget that first meeting with him," says Fraser. "The first thing I said to him was, 'Mr. MacDougall, you and I have a hell of a problem.'

"He replied, 'You and I, what do you mean?'

" 'Well,' I said, 'we've borrowed more money from you than

we're entitled to, and the unfortunate part of it is, we are totally out of cash. I need some more time to get this thing turned around, and if I don't get some more money, then I go back to where I was, and you own yourself a diversified management company.' "

MacDougall granted Fraser the necessary breathing space, and he rushed back to Winnipeg to try and sell off two business units to generate some cash flow.

His immediate strategy consisted of trying to understand the complexities of the many businesses that comprised the Federal empire, to know where to begin the turnaround strategy. Fraser spent months on the road, visiting all the outposts. He was frequently away from home for as long as four weeks at a time. At the end of the first six-month period, Fraser had visited and assessed all the operations, talked to all the managers, and listened to workers down the line and on the shop floor.

Flying back to Winnipeg after visiting the last business on his list, Fraser outlined his blueprint for the turnaround. On a single sheet of foolscap paper he itemized, one by one, all the things he had to do to get Federal Industries back on the rails and profitable once again. That single sheet of paper became his scenario for success, and he carried it with him wherever he went. Every time an objective was achieved, Fraser would pull out the increasingly dog-eared sheet of paper and tick it off.

"The strategy consisted of first stopping the cash flow hemorrhage by closing or selling off unprofitable business units. Then I concentrated on restructuring, reorganizing, building up the good business units, and then changing the management style, and then the management team. When I actually finished the initial turnaround, I just threw the paper away."

The White Pass Turnaround

The situation at Federal was much more complex and troubled than any outside observer would have suspected. At that point in 1978, Federal's future and fortune were both inextricably linked to the well-being of one of its major subsidiaries, the White Pass and Yukon Corp. Its $60 million in sales accounted for half of Federal's total revenues.

White Pass's history is caught up with the mystique of the North. Even today, tradition, as well as nostalgia, play a role in determining the company's future.

White Pass started life in the heady days of the Klondike Gold Rush of 1898. The construction of a 178-kilometer narrow gauge railway linking Whitehorse, the heart of gold-mining Yukon, with the Pacific port of Skagway, Alaska, provided essential transportation to bring the gold to market. Additional transportation services, including riverboats and horse and sleigh services, were soon added, creating a complete northern transportation network. Over the years, other innovations were pioneered, including the construction and operation of the world's first container freight ship. After construction of the Alaska Highway, a trucking division rounded out the increasingly comprehensive transportation services. And finally, a petroleum division distributed Chevron products throughout northern British Columbia and the Yukon.

By the late 1970s the petroleum division was the largest part of the company, the highway division came second, while the railway itself came third in terms of sales revenues. The railway was the most important segment, though, because it was the heart of the White Pass system. It was the center from which all the other parts of the system emanated. Without a functioning railway, the other divisions had no business.

Things had already started to go very wrong at White Pass before Jack Fraser came on the scene. John Pelton, who joined the company in 1974, explains the situation: "White Pass was a fixed, capital-intensive company, governed by long-term contracts, all negotiated in the late '60s, before the Arab oil hikes, and inflation really took hold. Net cash flow and profit began to decline in all areas. The company couldn't renegotiate those contracts, so they began to defer capital costs. But inflation just kept climbing. Fixed-rate, long-term contracts were the undoing of the company."

Two additional events set the stage for further trouble.

"About six months before I arrived," says Fraser, "the management at White Pass entered into a new long-term contract with the Cyprus Anvil mine, White Pass's second biggest customer. First, it was a bad contract; Federal just got outnegotiated. But then Cyprus Anvil insisted on getting Federal's endorsement on the contract, and Federal agreed. If things went wrong, this one contract had the potential to pull [not just White Pass but] Federal down with it as well.

"White Pass's biggest customer was Cassiar, a big asbestos mine, which was the key to running the marine division. I was living in Toronto at the time, and I picked up the *Globe and Mail* one day and saw a notice that White Pass had lost the Cassiar contract. So I phoned Winnipeg and said, 'What's all this?'

"The reply came back, 'Well, it's not very good, Jack, but I don't think we ever made money on that.'

"In fact, it was going to put White Pass (and maybe even Federal) out of business. I spent 80% of my time in Vancouver and the Yukon in '78 and early '79 trying to straighten out that mess."

"White Pass was the most complex problem I have ever faced, then or now," says Fraser, "because it was so fraught with politics—big 'P' politics. Why, there was a different regulatory body for every 8 miles of railway! Imagine, it was only 110 miles long, yet it passed through three different jurisdictions [Alaska, British Columbia, and the Yukon]."

Fraser's first major act was a ruthless downsizing. As John Pelton remembers, "It was clear we had to reduce costs everywhere if the company was to be saved. There was too much of everything—magnificent offices in Vancouver, more beautiful offices in Whitehorse." On August 15, 1978, Fraser and Pelton started the process that would result in a 1500 employee group being eventually reduced to a skeleton staff of 90, five years later. Announcing the closing of the Vancouver head office, Fraser personally fired the president, while Pelton fired the nine vice presidents. Pelton told the rest of the staff of 150 that they would all be terminated within six months.

Fraser took on the job of president of White Pass himself. He moved the head office to Whitehorse, the center of the company's operations, and began to look for a suitable manager to take over the struggling enterprise.

At the same time he turned his attention to another money-losing part of the venture – the marine division. The White Pass railway was just one small part of a complex transportation system that saw ore from mines such as Cyprus Anvil and Cassiar shipped on the train from Whitehorse to Skagway. Containers were offloaded from the trains directly onto ships, which then took the ore south to Vancouver for sale. White Pass ran two 6600-tonne freighters up and down this coastal route. Each ship ran with a crew of 35. Fraser soon changed that.

Sverre Kollbaer, the president of the marine division, approached him and explained that it might be possible to run the same ships with a crew of 12. Fraser was skeptical: "At this time I wouldn't have known a container ship if it had come by floating in my martini." A bold new concept was outlined to Fraser; it involved turning the present fully operational ships into dumb barges and towing them up the coast. A tugboat would be equipped with a new computerized steering mechanism, and a $50 000 bow thruster would also be needed to make the scheme possible.

Here was Fraser, the new guy in the president's chair, being asked to participate in what sounded like a harebrained scheme, delivered by a group of men he had only met for the first time that day. In typical Fraser fashion, he got to the heart of the matter immediately.

"Are you guys bullshitting me?" he bluntly demanded.

The reply came back, "Mr. Fraser, it will work."

Fraser gave the group the green light, but cautioned them against failure: "You see that," Fraser gesticulated, holding up his hands as if grabbing two invisible cylindrical objects "I've got one of your balls in each hand. Got that? Well, you make it work."

And work it did. The process was long and involved; it took more than a year to lay everyone off and re-rig the ships for towing. Then they towed the ships up and down the coast. Eighteen months later, the union was back, begging for their jobs back. Fraser struck a new deal limiting the crew to 12.

"That put the profits back into the marine division, because it was impossible to make money with a crew of 35. Those are the kinds of things you do in a turnaround – it was gutsy, it was risky, and it worked like hell," concludes Fraser. The incident remains "one of the highlights of my life."

Renegotiating unprofitable and unworkable union contracts was a key element in making White Pass successful. There were 14 different union contracts within White Pass, mainly with the tough Teamsters union, five alone on the railway. Overmanning was the standard, not the exception.

Fraser's response to the problem was to bring in "the toughest negotiator" he'd ever met as new manager of White Pass. Tom King had spent all his working life in the transportation business, buying failing companies and nursing them back to life. Starting in January 1979, he immediately moved up to Whitehorse, rolled up his sleeves and got to work sorting out the mess. But he started with a disadvantage. Northerners viewed White Pass as a vital part of the tradition of the North, and King represented a threat. He was viewed with suspicion – a southerner sent up by corporate management to meddle and take away people's livelihood. The scenario that developed was like something out of the Wild West.

"Some union members tried to burn down one of our bridges and sabotaged railroad equipment," King says. "And then there were strikes. My wife was verbally abused on the streets, and we were threatened. It was so bad that the manager was only going from home to work and back, and he kept a .38 by his side at all times."

Tom King's management techniques for mending White Pass were straightforward:

- Restructure management
- Listen to employees and give leadership
- Be aware of the needs of customers and stakeholders

He describes how he actually carried out this self-prescribed mandate: "I worked day and night, seven days a week, up to 20 hours a day. I rode trucks, I was on the railroad. People were totally unaccustomed to this. I talked to people, about what was going wrong, how to fix it, listening to people."

One day King held a combination pep rally and information meeting for all the 60 truck drivers in the trucking division. "I got a blackboard and told them, 'Here's what we're going to do with this company—and I expect you all to help.' "

In the meantime, King hired a new mechanic, who set an example by working long hours, more than the others. The new employee was soon called aside by his co-workers and told to slow down and stop working so hard. King heard about this and called a second meeting. He told the employees bluntly: "Listen, I'm working my ass off so you guys will have a job. I can always get a new job if this place closes, but I don't know about you guys . . . If you're not with me, then get the hell out—leave now." Productivity improved dramatically after that confrontation.

King rationalized operations everywhere. New, accountable managers were put into key positions, unprofitable divisions were sold or closed, many workers were laid off or terminated, inventory was checked and updated, and most union contracts were eventually renegotiated.

"It took courage to sell things off and to terminate people. That was the toughest part. Whitehorse is a small town. You fire them, and two hours later you're in the supermarket lineup with their wife," explains King.

The Railway Story

The railway was still the least expensive way of getting supplies to the North, but White Pass wasn't costing things correctly. It was losing money, mainly because of the uneconomic labor agreements it was locked into. As Tom King says, "We had 24 different crafts, and yet people couldn't cross crafts—a plumber couldn't fix anything electrical, for example." Because the railway operated in two countries, it was required to have two complete train crews, one Canadian, to run the 135 kilometers in Canada, and one American, to run the remaining 40-kilometer stretch. Alaskan regulations required five-man crews, while in Canada two were sufficient. The labor contract specified every little detail, and all the details cost money. The crews had to be given a choice of two hot meals at Bennett, the last town in Canadian territory. "Even the length of carrots was specified in the contract," King remembers.

Initial attempts to renegotiate the contracts were not successful. As King relates, Cyprus Anvil added to the difficulties White Pass was experiencing: "While at White Pass the attitude to labor had historically been 'peace at any price,' Cyprus Anvil's attitude seemed to be 'cash will fix anything.' " So while King was trying to hold his people to a 12½% pay increase, Cyprus Anvil was giving 46% raises.

Federal finally decided to close down the railway. However, the government refused to allow this, citing a regulation stipulating that Federal had "an imposed public duty" to continue its operation. An alternative strategy was adopted: try yet again to renegotiate the unprofitable Cyprus Anvil contract. This long-term contract, signed in 1978 just prior to Fraser's arrival, made no allowance for cost escalation or inflation, but locked Federal into a lengthy agreement to provide transportation for a fixed price. Tom King recalls the frustrating process: "We had 57 meetings with Cyprus Anvil over an 18-month period." They didn't budge.

Finally White Pass hired a Vancouver lawyer by the name of John Pearson. John Pelton remembers: "He discovered an obscure regulation in the Railway Act regarding RR rates. The relevant section stated that a railroad 'must charge a rate not less than its variable costs.' Once you determine that rate, you file the rate, and once it's filed, that rate is deemed law. And (most important of all) after 30 days, that rate supersedes contracts." Accordingly, Federal determined a new higher rate, filed it and 30 days later sent Cyprus Anvil a bill which was 50% higher than that called for by the contract.

Federal thought it had won this battle. And, indeed, for a short while that appeared to be the case. By 1981, things were looking positively rosy at White Pass: new managers had been put in place, resources and inventory were being tightly managed, all equipment had been overhauled and was now being maintained, expenditures were way down, profits were up, and the company recorded its best year ever. Then events began to overtake good management techniques. Dome Petroleum acquired control of Cyprus Anvil Mine, through its purchase of the mine's parent company, Hudson's Bay Oil & Gas Co. Simultaneously, oil prices started to drop, inflation took off, and Dome found itself in serious trouble. In June 1982, HBOG announced a short-term shutdown at the mine.

White Pass kept the railway running, expecting the mine to reopen shortly. But the closure kept being extended, until finally in September, White Pass temporarily suspended operations. Tom King adds that he always knew that "God was really on the side of management," because three days after the closing, a boulder fell onto the tracks, allowing him to apply for a formal embargo and opening the way to an official suspension of operations.

Recession Survival Tactics

Management was forced to go back to the drawing board in 1982 in the search for new answers to the dilemma of how to keep a regulated industry profitable through a severe recession. Gary Goertz was vice president, finance, at White Pass during this period: "We had to restructure yet again, but we didn't know how to do it this time. We had to go back and re-evaluate the fundamentals. What will the company look like if the mine never reopens? Well, it looked pretty abysmal."

Goertz, King, and the rest of the management team gradually evolved a new business plan. In the short term, the answer was simple – ruthlessly pare expenditures. All unnecessary staff was laid off and terminated. By mid-1983, there were less than 100 employees on the payroll, down from the 1500 that had greeted Fraser in 1978. In fact, King and Goertz carried the logic of their plan through to its inevitable conclusion. At a November 1983 meeting of the Federal board of directors, they went so far as to propose the elimination of their own jobs, a suggestion which the board rejected.

In the long term, this second restructuring had to be based on a new premise: to become profitable without the mining operation. King and Goertz had to phase out the railway as the center of operations, and build up other, more profitable parts of the business, such as the petroleum division and the trucking operation. "We shrank operations to make profits on remaining businesses," explains Fraser. "And we made money – good returns, but on a smaller scale." The fact that management had already spent two years rationalizing operations at White Pass was key to surviving the recession. "We were a stripped-down version of the previous company, and actually made money in '82, but it was nowhere near the return that we wanted," says Goertz.

The mine reopened in 1986, but by that time White Pass was profitable without it. In fact, White Pass did not win the major freight contract when Cassiar put it out for tender. However, it did benefit from the mine reopening through two subsidiary contracts; Neptune Terminals became busy once more, and White Pass did win the contract to take general freight and supplies into the mine.

The railway remained closed for six years, finally reopening purely as a tourist attraction in May 1988. It made money in the first year of operation, mainly because it had negotiated a much better union contract. The opening of the railway also encouraged more cruise ships to visit Skagway, thereby helping White Pass to make docking profits there.

Today White Pass is a thriving and profitable operation, with sales of $85 590 000 and healthy profits of more than $12 million.

White Pass was not the only operation in the Federal family to be hard hit by the recession that rocked western Canada so badly. It hit the company as a whole a reeling blow, just when it appeared to be up on its feet again after the initial turnaround. Earnings declined 50% in one year. Fraser explains what he learned from the experience: "That recession led us very clearly to say, 'We've got to have better regional representation.' It became strategically important for us to improve our geographical balance. That's why we eventually acquired Canadian Corporate Management, an organization with the great majority of its assets in Ontario and central Canada."

A look at Federal Industries in 1989 reveals a totally transformed company, bearing little resemblance to the struggling company Fraser took over in 1978. Thunder Bay Terminals is the only remaining operation that has not changed significantly. Both Citation Cabinets and Standard Aero have been sold, and White Pass has been totally restructured and reconfigured. Federal Industries is now a completely different mix of diversified companies, grouped into four broad general categories—consumer, industrial, metals and transport. It is a $1.9-billion company, with net income of $48 million, a far cry from the $40-million company Fraser started with.

The new company structure is a direct result of the series of lessons Fraser learned from the recession. But the key lesson, which would put a unique stamp on the Federal management style, was his emphasis on planning.

The importance of planning had already been impressed on Fraser earlier in his career with Norcom. When the bottom dropped out of the mobile home industry, "that turned us into a planning organization," explains R.J. Vahsholtz, a long-time Fraser associate. Vahsholtz, an American industrial designer, had done some consulting work for Norcom and eventually went on staff there. He was impressed by Fraser right from the start. "This guy was a world-class manager. I couldn't understand what he was doing in a cruddy province in a little biddy business," says Vahsholtz.

As soon as the initial turnaround had been achieved at Federal, Fraser invited Vahsholtz to join the organization as its senior vice president, planning. Vahsholtz rose to the challenge of helping turn Federal around. Fraser gave him carte blanche to set up the department as he saw fit. So, in the middle of 1980, Vahsholtz started an entirely new planning process within the organization. Although a large planning department already existed, according to Vahsholtz "it had little correlation with operations."

Vahsholtz's first task was to fashion a corporate long-range plan in just six weeks. This first plan, all 107 pages of it, was Federal's first attempt to quantify itself. It summarized each business unit, listing both strengths and weaknesses, and projected not only future earnings, but strategic plans as well.

This long-range plan is now rewritten every year. Due to Federal's tremendous growth and diversification since that first plan was written, current models have become more generalized and give a broad overview of the organization rather than specific operational commitments.

"We have to keep the responsibility for planning in the individual company manager's hands . . . Now the plans are more statements of what we do in our business," explains Vahsholtz. The evolution of the planning system means that "our planning is now more of a communications technique," Fraser adds, "more a management technique that it is in the pure planning sense." Because the planning process has become an intrinsic part of the way Federal does business, today its value lies more in the information it communicates to employees about future plans.

Fraser describes Vahsholtz as the company guru, and it is clear that he relies on his judgment. Vahsholtz himself sums up his role in cruder fashion: "I am the official pee-er on parades. I bring Jack down to earth and act as an anchor to curb his extra enthusiasm." Vahsholtz sits on the executive management committee, acting as official company contrarian, and clearly it is an approach that has been successful. Fraser is a strong advocate both for teamwork and consensus-building, and committee meetings are often argumentative free-for-alls. Fraser usually goes along with the consensus when an agreement is finally reached. Vahsholtz adds, "We rarely end up doing what Jack really wants, but usually we come up with an agreement that he finds acceptable."

Jack Fraser's Management Philosophy

One of the keys to Jack Fraser's success as a turnaround artist, and indeed as one of Canada's most interesting business leaders, lies in the development of his management philosophy. Gradually developed throughout his early business career, it crystallized, out of necessity during his first days at Federal, into a specific set of management principles. Fraser describes their genesis: "I remember flying to Winnipeg for my first meeting with Federal. It was a big company with ten or twelve subsidiaries, and I wondered, 'How the hell am I going to get through to these managers?' You need a quick way to let all the different managers know how you're going to run the company. . . . so I'll use my management principles."

When he arrived in Winnipeg, Fraser got a flip chart, had the principles printed up on the pages, and took them with him on his visit to all the Federal subsidiaries. It was his way of quickly summarizing his own views to the company at large, but also a means of initiating two-way dialogue with his new work force.

The principles have become embedded in Federal tradition, are reprinted in each year's corporate long-range plan, and are communicated to each employee in the 9000-member work force. They are simple, straightforward, and easy to understand:

1. Keep it simple
2. Set clear goals
3. Make it happen
4. Unquestionable ethics
5. Smell smoke
6. No surprises
7. Respect your hunches
8. Get the right information
9. No politics
10. Set high standards
11. Keep trending right
12. Maintain harmony

The principles are a natural extension of Fraser's own highly developed sense of personal moral values. As Vahsholtz sums up: "Jack just exudes ethics—it's part of his Prairie, Presbyterian, lumpy porridge background."

Accompanied by engaging cartoon illustrations penned by Vahsholtz, the principles come across as a light-hearted guide to corporate culture, an image which belies their importance. Behind these seemingly simple phrases lies a basic, underlying principle, which has driven Fraser since his early days in business. Put simply, his goal both in business and life (interchangeable in his case) is to "build a great Canadian company." Fraser had had this vision in his days in the mobile home industry, but it wasn't until he had turned Federal around that he really got a chance to try and implement his dream.

This aim to achieve greatness was first articulated in March 1982 in the corporate long-range plan, and the company actually identified a target date of 1995. Since that first bold statement, the company has done some significant soul-searching in its attempt to quantify with concrete criteria what this abstract concept really means, but with limited success. Federal is hardly a household word, let alone known as a great Canadian company. However, this lack of public success does not deter Fraser and his ambitious management team. They are continuing their efforts to achieve their quasi-metaphysical goal. In their 1988 corporate long-range plan, success is measured as follows: "We define a Great Canadian Company as being a publicly traded company headquartered in Canada that we and senior members of the Canadian business community could agree upon as being one of Canada's 25 greatest companies."

For purposes of comparison, Federal monitors its own progress against those companies listed in the TSE 300 Composite Index. It intends to conduct a survey in 1995, asking Canadian business people to choose the top 25 great companies "according to their own criteria of greatness from the TSE 300 list."

But a purely financial yardstick does not do justice to Fraser's broader vision, which involves more than just dollars-and-cents goals. Fraser is building for the future, for greatness in the larger sense—to do the best, to achieve the highest standards, as well as the best results. His prime objective of building a great Canadian company is bolstered by six additional objectives, which include nonfinancial aims such as:

- To consistently manage with excellence
- To contribute positively to every endeavor in which we are involved
- To be a responsible employer and corporate citizen

Federal believes long-term planning is vital to any organization. "Too many companies (and this is particularly true of conglomerates) grow rapidly and successfully for a few years and then fade in the stretch. There are great temptations for management to seek short-term profitability at the expense of long-term success. . . . By the end of this century, Federal is certain to face some difficult challenges, and the intent of this objective is to keep our attention on managing them well . . . Federal Industries intends to be a great Canadian company for a long time."

Anatomy of the Federal Turnaround

Jack Fraser took a small, struggling, and unknown Western company, and turned it, in the space of a decade, into a large, successful, diversified management company which is recognized by the business community. And by 1995 he may well have achieved his cherished goal of greatness. But why and how did it work?

The initial turnaround was "quick and dirty," and involved "applying Band-Aids to the spots where the bleeding was worst," according to Vahsholtz. A second, no less important measure was "to jam some life into the moribund organization." The second phase, once the immediate threat to life was removed, was restructuring, rebuilding, and planning, planning, planning.

"The process has to start at the top!" Fraser exclaims. "If you want planning to work, the top man has to be totally committed to the concept, be involved in it, and let everyone in the company know he's committed."

In the early years of the turnaround, Fraser was involved in all operational aspects of the turnaround. He visited struggling factories, talked to employees, conferred with managers, fired incompetents, closed unprofitable operations, hired new managers; in short, he was a one-man turnaround artist. But he soon recognized that this style couldn't continue, and that the company would not attain his high goals if he continued to manage in the same way. "There is a quick fix in a turnaround, and you need a certain type of individual to do the turn. But sometimes those people don't succeed once the turn is complete, because, although they have operational experience, they don't have the long-range view," says Fraser.

Having put together a highly competent team to manage the operational side of the ever-expanding business, Fraser now spends as little as 10% of his time on operations and as much as 75% on strategic issues. "It was the toughest thing I ever had to do – to ease back on my operational role . . . I'm like an old firehorse; once the bell rings I want to go out there and fix it. I still miss it.

"Now my time is spent on strategy, organizational matters, dealing with turn of the century matters . . . Many of the things I'm doing now, I won't even be around to see the results."

Fraser's success is certainly attributable in large part to his own remarkable personality. An unusual combination of street smarts, entrepreneurial ability, excellent communications ability and intuition, plus a prodigious capacity for work, coupled with tremendous enthusiasm make Jack Fraser a hard act to follow. And then there's his nose for a good deal. "So much of it is common sense. If it feels right, do it." Fraser's intuitive sixth sense has saved him from making a few mistakes too: "Don't go through with a deal if it just doesn't feel right."

A workaholic who regularly puts in 65 to 70 hours a week, Fraser says he's having "the time of his life. I love it." The enthusiasm for work is undoubtedly real and seems to permeate all parts of his life. When he does have a bit of leisure time, he relaxes by reading business management books, and admits that Peter Drucker is his hero.

"The secret of success," according to Fraser, "is knowing what you're good at, and what you're not good at. It's just that simple. If you have the courage and the desire, first you self-analyze yourself. Then you hire around your weaknesses." Taking his own advice, Fraser believes his strongest asset is communicating, and so that's what he spends "more time doing these days than any other single thing."

Snapshot of Federal Industries

Crisis (May 1978):

Company has assets of $40 million, but is showing net losses of $2.5 million on sales of $123 million, and has used up its $50-million credit line.

Turnaround Strategy:

- Arrange temporary financial support
- Sell off losing businesses, close others
- Cut expenditures across the board
- Fire unproductive managers
- Hire new managers
- Communicate management principles
- Make planning a way of life
- Consolidate gains
- Diversify and buy new businesses
- Build a strong management team
- Luck and good timing
- Plan, plan, plan

Result: Federal Industries is a highly successful diversified management company with $950 million in assets and sales of close to $2 billion. In 1988 it was ranked as the sixty-second largest company in Canada in *The Financial Post 500*.

Hospital for Sick Children:

A Business Injection

The history of change at Toronto's Hospital for Sick Children finds its roots in a series of baby deaths on the cardiac ward of the hospital from July 1980 until March 1981. Twenty-eight infants died in unexpected and mysterious circumstances due to overdoses of the drug digoxin. After a detailed police investigation, nurse Susan Nelles was charged with murder. However, the charges against Nelles were dropped in May 1982, after a preliminary inquiry concluded there was insufficient evidence for the charge. To this day, no one knows for certain what happened at the hospital, or who was responsible for the baby deaths. Until the time of the deaths, the HSC had had a superb reputation as a world-class medical institution, delivering superior care to sick children.

Several inquiries were held, both to delve into the mysterious deaths and to look at the administrative structure of the hospital. The Ontario government appointed a Royal Commission to examine the events surrounding the baby deaths. The Grange Commission, headed by Ontario Supreme Court

Justice Mr. Samuel Grange, concluded that eight babies were probably murdered due to overdoses of digoxin and that fifteen additional deaths were possibly murder cases as well. But the commission was unable to lay blame on any one individual.

The Ontario Ministry of Health commissioned another review, chaired by the Honorable Mr. Justice Charles Dubin, to inquire into the quality of management and administration of the hospital. This detailed and comprehensive committee studied the whole institution and submitted its report in January 1983. The Report of the Hospital for Sick Children Review Committee made some specific comments and recommendations about changes needed in the administration of the organization. Within the committee's comments lie the seeds of the major changes that occurred within the HSC over the next four to five years. For example:

"There is no single accepted structure for organizing the administration of a hospital . . . [but] the less complex the structure, the better it will serve its intended purpose."

"There is no identifiable management or executive committee."

"The chiefs of the clinical departments report to the Administrator on administrative matters, while the chiefs of diagnostic services appear to report to the Assistant Administrators. The Royal Commission does not understand the reason for this dichotomy."

"There is still lacking a medical presence in administration. All other activities of the hospital are represented by some administrative officer. . . . Yet there is no one of comparable status or expertise to co-ordinate the clinical activities of the medical staff and to advise the administration on medical or patient care matters."

"There is a very strong feeling within the hospital, among the medical staff below the rank of department chief or division head that they have no input into Administration. . . . The restructuring of administration to provide a medical presence within it, we think, is essential to improve the patient care monitoring ability of the present administrative staff and will go a long way in improving the morale of medical staff."

"There exists a difference of opinion as to who is the

chief executive officer: the Board Chairman or the Executive Director."

"The Medical Staff organization . . . encourages the development of individual fiefdoms . . . there appears to be no 'collective' responsibility with respect to review, analysis and evaluation of medical care in the hospital."

"It is the opinion of the Royal Commission that effective communication is a very major problem in the HSC."

Here was an organization dedicated to the highest goals — saving the lives of children — which had recently undergone the worst kind of trauma — the possibility of murder within its walls, followed by an exhaustive and microscopic public scrutiny. In addition, the hospital was saddled with a complex, unwieldy administrative setup: there was no overall control over medical staff, the physicians felt left out of the decision-making process, and it was even unclear who held the final reins of power, the executive director or the chairman of the board. No wonder morale was low and communications poor. Throw into this unsettling mix of ingredients the ever-spiraling costs of health care, together with a government determined to put a cap on health care expenditures, and you end up with a hospital in crisis.

During the 1970s and early 1980s, hospitals in Ontario consistently overspent their provincial budgets, and at the end of each year, the government usually found some extra money with which to pay off the deficit. By 1985, however, tougher guidelines were in effect; no more deficits were to be allowed. Hospitals were being forced to learn to budget effectively. But the HSC, like so many hospitals, was having real trouble achieving a balanced budget. By the end of 1985, its accumulated deficit was around $8 million.

The Dubin Committee's comments on the question of who ran the hospital underlined one of the organization's problems. Its decision-making processes had been influenced for many years by two important administrators: board chairman Duncan Gordon, who in effect acted as chief executive officer for 12 years (from 1972 to 1984), running both the board and the hospital, and Douglas Snedden, the executive director, whose administrative career spanned 34 years, 16 of those years as chief operating officer. Gordon retired in 1984, handing over the chairmanship to lawyer Jim Tory. At the same time, Doug Snedden indicated to the board that he wished to retire as well. The board considered the question of a replacement for Snedden for almost 18 months before filling the job.

According to Dr. Robin Humphreys, associate chief of surgery, who has been at HSC for 18 years, "It became obvious in the 18 to 24 months prior to Doug Snedden's departure that change was needed at senior levels. Our medical shop was in order, but we were being swamped by information and new technology, particularly high ticket diagnostic aids. For the first time ever, people started whispering about our ability to live up to our creed, 'Where no child knocks in vain.' We could no longer be all things to all people.

"Doug Snedden had an extraordinary hands-on approach. But by the early 1980s, administration had become so complex, that no one person could be so hands-on."

Bill Davis summarizes the administrative style when he started as an administrative assistant in 1984: "Doug Snedden's style was the industry standard at that time: highly autocratic, bureaucratic, slow to make decisions." As Dr. James Phillips, pathologist-in-chief, says, "The top-down system fell apart at the end. There were many more demands being put on management. Once they ran into the fiscal problems, the management skills needed to deal with it just weren't there, and they just fell apart."

The Board of Trustees, also adapting to the changing environment, was reevaluating its own role and that of the hospital's executive director. Even before Doug Snedden retired, his job title was upgraded to that of president. According to current chairman Allan Beattie, who assumed the title in June 1988, the board realized that the day-to-day running of the hospital had to be put into the chief administrator's hands, while "the board's role today is increasingly one to create and monitor policy."

"The key to hiring the right person to run the hospital," says Beattie, "was to hire someone with a broad overview, combined with passion and warmth."

In early 1986 the board announced the hiring of 53-year-old

David Martin. Martin came to HSC with impressive credentials. Although trained as an accountant, most of his work
experience lay in the field of hospital administration. At age 27,
he had taken a position with Mississauga Hospital, where he
was quickly promoted to associate administrator. A number
of increasingly senior positions saw him move to National
Nursing Homes, the Ontario Crippled Children's Centre, and
Variety Village before taking up the job as president of Toronto
East General Hospital in April 1982.

In his four years at East General, Martin had turned the
flagging institution into a first-class organization. When
Martin arrived at East General in 1982, the institution was
suffering from both a serious credibility problem, as well as an
escalating budget deficit. Accusations of deteriorating medical
care and conflicts of interest, combined with a projected
$5.2-million budget deficit, resulted in a severely demoralized
staff, maintaining an uneasy truce with their public. The
situation had deteriorated to such an extent that the Ontario
Ministry of Health had invoked a little-used provision to place
a government-appointed supervisor in charge, with authority
over the hospital trustee.

Martin brought in a fresh approach, participation, consensus-building, and strict budgetary controls. His renewal
process involved developing an effective management team to
get the basically sound institution back on the track again.
The marked change in East General's fortunes made David
Martin's name synonymous with "turnaround" in health care
circles, and he was a natural candidate for the post at HSC.

One of the reasons Allan Beattie believes that Martin was a
good choice is "that he has a vision of the hospital. Too many
people don't see the big picture."

"The hospital has to provide the highest level of medical care
possible," explains Martin. "Diverse medical groups should
have as much input as possible, and physician involvement is
the key to the process. We have to create an environment to
attract the very best physicians, and allow them to become
leaders in their fields.

"My job is not to come in and tell people what to do. Instead,
it's a form of consensus-building with guidance. We're moving

towards definable goals and creating a process that can make that happen."

Martin's vision of HSC was very different from that of his predecessor. "The previous management style had rewarded long service, and no one was ever fired, because no one was ever held accountable," explained vice president of human resources, Don Chiro. "Martin's vision was of a participative institution, where managers were held accountable for their actions."

Even before actually taking over the HSC reins of command, Martin began to plan changes. Two months prior to his official start at HSC, Don Chiro, who had worked closely with Martin as his director of human resources at East General, started as head of personnel at HSC. Martin, assisted by information provided by Chiro, began to assess the whole organization.

High on the list of priorities was the reorganization of the cumbersome administrative structure. Under the existing organizational hierarchy, the president and the administrator (a vacant position at this time) had 22 different administrators and senior medical staff reporting to them. Martin streamlined all that. The administrator role was eliminated, and the senior administrative group was reduced to five vice presidents, who were placed in charge of medical services, finance, nursing, diagnostic and support services, and human resources. As a result of the changes, a number of senior administrators left almost immediately; one retired and two others departed within the first couple of months, even though two of them had been with the hospital for longer than 40 years.

Martin admits that every senior staff member was reviewed and "assessed for their ability to adapt to change." Many didn't make the grade. In the two years immediately following Martin's appointment, 55 senior and middle managers left the hospital, a combination of early retirements and dismissals. These firings were particularly traumatic at HSC because of the earlier paternalistic environment. And although generous severance and relocation packages were offered to departing employees, many scars were created in an already fragile organization. Criticism of the "clear your desks and be gone by tonight" approach caused additional anxiety for employees who remained. By emphasizing the need for change, perhaps too much attention was focused on the dismissals.

On the senior level, Don Chiro explains, "people were not incompetent, they just didn't fit in with the new culture. One person we fired, in fact, is now the chief executive officer of a larger hospital. We were paying for the sins of the past, when no one was ever fired. Many of these people's continued existence at HSC was born out of paternalism. Because nothing had been invested in the development of these people, by age 50, they had either burned out or become set in their ways. There was no environment for management creativity."

The lack of employee development is clearly demonstrated by the budget for staff development. On Chiro's arrival, it stood at $8000, for a staff of 4400 people. Today, the fund is a healthy $750 000, and is spent on a variety of training and upgrading courses, up to and including management training courses for physicians.

David Martin faced a tremendous challenge when he arrived at HSC. "It's a huge, complex organization, and I had to try and turn it around quicker and in a more fundamental way than anyone thought possible.

"The key difference between the hospital and a regular corporation is that the president has no control over the physicians. I had to persuade them to change, persuade them to get involved. In other words I had to change the process without destroying it. If I hadn't been able to get the physicians to go along with the concept, none of it would have worked."

Martin's first full day on the job was April 22, 1986. Nine days later, the six other members of the senior management met with Martin and Ian Percy—a management consultant specializing in health care institutions who had been working with HSC for the past couple of years—for a two-day meeting to map out problems and priorities for change. The first item on the agenda was "senior management and management philosophy." A quote from the minutes says: "It was evident from examples expressed that frustration was experienced throughout all levels of the organization." Problem areas to be addressed were listed—29 of them. A partial list includes:

- Lack of consistency in decision-making
- All decisions made at the top
- Delegation not encouraged
- No planning concept, and plans that were made were not followed
- "Godfather" management resulted in reduced management confidence
- Lack of trust and consistency
- Little value of human resources

The group discussed and initiated a management philosophy that would attempt to deal with the problems outlined, and try and "promote a climate of positive change throughout the organization." A list of 14 statements that formed the core of their new management philosophy was outlined. This new approach was centered around the concepts of participation, delegation of decision-making, staff development, accountability, open communications, planning, and constructive change.

This executive planning session was followed, three weeks later, by an all-day management conference for the 120 senior managers of the hospital. At this session, Martin briefly described both his role and his vision of change for the organization: "to provide an environment of opportunity, innovation, and accountability, in terms of management style; that decision-making emanate from the lowest level possible to encourage ideas and to bring change into the organization; that the delegation of decision-making be a commitment at all management levels; that communication of ideas flow in both directions, from the top down and from the bottom up."

Out of this session came the request for a clearly defined mission statement for the organization. One month later, June 25 (only ten weeks after Martin took office) all department heads and senior administrators met for another all-day session. After a discussion of external factors with an impact on the organization, and budgetary issues, the question of management problems returned again. In this session, 40 problems were identified.

Change was underway, more change than the venerable institution had seen for many years. Autocratic, paternalistic, top-down management was out; participative management and collective decision-making was in, along with communication, communication, and more communication. Discomfort, exhilaration, anxiety, excitement, and fear all coexisted in various fashions. No one could escape the effects of the changes sweeping through the hospital. Some staff members thrived under the new, more participative, and accountable style of decision-making. Others were suspicious of the new approaches. And a number simply couldn't cope with the new demands placed on them.

Anne Evans is a poignant example. Evans had spent most of her professional life at HSC, beginning there as a nurse in the early '60s. She worked her way up to the position of head nurse, and then returned to university for additional training. Upon her return to the hospital, Evans's promotions continued – project supervisor, associate director of nursing, then in 1982, director of nursing services. After a second return to school, this time for an MA, Evans returned to the hospital as vice president, nursing, just prior to David Martin's arrival.

While she admits that change was necessary at HSC – "the charitable, paternalistic style under the old regime, together with the favoritism, were not ideal qualities in management" – Evans found herself caught in the middle. "I was one of the only ones in the old guard with credibility with the troops. I found myself straddling the middle ground between the old and the new."

Evans constantly found herself saying, "Go slow. Don't change everything. And before you change it, see if there's still some value there." The tension between what she perceived as medical values versus business values became almost unbearable. She felt she could see things from both sides, from the patient care viewpoint and from the administrative need to tidy up a system that was no longer working. However, she just couldn't make decisions that would compromise either point of view. She seemed to have spent too long under the previous system to be able to alter her routines. "It's like a form of schizophrenia," she admits. "They were running a business, and I was just trying to be a human being. My personal warmth and values were in conflict with business values." Although she believes that patient care has not suffered under the new administration, she herself was unable to function effectively within the new framework.

Evans's solution was to leave the hospital and take a less demanding job with a gerontology center. Although she clearly found the situation at HSC too difficult to remain, she's not sure her present move was the right one either. "I wonder if I haven't copped out by going into gerontology and avoiding some of the thornier issues in modern medicine. I'm no longer at the cutting edge of health administration."

Tackling the Budget Deficit

"The first challenge was to deal with the budget deficit – to try and get better value for our spending dollars," said Martin. The hospital had to be put on a more stable financial footing. To this end, the whole budgeting process was put under close scrutiny. A number of glaring weaknesses had to be set right immediately. Specifically, the old system for allocating money for new capital expenditures was clearly outmoded and ineffective. As Dr. Robert Freedom, head of the division of cardiology, explains, "The person who got what he wanted under the old system was the person who shouted loudest and screamed the most." Money was allocated for additional, unbudgeted expenditures without much thought about where it was going to come from, or if there were sufficient funds in the budget to meet the expenditure. Clearly this had to change.

In addition to instituting a review of the budgeting process, Martin established a rigorous planning process, asking all departments to prepare lists of equipment requirements and new capital expenditures, as well as regular budgetary outlays.

A new head of finance was hired in the middle of 1987 to implement the new budget system. Martin went to industry to look for the person with the right credentials to put the hospital on a businesslike footing. Michael Strofolino, a former linebacker with the Los Angeles Rams and the Hamilton Tiger Cats, had gone on to a promising career in public accounting, first with Clarkson Gordon, and then as vice president, finance, of the Canadian division of American Hospital Supply (a distributor).

Under Strofolino, the budgeting process started at the bottom of the organization. "The process used to be done in January, February, March of the year in question. I moved it back to April/May of the previous year. I gave all departments a range of what increases would probably be, and supplied them with new forms to fill out. Finances were not the issue— rather it was a question of the qualitative standards that each department wanted to achieve."

In the first year of the new process, by the time it had worked its way through the entire hospital to the top, the budgetary wish list was $18 million over budget, and the senior management group had to make some tough decisions to bring it back under the allotted amount. The second year, budgetary requests were more realistic, ending up only $4 million over budget.

The new planning system meant that every group in the hospital had a chance to submit its wish list for new equipment and funds for consideration by the capital equipment committee. All requests were not granted, but at least they were all reviewed and considered, before decisions were made about priorities. Although in the past everyone had engaged in shouting matches to achieve their individual aims, a system which was universally criticized as unsatisfactory, it still took the physicians some time to adjust to the new, more democratic process. They suddenly found themselves involved in decision-making which would affect the future development of their respective departments.

Unanimity of support for the new system is unqualified. Even some of the new administration's harshest critics can't fault the budgetary and planning structures. According to a former head of the division of endocrinology, Dr. Robert Ehrlich, "The former financial systems were very poor, and now we're financially sound. The administration has done a very good job on that level."

The department of environmental services (maintenance and cleaning services) is a good example of the ad hoc and unbusinesslike approach that had gradually developed in the hospital. When Joseph Mancuso was hired to take on the job of director of environmental services in 1984, he was excited and challenged at the prospect: "This hospital is a world-class organization. I expected everything to be in place." Instead, he found an institution "50 years behind the times."

Imagine his surprise on the first day on the new job when he set out to discover the extent and scope of his new responsibilities: "There were no previous records. I didn't know who was in the department or how many people worked here. There were no capital records either, and for more than a week, I wasn't even sure how many pieces of equipment were in existence. In fact, there were only 15 pieces to service 1 200 000 square feet of floor space."

Other inadequacies soon surfaced. Budgets were prepared by one person in a budget office with little or no input from the environmental services department. Staff was segregated into male and female, and meetings were rare. Salary anomalies also existed, with male staff sometimes making as much as $7000 more per annum than female staff in similar positions.

Today there are regular staff meetings with open agendas, lots of communication, and equality in both pay and scheduling.

Just one year after taking over, Strofolino had turned the deficit into a surplus. When Strofolino first arrived at HSC, the projected deficit for 1986/87 was a staggering $16 million. But instead of a deficit, the hospital showed a $2-million surplus, an amount that was quickly allocated to one of the areas of greatest need. By the 1987/88 fiscal year, the surplus had increased to $2.9 million. Strofolino explains: "When I arrived, there was a deficit, but the board wasn't worried. But the problem was that decisions were being made in a very top-down fashion. In reality the bottom line was so bad that if this had been a corporation, shareholders would have been jumping up and down with rage. The problems were many: 80% of the accounting employees had less than one year's (accounting) experience and very few had accounting degrees. The financial results were inaccurate, untimely, and ultimately not meaningful. In short, the financial systems were archaic."

Strofolino decided that the first step in solving the problem had to be the development of an operating plan for the hospital. "An operating plan would enable us to build participation into the system. A strategic plan, which would deal with long-term planning, would come later." The plan was hammered out. Every department identified planning objectives, which were compared against the financial plan. For the first time, managers were being held accountable for their decisions. This meant living within plans, following priorities established within the budgetary process. It was no longer possible to hire a new person and worry about where the money for the salary would come from later, as had often been the practice in the past.

The shift to a corporate approach brought its own share of problems. "When I first started talking about running a hospital as a business," Strofolino explains, "the doctors practically cut my throat. They automatically assumed that meant a cut in services. But they're starting to understand now that the system works if you use the money effectively." The tension between business and medical values is very real in a hospital. "It's easier in business – if you make a wrong decision, you lose a few dollars. Here, if you make the wrong decision, you lose a patient!" says Strofolino graphically.

He also adds that clinical input always drives the business decisions, not the other way round. Nevertheless, many members of the hospital staff remain highly skeptical about the order of priorities. Chief of medical staff, Dr. Anna Jarvis, says: "Management style has become more important than training and knowledge of pediatrics."

Many of the physicians are still grappling with this thorny question of business versus medical priorities. Dr. Robert Filler, surgeon-in-chief, asks, "What is success, and how do you measure it in a hospital?" Chairman of the Medical Advisory Committee, Dr. Geoffrey Barker, adds: "Do you measure success in terms of dollars?" Both believe the ultimate criterion still has to be effective patient care, and that on this basis, the hospital is on an upward curve and improving all the time. Barker says, "There is a difference in style under the current administration, but I'm not so sure the end result isn't still the same."

Barker and Filler, like other physicians who head up a

department or division, find their time increasingly taken up with administrative duties, creating conflicts between their medical and administrative functions. "My administrative duties have increased by a factor of five in the past 12 years, although the department has remained the same size," Filler says. "I believe the hospital has to come to grips with the time commitments necessary for administrative duties and arrange appropriate financial compensation."

For Barker, the additional administrative duties have brought on a kind of mid-life career crisis. "I feel as if I'm moving away from the core of my job, which consists of clinical practice, and yet I can't advance into the front tiers of my profession unless I'm involved administratively. The profession now requires us to be triple threat people, combining teaching and research, administration and medical practice. But at the core, my main aim is to remain a physician."

"All this administration carries a big-time price, but in the end it's probably worth it," Filler admits.

Once the budgetary problems were reduced in size, other issues were dealt with. Bringing physicians into the decision-making processes throughout the hospital was an essential objective. Doctors assumed the chairmanship of three key committees: Facilities Planning, Capital Equipment and Program Review. Under the old system, doctors did not make many non-medical decisions. But in the new scheme, input from physicians became mandatory in almost all areas of decision-making, from equipment purchases to running the operating rooms.

New systems, such as the physician-manager model pioneered at Johns Hopkins Hospital in Baltimore, Maryland, were introduced. The hierarchy within operating rooms used to function on very traditional lines. Ultimate authority rested with the head nurse, who worked with the surgeon, anesthetist, and other nurses to ensure the smooth running of the team. The new system, initiated in July 1988, puts a physician-manager—in this case Dr. Robin Humphreys, associate chief of surgery—in charge of all 14 operating rooms at HSC. He works with the nursing unit administrator (the new title for head nurse), plus the director of administrative services (operating rooms and patient services), to oversee all operations. Humphreys spends time each day examining all immediate activities in the operating rooms and dealing with any problems, such as scheduling and emergencies, and reviewing the next day's rotation. Long-term issues are addressed at twice-monthly meetings, and a report is presented monthly to the operating room committee.

The new system seems to be functioning smoothly and has "put in order the nursing hierarchy which had gone asunder," according to Humphreys. "This is just opening the window to get physicians more involved. In the old days you had just two or three people doing all the work, taking all the flack, out of a medical staff of over 500 people. Unfortunately, doctors seem to have an instinct to hide behind the need to care for their patients when push comes to shove. But doctors have to become more involved in all aspects of administration. As long as 'what's best for the child' remains foremost, we'll be all right." Humphreys is convinced this is the trend of the future, and that "before the turn of the century, we'll see huge numbers of doctors with MBAs."

Another senior staff member who is convinced of the need for doctors to combine administration with medicine is pediatrician-in-chief (and chairman of the department of pediatrics at the University of Toronto), Dr. Robert Haslam. "I've been in management since the beginning of my medical career," he explains. Although originally from western Canada, Haslam's training and early career all took place in the U.S. He returned to Canada about 14 years ago as chairman of the department of pediatrics at the University of Calgary, before moving to his present position at HSC in July 1986.

Concern about management problems at HSC had spread as far as Calgary, and Haslam didn't want to move at first. "The senior management's main concern was to keep the hospital a world-class institution. As a result, those with the best skills at getting to Doug Snedden really got ahead, and two or three strong departments developed. But I saw tremendous morale problems developing – dissension in the ranks, combined with a strong sense of unfairness." After meeting David Martin and becoming convinced "his money was where his mouth was,"

Haslam agreed to come to HSC. In his three years with the hospital, he has seen Martin's management style put in place at HSC, and firmly believes that it's a positive advance for the institution. "It's vital that the hospital be viewed as well run. Medicine and administration go hand in hand. It's even more vital in a monopoly situation (as we have with health care here in Canada). There will be increasing competition as other hospitals improve and become more aggressive. We've been sitting back on our laurels for too long. We must learn to provide good service, or we won't have any patients in 20 years' time."

Haslam echoes a refrain more commonly heard in business circles: "We're all in marketing." He sees good customer service as the cornerstone of hospital care of the future. As a result, some of the issues currently being addressed at HSC revolve around customer service. Waiting times are being examined to try and set standards. How long is too long to wait for emergency treatment, for example? How much medical information should be provided to an increasingly sophisticated and educated parent group? What are parents' needs when their children are hospitalized, and how can they best be addressed?

Changes in these areas may revolutionize health care in future years. The new planning mode at HSC ensures that these issues will be anticipated and acted upon before they become crises.

Cornerstones of Change

Three years after David Martin's arrival, the Hospital for Sick Children is a very different place. Rigorous budget processes are firmly in place; a clear set of management principles have been enunciated and a mission statement expressed; planning is part of everyone's responsibilities; staff are all held accountable; job evaluation and performance appraisals are conducted annually; communications have improved throughout the institution; training programs on a wide variety of subjects are available on many levels, including management courses for physicians. Decision-making is much less top-down oriented. Much more input comes from the bottom-up, although there is still considerable room for improvement in this area.

A small, yet significant example of this change is given by cleaner Josephina Visconti, who has been with the hospital for 17 years. She is very proud of the fact that she and other cleaners were consulted before new staff uniforms were selected, and they were allowed to choose both the color and the fabric. "We're much more comfortable now than before. We have meetings every month, and we know what's going on now."

The majority of the staff believe the new system works, giving them confidence for the future. Dr. James Phillips, head of pathology, sums up what the changes have meant to him: "It's a business-type approach and very different from what we had before. It's hard-nosed and was not easy to accept at first. But I personally like it much better. It gives one a great sense of achievement and belonging. This is now a well-managed place. And it's more than just a well-balanced budget. There is also a reinvestment in the institution, to the tune of tens of millions of dollars. I have tremendous confidence about the new management style."

One of the hospital's more remarkable achievements is its five-year strategic plan. In spite of the handicap of a fluctuating yearly budgetary allocation from the province of Ontario, which complicates attempts at long-range planning, HSC has attempted to map its course for the next five years, to better plan its future, and to adjust to changing conditions in the outside world. This has involved reaching an understanding that the hospital can no longer try and remain all things to all children. The administration have made some hard decisions about the focus of the hospital and of its many medical programs. For example, the hospital will continue to support and increase its expertise in areas such as transplants, trauma, cardiology, and neonatology (infant care). Ambulatory and outpatient services will also be increased. Other areas will decrease in importance; for example, generalized care for all sick children (specialization will increase and other hospitals will assume more of these types of patients). There has also been a major thrust to dramatically increase public fundraising to supplement government funding.

Chief Pediatrician Dr. Robert Haslam, who was brought in to HSC after the change was launched, has some insights into both the best and the worst of the process: "The impact of the firings was very scary. Somehow you have to prepare people for changes to come. Too big a deal was made of the firings by the senior level. You shouldn't remind people that they were ineffective and that's why they're gone. It was overkill, an over-emphasis on change.

"The kind of communication was too negative. It had an impact on the tradition of the place, causing a loss of commitment to that tradition.

"At HSC there is too much suspicion between administration and physicians. It's an adversarial setup. But on the positive side, management really is leaning over backward to get physicians involved. Doctors really are in a very favorable position here."

The dramatic turnaround at HSC has been recognized within the Ontario Ministry of Health. The Ministry's 1988 accreditation report summary on HSC states: "This is a superb hospital, unique in Canada, and one of the best children's hospitals in the world. In almost all areas, HSC satisfies or surpasses Council standards.

"The Board, medical staff, senior administration, and especially the department heads are to be commended for their demonstrative ability to successfully initiate, implement, and manage change."

Board chairman Allan Beattie believes the hospital is "over the hump, as far as change is concerned. It's like a snowball; once you've built it up to a certain mass, the acceleration moves it along. Now there's a fair amount of acceptance of change, and the main goals of the change are being understood now."

Without David Martin and his specific vision of a participative, accountable hospital community, very little productive change would have occurred. As with many good administrators, his uniqueness is hard to describe, partly because his style has become adopted to such an extent that it is almost indistinguishable from that of the hospital.

"Martin heals organizations; he's a real changemaster," says former vice president, medical, Mary MacDonald. "He really gives away the responsibility for change. Martin hides his ego in his pocket so you don't even see it."

These sentiments are echoed by other senior members of the administration. "David can be a leader and yet not be a leader," says vice president, finance, Mike Strofolino. "Even when he's critical he's so nice, you don't even notice. He has a quiet, reserved, non-threatening style. Another vice president facilitates at meetings, but when David does talk, everybody listens."

Martin's strengths are drawn from his personality: a calm, unruffled yet businesslike manner that allows him to deal with everyone impartially. His ability to delegate responsibility is important, as is his skill of attracting talented people with complementary skills around him, and forging them into an effective team. His quiet manner belies the toughness and determination to succeed, which lies just below the surface.

Not surprisingly, everyone isn't uniformly enthusiastic about Martin. Although there is unanimous praise about his efficient solving of the budget crisis, there are others who don't approve of many of the changes he has implemented, or the style in which they were accomplished. Former vice president, nursing, Anne Evans believes, "The team wouldn't be a team without David. It's merely five individuals held together by David. If he left, a more human, caring approach might come back." Another doctor in the division of endocrinology adds, "Martin is great at raising money, and he's done a good job in many ways, but he's forgotten the human element . . . they're trying to run it like the Ford Motor Company, and it doesn't work because we're not making cars."

Pushing through dramatic change in a relatively short time span has been accomplished without any deterioration of patient services, which is in itself no small achievement, and although there are pockets of disaffection, they are relatively few. Mistakes have been made, and in some areas more change is badly needed. More doctors have to be convinced of the vital role effective administration plays in maintaining the hospital's traditions of excellence in patient care and research. But in general Martin has accomplished a remarkable transformation of a large, complex, and unique organization very quickly.

Snapshot of Hospital for Sick Children

Crisis (1985):

The hospital has built up an accumulated deficit of $8 million and projects a $16-million deficit for 1986/87.

Turnaround Strategy:

- Ask senior staff for input
- Reorganize administrative setup
- Fire unproductive staff and rehire
- Institute new budgeting process
- Persuade physicians to participate in decision-making process
- Implement new communications programs
- Organize hospital-wide planning process
- Develop mission statement
- Create yearly operating plan
- Institute long-range strategic planning

Result: Today the hospital operates with a balanced budget, and its new planning procedures allow it to anticipate and deal more effectively with both financial and medical problems when they occur. Involvement in decision-making is encouraged at all levels, physicians are much more involved in administration, and morale levels have improved.

Canadian Pizza Crust:

Indomitable Spirit

On September 22, 1987, Henrietta Virga, 42, stood proudly in the World Trade and Convention Centre in Halifax, Nova Scotia, to receive the Bronze Award for Entrepreneurship, one of the Canadian Awards for Business Excellence. The award was being given in recognition of her company's dedication to excellence in management practices, productivity, and innovation. A congratulatory letter from Prime Minister Brian Mulroney further highlighted Virga's efforts: "You may take great pride in your accomplishments in transforming a failing company into a significant competitor in the manufacturing of pizza crust. You have made a contribution to Canada's competitiveness."

When Virga assumed control of the company in June 1983, the once healthy profit sheet of $200 000 realized in '81 and '82 was on a downhill slide. In 1983 Canadian Pizza Crust reported a substantially lower profit of $88 000. In 1984 the company registered a $64 000 loss. This was a crushing blow for the family business that produces and sells pizza crusts and sauces throughout North America. Their customers range from prisons, schools, bowling alleys, and bars to large grocery chains, parks, and pizza chains. Canadian consumers know their products as Marco Polo Pizza Crusts and Virga and Luigi sauces.

Like many companies, the Virga Pizza Crust Company didn't start out as a pizza crust manufacturer. Not content with the bakery he had established in 1945, Andrew Virga, a Sicilian immigrant, wanted to expand. He identified an opportunity to capitalize on the large Catholic population in New York City and their tradition of meatless Fridays. He cut large bagels, known as "pizza bread," in two, covered them with sauce and cheese, and sold them as an appetizing meatless alternative. It wasn't long before the production capability was unable to keep pace with customer demand. To meet this challenge, he began producing his "pizzas" throughout the week and freezing them for the heavy Friday traffic. His business, Virga Pizza Crust Inc., thrived at a time when the fast food industry in North America was experiencing an explosion. During the '50s and '60s, Virga expanded, adding subsidiaries in Baltimore, Maryland; Portsmouth, Virginia; Jacksonville, Florida; and Mississauga, Ontario.

In 1971, when Andrew Virga was over 70, a Vancouver subsidiary was added to the Virga network. To run their far-flung subsidiaries efficiently, the New York-based Virga family realized they needed on-site, committed managers in each location. Since Andrew Virga, the sole owner, didn't have family members available to run the two Canadian companies, he sold 27% in each of these subsidiaries to their respective business managers. This equity strategy, which at first appeared to be the key to the company's business growth in Canada, backfired ten years later. Virga's hands-off management style had allowed both the Mississauga and Vancouver business managers to make decisions that went beyond their minority share position, jeopardizing the financial security of both Canadian companies.

In 1980 the Virga family sold off the Mississauga subsidiary to Gino Molinaro. In late 1982 the Vancouver company minority shareholder and business manager decided to diversify beyond the frozen pizza crust market into the finished pizza industry. The result was a 15% increase in sales and a 56% drop in profits in 1983. This change in the company's financial security forced Henrietta Virga to assume control.

In late 1981, Henrietta Virga visited the Vancouver-based company to find the business lacking in leadership and control. She decided to move to Vancouver to run the subsidiary herself. "It came at a point in my life when I wanted a change," reflects Virga. "I am a very good cook and I like doing it. Since my background had been largely on the creative side, and we were going to diversify, I thought it would be a good opportunity . . . a change." She had started working in her father's bakery as a teenager, and then moved into marketing and product development positions in the Virga Pizza Crust company. Newly divorced, she had only recently returned to the business. Although her decision to move was made in 1981, it took until June 1983 to arrange the immigration papers to allow Virga to work in Canada.

Having decided to take charge of the operation, Virga approached her brother Jack and sister Anita to discuss how she could gain sole ownership of the 63% of the Virga-owned shares in the Vancouver-based subsidiary. On his death in April 1982, Andrew Virga had left his three children the shares of the New York-based Virga Pizza Crust Inc. and its subsidiaries. After a number of tense and sometimes heated family discussions, the subsidiaries were severed from the parent company. Virga assumed ownership of the family shares in the Vancouver company; her brother took over the operations in Florida, Maryland, and Virginia, and her sister gained control of the New York plant. Jack Virga was appointed chairman of the board for all the Virga companies.

Henrietta moved to Vancouver in June 1983 and changed the company's name to Canadian Pizza Crust (Western) Ltd. to reflect the new Canadian ownership. It didn't take long for her to realize that the diversification into the finished pizza business was backfiring on them. Not only was the company alienating many of its packers and distributors by bypassing their services, but it had also converted the mainstay pizza crust customers into competitors in the finished pizza market.

"Before we got things turned around," says Virga, "we must have lost at least 75% of our original customers, including Snackery Food Ltd. [now called Chef Ready Ltd.], an account that represented 30% of our overall sales. What made this worse was that this loss could have been averted. Customers had informed the company on a number of occasions that unless it moved out of the finished pizza business, they would be forced to find another pizza crust supplier." The Vancouver business manager had chosen to ignore these warnings. Virga continues, "One Monday morning in early '83, Snackery Foods were gone. They'd moved their account to Orroro Ltd., our main British Columbia competitor." Added to this loss, the once wide-open finished pizza market had become highly competitive. Promises that had guaranteed "exclusive shelf space" for the company's finished pizza products fell through and a competitive price war ensued between Canadian Pizza Crust and other suppliers.

The business manager tried anything and everything to win the war. One plant supervisor recalls, "He would do just about anything to make our finished pizzas more marketable, no matter what the cost." "He tried to do everything in a Cadillac fashion," continues one of the plant workers. "His boxes were real eye catchers, I must admit that. But as a customer, I'm going to pay for what's inside. For the dollar more we were charging for our finished pizza, our customers would have just as soon put their own toppings on!"

When Virga later reviewed the operating expenses, she discovered that they were providing most of the customers with personalized boxes, costing the company between 20 and 30 cents more per box than its competitors. It took her almost two years to consolidate the packaging process, selling the existing inventory as scrap.

The 1983 "Grey Cup Special" represented another example of the company's overzealous efforts to take an aggressive hold of the finished pizza business. For this one-day event, the plant produced 4000 cases of Deluxe and Hawaiian pizzas. This translated into 38 000 pizzas to be sold in the B.C. market alone. Plant workers remember, "It took over a year to get rid of them. In the end we practically gave them away!"

Although the company's diversification efforts had started off slowly, increasingly large amounts of capital were being drained from the frozen crust side of the business. The finished pizza line was not only affecting the company's financial security, it was also diverting management's attention away from the mainstay of the business—the frozen crust operation. Frozen crust production was running at an all-time low of two to four shifts a week.

The manager's emotional involvement in the new finished pizza product also affected his perception of the role he played in the company. "He had three business cards in his desk," recounts one of the plant's employees. "Together with those that said 'General Manager,' and 'Sales Manager,' he also had a set of cards with 'President' written on them." Because he wanted to control everything himself, he was never where he needed to be. This one-man show eventually led to customer irritation according to Paul Royce, the company's auditor and financial consultant. Marvin Salvail, plant shipper at the time and currently bakery manager, adds, "He was on the road most of the time, getting orders, talking to customers. If he was here, it was first thing in the morning, to do whatever work he had to get done, then he was gone. He would phone in to make sure the company was doing okay . . . pretty well doing the whole show himself." In 1984, not one of the 26 people employed by the company had any responsibility; nobody made a move without "the boss."

Crisis #1

Plant personnel remember Henrietta Virga's arrival at the company as being very quiet. Gwen Jorgensen, the office supervisor, was the only employee who knew about Virga's ownership position. It appeared that both the autonomy given him and his 27% share in the company had led the business manager to believe he really did "own" the company. Marvin Salvail further explains, "Our manager had driven into us that Henrietta was 'just' a business partner and to more or less disregard her. We were told that she was not the owner. Whatever he said was to be a 'go'; whatever she said was to be a 'no go.' " Gwen Jorgensen adds, "Our boss never showed Henrietta anything. She was treated as if she wasn't here."

Over the next couple of months, there were countless shouting matches, arbitrated when necessary by Virga's brother Jack. As chairman, Jack made a point of visiting the various Virga businesses. It was, however, as Henrietta's brother that he now came to help. Employees started to avoid all contact with the office, fearing they might be caught in a cross fire. "The way they were yelling at each other, I thought for certain this company was going down, but I certainly wasn't going to go in there pointblank and ask them if we were about to close down the operation!" says one plant worker. Finally, the tension reached the breaking point. "Henrietta came into the lunchroom and told us who she was . . . we were totally shocked!" recalls a plant supervisor. "We thought, 'Oh no! We've been treating her like a nobody, and here she is our boss!' It was hard to believe, given all the years our manager had told us that he was the owner . . . the boss."

The immediate reaction of the employees was one of great uncertainty. Many of the workers had been with the company for years and had built a steadfast loyalty towards the manager. There were husband and wife teams on the line who greatly feared the loss of their total family income. "For most of us in the production area, we didn't know if this meant the company was going down . . . if we were going to lose our jobs, or what." Added to their concern over the change of management was the suspicion that the company would be moved to the U.S. Virga was quick to reassure them. "She came and told us not to worry. 'The business manager will be going, but you will still have your jobs here. If he starts his own company and you want to go to work for him, that's fine. But you still have your jobs here. You've been doing a good job, so I want you to stay.' "

Rumors that the company was losing money also spread throughout the plant. Virga worked hard to quiet their fears. One of the plant workers explains, "Things were a little slow at first, and it did get a little hairy, but she promised we would all be working here and things would be taken care of. She took it over and we started to get back into business."

By April 1984, Virga had bought out the business manager's 27% with a bank loan from the Royal Bank. Her rebuilding could now begin. As president, she immediately went on the road to repair the company's tarnished relationship with the major distributors, packers, brokers, and suppliers. As she explains, "I had to get them to trust the company again." It wasn't only the company that these people had to learn to trust, but its new president too. She found herself struggling with an old-boy network that included the former business manager. Wherever she went, Virga was confronted with the fears associated with her American citizenship and the rumors associated with the company's change in management. In her first few months of presidency, Virga's trademark charisma and diplomacy were put to the test.

Slowly, she managed to win over her customers, brokers, and suppliers, until the words "trust" and "Henrietta Virga" became synonymous. With the customer recovery strategy in motion, a four-point corporate recovery plan was put in place. It involved:

1. Establishing a new management team
2. Paring down of the finished pizza line and re-establishing the frozen crust business
3. Cost cutting
4. Rebuilding the customer base

Virga realized that staff morale was at an all-time low. "I believed everybody was trying to do the best job possible for the company . . . but they just weren't going about it the right way." She knew she had to start delegating more responsibility, especially to those employees who had been with the company for many years. The new president began to emerge out of the office the former manager had hidden in, to spend hours listening and talking to her staff. It soon became clear that the establishment of a strong management team was critical to the company's recovery. The answer lay in the Virga family's traditional response to crisis—pull in the family. In early 1984, Virga asked her 24-year-old daughter, Aurora Deluca-

Weinlein, a newly graduated pharmacist, and her husband, Bill Weinlein, a jewelry designer and home remodeler, to come to Vancouver to "take a look around." Having been involved in the family business all her life, Virga had encouraged her children to go into totally different fields. This was a difficult request for Virga to make as she had vowed "never" to involve either of her daughters in the family business.

Echoing her mother, Deluca-Weinlein recalls that she too had often remarked, "Never, never, never, am I going to make a pizza crust. My grandfather had constantly asked me to come work for him. Whenever things are breaking one after the other around the plant, I tell the guys that this is my grandfather getting back at me for every time I told him I would never make a pizza!" Bill Weinlein remembers talking to Aurora's grandfather: "He would say to us, 'Why don't you and Bill come to work for me?' We would look at him and say, 'You're crazy!' "

Before deciding to put their own professions on hold, the newly married couple realized they needed a greater understanding of the pizza business. After visiting the Vancouver plant in April 1984, Deluca-Weinlein moved to Virginia for a 12-week crash training course with her uncle, Jack Virga. In November 1984 she arrived in Vancouver to make a comparison between the Virginia and Vancouver plant operations. Only after she had reviewed the situation and had discussed it with her husband was she prepared to make the decision to join her mother. During this November trip, Aurora accepted her mother's offer to become the general manager of the company while Bill assumed the position of Canadian sales manager.

Meanwhile, Virga was adding other members to her team. Frank Medrano, who had resigned under the previous management, rejoined the company as the U.S. sales manager. A Canadian sales manager, Jim Dartnell, and his assistant, Shelly Brown, were hired to replace the retail food brokers they had hired to market their products. A computer consultant and an accountant were then added to the team. As 1984 drew to a close, Virga felt she had all the necessary players in place ready to pull off the recovery.

Crisis #2

It was during her November 1984 trip that Aurora sensed something was wrong with her mother. It wasn't long before she discovered how ill Henrietta really was. Aurora explains, "My mother called me the week before Christmas to tell me that she was ill. She and my Uncle Jack wanted me in Vancouver right away to run the business. I came to work in the Vancouver plant at seven in the morning on January 5, 1985, as my mother went into surgery. I was now on my own."

By this time, Virga had built a strong bond of trust between herself and the employees. Her quiet, trusting manner attracted people, as did her never-ending confidence in what they could do. Her daughter comments, "She leads with diplomacy. People always want to follow her and do the best job they can."

Only seven months after Virga had assumed the leadership of the company, the Canadian Pizza Crust employees were faced with another management crisis. At the same time, Deluca-Weinlein was facing her own personal upheaval. "I came to work every day and quietly sat here, assessing what was going on. I tried to get to know everyone. I didn't know the business well enough to do two things at once."

Since Virga had spent most of 1984 rebuilding her customer base, she had had little time to focus on the plant operation. Due to the significant reduction in production shifts, the urgency of this situation had not become apparent. Aurora's immediate focus as general manager became plant operations and administration. She knew that she could not accomplish this without first gaining the acceptance and trust of the employees. Her fears were confirmed by the silence that would fall over the lunchroom whenever she walked in.

"Who was I – this 24-year-old woman who had just dropped in on them? Most of them had been working here for ten years. I couldn't tell them how to run their bakery . . . they certainly weren't going to take orders from me!" This newcomer's remarkable sense of humor and straight talk played a strong role in gaining her employees' respect. She responded to the lunchroom silence one day by saying, "You know, you guys must be talking about me, if you stop talking every time I walk in!"

When they questioned why she was coming in so early in the morning, her reply was, "What time do you start working?"

"Seven o'clock," they answered.

"Well," she said, "that's when my job starts, or are you taking a video tape for me and am I going to watch it at ten?"

When they asked why she wasn't coming into the office "dressed up," she replied, "Oh, am I supposed to stand around the bakery in a suit?"

When they asked somebody to drive the forklift, she volunteered, having learned to do so from another employee. She worked along with them, continually showing how interested she was in learning everything and anything about the plant operation, from the office work to the equipment maintenance. When she asked them why they performed their jobs the way they did, she discovered that no one had ever told them what to do or why. They had no idea that the "customer" paid their wages. As Deluca-Weinlein concludes, "One of the things we had to teach them was where the product was going . . . the kind of customer we were dealing with and that we were not the only people selling pizza crusts."

Early in 1985, the calculation of the 1984 financial statements confirmed the negative impact the company's production and marketing problems were having on the bottom line. They showed a net loss of $64 000 on total sales of $2.6 million. This was in spite of the '84 increase in finished pizza sales from $470 in 1982 to $1.2 million. Pizza crust sales, however, had dropped from making up 82% of total sales in 1982 to 60% of sales in 1984.

Much of the financial loss was due to low margins that were, and still are, characteristic of the finished pizza business. It requires high overheads, a large inventory, and aggressive and competitive marketing. The pizza crust business, on the other hand, generates significantly higher margins due to the controllable overhead, fluid inventory, and less competitive market.

Aurora spent a great deal of time discussing her growing concerns with her hospitalized mother. Finally she told Henrietta, "Let's just take this company back, and do what we know how to do best. We've been in the pizza crust business for over 40 years and have somehow managed to survive. Let's develop the business, make a better product, invest money in the bakery . . . then we'll be ready to get our customers back and get rid of our tarnished image." Sacrificing a significant investment in equipment and inventory, the company undertook this redirection, and by mid-1985 was well on its way to recovering its losses.

From Virga's point of view, "The return to the pizza crust business was the turning point for the company." The company's product line restructuring won praise from its customers. Dick Howard, president of Western Foods, a food packaging and distribution organization, in Richmond, B.C., says, "When the previous management started producing finished pizza, we found ourselves competing with them in the finished pizza market. Fortunately, when Henrietta took over she reversed the process. Now we are their exclusive distributor in B.C. again, and we have a good understanding. Henrietta's not only a reliable supplier, she's a good friend. And I can tell you, I'd rather be working with her than as her competitor."

While re-establishing the frozen pizza crust line, the management team uncovered a large number of operating and administrative problems. There appeared to be a complete lack of systems and controls for most of the key plant functions such as:

- **Customer order taking.** Orders were being taken by anyone who was walking by a ringing phone. The wrong orders were being recorded, shipped, and invoiced. Reshipping and re-invoicing had become an expensive undertaking.
- **Purchasing.** Purchase orders could be created by anyone, and the items would be purchased with no questions asked and no price comparisons made.
- **Accounts receivable.** No one was overseeing the administration of the receivables. Significant amounts of money were outstanding well over 60 days.
- **Inventory.** The excessive inventory was allowing a turnover of only 5.2 times per year (an average of 70.2 days) compared to the industry average of 12 times per year (an average of 30 days).
- **Product accounting.** Inaccurate product accounting was

providing little to no information for informed decision-making. A blatant example was a recorded $60 000 profit for a product that was actually operating at a loss. On further investigation, it was discovered that slow-moving products were exceeding their shelf life due to the lack of product rotation in the grocery chains.

Aurora responded to the chaos by taking over the purchasing, inventory control, costing, production planning, and shipping; while Bill took control of the office responsibilities including the order taking, invoicing, and receivables.

The management team then embarked on a cost-cutting campaign. Their goal was to reduce costs without layoffs or labor concessions. Those that lost their jobs on the finished pizza side of the business were offered shift positions on the expanded pizza crust shifts. Inventory was cut from $360 000 to $176 000, and better terms were negotiated with suppliers. Many suppliers cut them off when the company asked for a 60-day payback period. This brought Virga back into action. She renegotiated payback terms with the suppliers who were willing to stand by her. To repay their goodwill, Canadian Pizza Crust strictly maintained its payment schedule and kept them on as their main suppliers, even when their prices exceeded the competition's. As a result of these initiatives, Canadian Pizza Crust was able to cut its net operating costs in 1985 by 10%, despite facing increased prices for raw materials.

During most of that year, Aurora and Bill ran the operation on their own. Yet, Henrietta was only a phone call or visit away. "The doctor told her to slow down, but we had to deliver rolls of change to her at the hospital so she could phone us at the plant. I think the work probably kept her alive. She just decided she wasn't going to die and that was that." Aurora continues, "Mom was like a general and we were her foot soldiers . . . a general who stayed in the back and directed her soldiers from behind. She never lost faith. We just had to keep going."

Nevertheless, it was a difficult time for the new management team. As Bill says, "Aurora was always at the plant. Henrietta was ill, and I was adjusting. I packed my bags eight times during the first six months. It was a really tough time." Meanwhile,

Aurora was struggling to imitate her mother's soft and diplomatic style, a manner she found difficult to adopt. "I did have, and I still do have, a tendency to overkill . . . to take everything I don't want to the front door and chuck it out. My mother is a little more rational. I was lucky that when I started to come on as a pile driver, my mother would hold onto my shirt."

Expansion

The renewed efforts in the frozen pizza crust line created tremendous customer response. To capitalize on this market potential, the plant required a major overhaul to meet the increased production demands. Although the company was in the midst of financial recovery, both Aurora and Henrietta realized that the company had to launch a capital expansion program if they were going to aggressively rebuild their business. "Mom is a real risk-taker," says Aurora. "When all her wheels are off the cliff, she steps on the gas." The bulk of the program was dedicated to a new $250 000 spiral cooling system for the 1400-square-meter plant. This would allow the plant to operate around the clock, increasing the number of shifts from five to seventeen a week. Production increased to over 20 million (whole wheat and white flour) crusts a year in ten different sizes, from 13-centimeter rounds to 30-centimeter $\times$ 40-centimeter rectangles.

However, no one realized how complex the project was going to become. It began to raise more questions than answers. How were they going to get the new conveyor belt into the building? What were they going to do with their existing freezer space? How were they going to store their inventory now that the spiral cooling conveyor belt had taken over their storage area? As Aurora says, "What started off as a change in equipment, ended up being a total plant overhaul. As we started to put in the spiral, we realized that we were going to have to change the building and the entire production setup."

The management team decided to go to the employees for suggestions, and they were amazed at the quality and quantity of ideas they received. Through this process, the staff became reassured that this new system was not going to replace any workers. Deluca-Weinlein continually emphasized how the increased production capabilities of the spiral cooling system would improve the efficiency of the plant, and therefore, its productivity. "The more involved style of leadership created 'mixed reviews' among staff at the time," says Aurora. "However, by the time I started doing these things, people knew that I was here to help. The minute this crew knew that I wanted to rebuild the pizza crust line, they would do anything I asked." The employees did not feel any real impact since they had never had much responsibility for any of the plant's operations. "I didn't really take responsibility back from them," Deluca-Weinlein says. "I oversaw it with them." In the end, there were no staff casualties. Instead, the company had to hire more staff to man the additional shifts.

Their planning had also underestimated the unforeseen costs such as a new $20 000 transformer box that was needed to power the new equipment. Initial estimates of $160 000 ended up costing $250 000. In the end, Virga financed the project with $125 000 of her own money and a $125 000 loan from her flour supplier, Ellison Milling. This latter arrangement is a tribute to the type of relationship Henrietta had built with those around her.

Looking back at the expansion, everyone believes it could not have occurred at a better time or in a more efficient manner. As a result, the spiral cooling system achieved a two-year payback. Pizza crust sales rose from $1.8 million in 1984 to $2.3 million in 1985. That year the company was able to show a slim profit.

With the core business improving, along with Henrietta's health, the management team moved ahead with their expansion plans. These included further product diversification and market expansion. Virga decided to revive the mission she had entered the business with—to diversify the company into a related product line. The product that most interested her was fresh pasta, which enjoyed a wide-open and untapped market. To mass retail her light "homemade" pasta, Virga used a vacuum pack called Controlled Atmosphere Packaging (C.A.P.). This involved removing the original air and replacing it with an 80/20 nitrogen/oxygen mix.

She soon realized that her innovation was not without problems. Her original formula created too much moisture in the package, causing the pasta to become moldy. By the time she realized this, her competitors had caught up. Olivari Ravioli Mfg. Ltd., a major competitor, solved the moisture problem and contracted a food broker to take the pasta to the retail market. Canadian Pizza Crust's ability to respond in a similar fashion was inhibited by the cash drain from the finished pizza business. Although Virga took pride in being the first to experiment with vacuum-packed pasta, she concludes, "Sometimes it doesn't pay to be first. Our competitors usually follow us in ideas; however, you need to have strong financial backing to take these ideas to market in a big way."

It appeared that Dartnell and Brown were sending conflicting messages regarding the pasta's potential success to Aurora and her mother. This growing concern led the management team to further analyze their sales information. In an out-and-out confrontation involving all parties, it was decided to replace the two sales positions with outside assistance – in the form of Perco Sales, a well established and trusted food brokerage company. Henrietta was forced to abandon her fresh pasta product.

The company then cautiously set about developing two new products – a microwave-compatible pizza crust and a pizza sauce. Virga notes, "The pasta experience forced us to dig deeper into the crust business, to really go out after it and other products we knew to be successful. We decided to stick with what we knew best."

In 1985, Bill, a gourmet cook, had joined Henrietta in the kitchen to develop a pizza sauce that was different from the Virga Pizza Sauce. He had come to the conclusion that Canadians preferred a sweeter-tasting sauce to the more tart Virga product. One of the challenges facing the two cooks was how to create a sauce recipe that had to be modified each time the volume was increased. As Bill recalls, "It got to the point that you dreaded lunch because there was going to be another pizza test for the sauce."

They finally agreed on a recipe they believed to be a winner. Their guess proved right; the sauce went on to win every competitive taste test in which it was entered. Rather than continue with the production of the sauce in outside kitchens, they invested in the equipment to produce the sauce in Canadian Pizza Crust's plant. In the fall of 1985, they took the sauce to market in 398-milliliter jars. It was so well received that they decided to attract more sales by using 5-, 10- and 16-liter reusable pails, rather than the Virga sauce tins. The longer storage capability of the pails and the fact that they can be reused have proved advantageous for their deli and restaurant customers. The company also capitalized on packaging the pails under the brand names of the grocery outlets.

Their strategy paid off. Over an 18-month period, their B.C. distributor jumped from ordering 100 pails to 500. In 1988, this product grossed a quarter of a million dollars, while the 398-milliliter jars registered over $300 000 in sales. As a result of the success of the higher margin Luigi sauce, the Virga sauce has been gradually phased out.

The company's product development projects have provided the Virga family with invaluable lessons. They have learned to go slow until the right product is ready and they have the necessary financial backing in place. They've realized that without a significant injection of funds, the packaging and marketing costs alone can bankrupt the very best of products.

The Canadian Pizza Crust's success in 1985 continued into the following year. With a clean bill of health, Virga and her management team continued the rebuilding strategies they had started the year before. Their efforts paid off in '86 with a 54% increase in pizza crust sales and a 22% increase in total sales. The crust business had increased from 75% of total sales in 1985 to 95% in 1986. The new sales high of $3.8 million brought the net profit back to the 1983 levels. As the company moved into 1987, it employed 60 people, compared to the 26 employed in 1984.

Spurred on by their growing success, Virga, Weinlein, and Frank Medrano went on the road visiting Europe, Australia, the Far East, and the U.S. to find new markets and distributors.

By September 1987, they realized that the U.S. market potential was too large to service from Canada. In an effort to establish a U.S. West Coast operation, Henrietta journeyed to Los Angeles to look into some bakery equipment that had been sold by a bankrupt manufacturer. She concluded her discussions with Zetlain Inc., the bakery that was storing the equipment, with an agreement to purchase the equipment, rent the bakery's unused space, and share their other equipment to produce pizza crusts during the day. The deal greatly appealed to the Zetlain bakery, as it would be able to use the Virga equipment for its night shift bread production. The agreement in place, the Virga Pizza Crust Company of California was formed with Frank Medrano, the U.S. sales manager, in charge of expanding the company's U.S. market. Frank hired a sales consultant, Joe Loopo, to assist him as well as Ralph Petrillo, a San Francisco food broker.

Aside from their existing American customer base, there was a large subsidized school lunch program in the U.S. that alone had the potential of $20 million in sales. The U.S. sales team optimistically estimated that the Virga Pizza Crust Company of California could make $10 million a year if it capitalized on the $20-million school lunch program. Even though the company conservatively downscaled the estimates to $3 million, the expansion appeared too risky for the Royal Bank, Canadian Pizza Crust's Canadian bank. The most they were willing to do was to back a letter of credit for an American bank.

Crisis #3

In January 1988, with the U.S. company on the verge of going into production, Henrietta's cancer flared up again. Her sudden illness took everyone by surprise, particularly Zetlain's management, who refused to establish a working relationship with the remaining members of Canadian Pizza Crust's management team. "The Zetlain people who had cooperated with my mother wouldn't talk to me after she became ill. I'm on the phone and they are saying, 'I only want to talk with Henrietta.' "

In March 1988 Weinlein decided to take a personal look at

the situation. On his arrival in Los Angeles, he quickly became aware that a crisis had developed in the U.S. company. Medrano's quiet sales style had produced scant results in the aggressive California market. Their sales consultant, Joe Loopo, had only sold 32 cases of pizza over a six-month period. The plant equipment, badly in need of maintenance, had created a complete production slowdown. Bill also discovered that their landlord was working in collaboration with Loopo to compete against them in the lucrative school lunch program contract. A hard lesson had to be learned when Canadian Pizza Crust's management realized that, regardless of the circumstances, they had to pay Loopo for the duration of his six-month contract due to a missing performance clause in their agreement.

Although Bill went into high gear to resolve the problems and gain new contracts, by June 1, he realized that both time and money had run out. As Aurora describes the situation, "When my mother became ill, that was the icing on the cake. What the Zetlain people didn't realize was that Bill and I were not about to let them take the U.S. company even if it meant shutting it down." They either had to close the California plant or risk bankrupting Canadian Pizza Crust. Henrietta sadly concurred with their decision to get out. There was now the problem of getting back their two million dollars worth of equipment. "Zetlain was essentially holding the equipment hostage," says Bill. After fruitless negotiations, Bill rented a truck and 'stole' their equipment back. He recalls, "It was like 'mission impossible' . . . black slacks . . . black sneakers . . . chain clippers . . . the works."

Putting the California situation behind them, the Canadian management team felt that the worst was past. However, they soon discovered that their bank was deeply worried about their financial security due to the failure of the American expansion. Deluca-Weinlein explains, "They didn't like the fact that we went in. They liked the idea even less that we pulled out!" To make things worse, their account manager had also changed. Their former account manager had understood their business, while his replacement was strictly a "numbers man." "This was the end of our relationship with the Royal Bank," says Aurora.

"Within a couple of weeks, the company had established a new banking arrangement with the Bank of Nova Scotia, who believed Canadian Pizza Crust could weather the near-term financial difficulties."

The jarring closure of the California operation brought home to Henrietta, Aurora, and Bill, the lesson that Andrew Virga had refused to learn. "You can't run a company from a distance," Aurora concludes. "You need to be on-site to control everything that is going on, at least until you have a management team in place that you have trained and have grown to trust. Only then can you believe that these people will operate the business as if it was their own."

Henrietta continues, "Expansion, whether it be in new products or new operations, requires solid financial backing. You will only fail if you do not have either a supportive, flexible bank that is willing to work as a business development partner, or a private investor/joint venture arrangement that will bankroll your ideas." It finally struck home that they needed management control and financial support if they were going to expand and increase profitability in a mature market.

Aurora knew that unless the company paid rapid attention to its overhead and profit margins, 1988 and 1989 would see them drop into the red again. Applying the lessons she had learned from the first turnaround, she reviewed all her customer accounts to determine her money-making and money-losing accounts. "I dumped our small margin accounts, including our largest U.S. customer," explains Aurora. "The Canada-U.S. exchange rates were starting to kill us. I knew it wouldn't be long before it would start costing us money to sell crusts to these customers."

These sales reductions had an immediate impact on the company's product schedule. "We dropped from an average of eleven shifts a week to an average of seven," says Aurora. "The night shift was the hardest hit since we went from five shifts a week to between two and three." Since the Virga family has always cared deeply for its employees, such reductions in take-home pay worried Aurora. To offset the financial concerns of her night shift employees, Aurora registered in the workshare program with U.I.C. This has allowed those employees forced to take a cut in pay to receive U.I.C. benefits for the evenings they no longer work.

To help the management team more rigorously oversee the operation and its overhead, two long-term employees, Marvin Salvail and Mike Lundregren, were promoted to the management positions of bakery manager and plant manager. Strict budgets were installed and the office staff was reduced by 50%.

Canadian Pizza Crust's cost-cutting measures paid off. Although the company experienced a significant loss in California, they realized a small profit in 1988 with 1989's figures suggesting an even stronger profit picture, despite the lower sales revenue.

The company revamped their entire retail product and in August 1989 will be replacing the traditional Marco Polo Frozen Pizza Crusts with a deep dish crust. A large sales effort is currently underway to add high margin accounts to their customer base especially in the U.S. They've hired Bruce Bouer, a master food broker, in Los Angeles to help the company broaden its sales out of the commodity market associated with school lunch programs. Bill has continued his marketing effort in the Pacific Rim countries and is putting the final touches to a large Taipei account. They have learned the hard way that success comes from having more than one strategy in motion. "You have to always be focused on your costs. But remember, you can only cut costs so far," says Aurora, "then you have to add aggressive marketing."

The couple are rigorously following every lesson they have learned from dealing with long-distance brokers, including written performance clauses that demand sales productivity from their brokers. Determined not to be caught again by fast-talking sales people and joint venture players, this older but wiser, management team have replaced their open, trusting attitude with a more cautious, skeptical approach to business. As to financial support, the management team are involved in an ongoing search for the right type of financial backer who will help them expand their horizons. "And I want to stop working 20-hour days," says Aurora with a touch of fatigue in her voice.

The Key to Success: Teamwork

Henrietta Virga attributes the company's ability to bounce back to teamwork. Deluca-Weinlein concurs, "My mother truly believes in people. She has a lot of trust in me and everybody here. She lets me make mistakes without pouncing on me . . . always telling me why she didn't like what I was doing."

Virga adds, "We have always run the business very much like a family. I have stressed that we have to help one another. We're lucky. We have people who really want to do the job right. It's not hard. It's the little things like sitting down and having lunch with them. It's treating them like they are human beings."

The mother and daughter combination of personalities and style has played a special role in and outside of the company. Henrietta's leadership focused Canadian Pizza Crust and its employees on the "big picture" of where the business was going, while Aurora's practical management style kept the day-to-day operations on track. In putting Aurora's role into perspective, Henrietta says, "My father would never have allowed Aurora to run the company . . . only if she was a son, and even then he would have stepped on her. I have let Aurora run the company freely. There are things I haven't liked, but you have to live with that."

In Tribute

Throughout all of the twists and turns of the business, Henrietta Virga remained totally committed and involved. She never lost sight of her goals. She never gave up the fight to continue the legacy her father had started. Her approach to her illness was the same: she fought all the way. On December 17, 1988, Henrietta died in Vancouver at the age of 43. Her warmth, sincerity, and charisma will be greatly missed, not only by her family, friends, employees, and customers, but by anyone who had the fortune to come into contact with her. Her daughter Aurora, the new owner and president, has large shoes to fill. Henrietta's legacy to her was probably the greatest gift of all—her indomitable spirit. "I probably learned more from my mother in a short time than most people learn from their mother in a lifetime. I've learned that being a little more patient is a better way to be."

Snapshot of Canadian Pizza Crust

Crisis (May 1983):

Company has experienced a 56% drop in profits and the loss of 75% of its original customer base due to diversification into finished pizza business. By 1984 yearend, it registers a $64 000 loss.

Turnaround Strategy:

- Assume 100% ownership of Vancouver subsidiary
- Rename company
- Bring in new management team
- Discontinue finished pizza line and re-establish frozen pizza crust business
- Install a $250 000 capital expansion project
- Implement cost-cutting and streamlining programs
- Rebuild customer base mostly through personal contact
- With base business intact, add a successful new product line
- Establish Virga Pizza Crust Company of California

Crisis (June 1988):

Virga Pizza Crust Company of California aborted due to lack of sales and problems with plant landlords. Royal Bank of Canada applies pressure due to lost revenue from U.S. plant closure.

Turnaround Strategy:

- Relinquish low-margin customer accounts
- Reduce number of production shifts
- Reduce office staff by 50%

Result: A streamlined, cost-effective operation with an increasingly strong profit picture despite lower sales revenues.

National Sea Products:

Refitting the Ship

"Have you ever been to sea, Billy?" For many Canadians, these words raise the image of a weather-beaten Captain as he alludes to the romance of the sea for the benefit of an earnest and all ears little boy. In the middle of October 1983, these same words were pounding in the ears of Bill Morrow, the president of National Sea. For Morrow, however, the "sea" was no longer a reference to the pulsing waves of tidal waters in a commercial for one of his company's products. It was the sea of debt that was washing over his 83-year-old family business. A total accumulated debt of $244 million, an inventory of $122 million worth of unsold fish, and a net loss of $17.3 million for 1983 all added up to a tidal wave that was about to drown Canada's largest fish processing company. The triple whammy, as Morrow refers to high interest rates, low prices, and high inventories of fish, triggered not only the worst crisis in the history of National Sea, but also in the volatile and troubled East Coast fishery.

Morrow's storm had been raging since 1981 when H.B.

Nickerson and Sons Limited, a major competitor and strangely enough NatSea's controlling shareholder, had overextended itself and had been using NatSea's assets and once healthy balance sheet as its lifeline. What had once been a simple business of harvesting and processing fish had turned into a corporate and political quagmire, which was about to turn a freestanding entrepreneurial organization into a pseudo-nationalized arm of the federal and provincial governments.

The struggle for survival that Bill Morrow and his management team now faced had as much to do with the complexity of the fishing industry as it had to do with corporate maneuvers. By the time the fishery collapsed in 1981, the Bank of Nova Scotia alone was sitting with close to $400 million worth of loans to the industry, without taking into account the financing provided by the federal and provincial governments. Rod McCulloch, a senior partner of Clarkson Gordon at the time, and now NatSea's senior vice president of finance, describes the series of events that led to the Dome Petroleum of the fishing industry as "a situation where free enterprise was carried out to the ultimate of ridiculousness."

The Canadian fishery involves a series of connections that begins with one of the world's greatest natural fishery resources and ends with one of the largest and most accessible markets to the south – the United States. It has always been an industry of great unrealized potential. Although Canada has significant fishing activity, our total catch represents an insignificant amount compared with the rest of the world. Uncontrollable variables, such as market price, interest rates, and exchange rates, have long since created an industry that is as unpredictable as the sea itself. Like the waves of the ocean, the only certainty is that each peak will be followed by a valley, thus creating a continuous cyclical effect. The economics of the industry give scant security to its workers or small producers. Short heady peaks in catch and market price followed by subsistence living have never allowed these people to maintain a lifestyle much above the poverty line.

In the years leading up to the 1970s, tough international competition from the large and technologically advanced Russian and European fleets further ate away at Canada's market position. Not only were these fleets able to outfish and outprocess the Canadians, they also were taking their resource from the lucrative fishing banks off Canada's shores. The 19-kilometer limit had become a meaningless restriction as the centuries-old tradition of distant water fishing by the international fleets had overfished Canada's banks. Canadian harvesting costs escalated as their out-of-date fleets had to sail farther and farther from shore. As luck would have it, costs were rising while market prices were softening.

By the mid-1970s, the Canadian fishermen's cry of rape was finally heard. Canada toughened its negotiating stance on the international level, and in 1977 established the 320-kilometer limit that at last forced out foreign fleets. Suddenly the Canadian fishery felt it had a new lease on life. With the boom to bust mentality inherent in the industry, many executives and entrepreneurial fishermen fell into the Klondike mentality of building fishing boats and processing plants. Negative interest rates induced more borrowing. This was spurred on by the Canadian chartered banks, eager to redeploy their oil and gas money. The federal government and the four Atlantic provincial governments were also not blind to the political advantages of revitalizing the fishery.

In the sober reality of today, such long-term debt-to-equity ratios seem totally irresponsible. The warning signs were there, but nobody was paying any attention. All around strange things were happening, including the takeover of National Sea by H.B. Nickerson and Sons Limited. As Gerald Regan, Nova Scotia's former premier suggested, it was a matter of "the horse swallowing the elephant."

The Horse and the Elephant

By the time Jeremiah Nickerson started his company in 1945, National Sea had been in the business for 46 years. After a brief period of joint venturing, Jeremiah declared his independence from the established corporate entity of National Sea. H.B. Nickerson and Sons remained a modestly successful Cape

Breton-based company until Jeremiah's son, Jerry, joined the firm in 1959 with aggressive growth ideas. The arrival of his brother, Harold, in 1969 added fuel to the corporate expansion plans, aided by large injections of government funds. During the mid-1970s, Jerry Nickerson began acquiring NatSea stock. By 1976 Nickersons had acquired ownership of approximately 10% of NatSea's outstanding shares.

Meanwhile, Sobey's, another large Maritime family business, had been doing its own fair share of buying – to the tune of 39% of NatSea. In the early spring of 1977, the same year that the 320-kilometer limit was instituted, Empire Co. Ltd., the Sobey investment entity, created a 21-year voting trust together with the Nickersons. The two Maritime businesses then assumed control of National Sea.

Takeover bids were not new to Bill Morrow, who had been with the company since 1953. When Morrow was appointed president in 1969, he represented the third generation of one of the founding families. It was in the midst of one such bid from Ward Foods, a Midwest U.S. bakery, that he had become president at 39 years of age. Morrow was part of the "new ideas" generation of NatSea, at a time when the older management shareholders were interested in liquidating their shares for a good price. He managed to skillfully stop the Ward deal by putting together a private share offering of the key block owned by Samuel Fingold, the owner of Salada and president of Slater Steel.

Morrow knew that he could not stop this takeover attempt. He had declined the invitation to join the voting trust, when it was made clear that the offer was extended to him alone. His sense of integrity would not allow him to make any agreement without the inclusion of his management group and major shareholders. In June 1977, Morrow proposed that NatSea's existing management join with Nickersons to buy out Sobey. Jerry Nickerson replied that he was not interested.

Morrow knew it wouldn't be long before one of the controlling shareholders would take charge. When the Nickersons bought out the Sobey interest in early August of 1977, Harold Nickerson was surprised by Morrow's response. "Harold walked into my office," recalls Morrow, "one Monday morning about quarter to eight. The door wasn't even unlocked. I kind of kidded him that he was up early, but I already knew exactly what he was there for." What the new owner did not know was that Morrow had been tipped off by a source in the Bank of Nova Scotia that the Nickersons and Sobeys had struck a buy-sell deal by which one party could buy out the other before October 15, 1977. The only joy that Morrow could muster at this point was his control of the situation, if not the company. "Harold," he said, "I know that you closed that deal last Thursday." Nickerson was indeed taken aback. "You can't have any secrets in this business," Morrow coyly told him. When Morrow was asked if he wanted to stay on, he replied without much hesitation, "I was born into the fish business and I'm too young to retire." Jerry Nickerson assumed the position of chairman of the board of National Sea and Harold was appointed a board member. Morrow was given the instruction to run NatSea as he always had, in competition to Nickersons.

The takeover sent shock waves throughout the Atlantic fishing industry. The Nickersons, relative unknowns in Nova Scotia's financial community, had been able to finance 56% ownership of National Sea with a loan from the Bank of Nova Scotia. "The only big fishing company the Bank of Nova Scotia did not have on the East Coast was National Sea," explains Morrow. "This is why they loaned the Nickersons 100% of the capital to buy the stock of National Sea." This financial arrangement would eventually trigger NatSea's financial demise in 1983.

Armed with National Sea, Nickersons continued its buying and expansion spree, building and acquiring vessels and processing plants throughout Atlantic Canada. In their rush to obtain existing licenses, all small fishing communities became targets for partnerships or buyouts. As one Newfoundland plant manager explains, "Their judgment became questionable. These may have been good places to catch rabbits, but there were no fish."

Nickersons was not alone in its haste to take on large capital expenditures. From 1977 to 1979, the big five East Coast fish companies (National Sea, H.B. Nickersons, Fishery Products,

The Lake Group Ltd., and John Penny & Sons) doubled their asset base from $200 million to $400 million. By the early 1980s, there were 600 fish plants throughout the Atlantic provinces, triple the number operating in the mid-1970s. NatSea also rode the high waves of the late '70s, despite the culture clash it experienced with its new owners over customer relations and product quality. The flamboyant and highly leveraged style of the Nickersons conflicted with the conservative and frugal philosophy of National Sea's founding families. NatSea met this challenge by continuing to do the three things it did best — producing a quality product, maintaining a firm customer orientation, and harvesting aggressively.

This phase in the history of the fisheries was the epitome of a free-for-all. Under the "Olympic" fishing strategy, each species of catch was allocated an annual quota, known as the Total Allowable Catch, or TAC. The Olympic system forced fishermen to harvest as much of the annual quota for each species as quickly as they could, before its TAC was reached by their competitors. As Maureen Yeadon, vice president of fleet, explains, "The result was that good ice and weather conditions along with high catch rates would find the whole fleet tied up by the end of February, with nothing to do. This forced the onshore fish processing plants into outrageous peak production periods that would fall off to nothing once the vessels were tied up." While the TAC system stimulated growth in the large offshore fleets (vessels of 30 meters or more), it had an even greater impact on the inshore fishing fleet (vessels under 20 meters), which increased by 82% between 1975 and 1981, mostly financed by debt. The boom in activity brought with it excessive amounts of fish for sale. Inventories of processed frozen fish started to build along with the interest rates, which were rising to a record high of 20%. The significant drop in poultry prices in American supermarkets, along with the flood of fish in the market and the general decrease of fish consumption, added to the already depressed fish prices. The increasing value of the Canadian and U.S. dollars against the European currencies, suddenly made Canadian fish more expensive than its competitors' fish in the vital American market. The result? Nobody was buying the fish National Sea was selling during the highest catch year in the company's history—1981. To make things worse, carrying charges on fish storage jumped past 20%.

Navigating through Troubled Waters

By the beginning of 1981, it became evident to the Bank of Nova Scotia that falling fish prices, escalating interest rates, and excessively high inventories were strangling the East Coast fish companies. The primary subject of the emergency meeting of the bank's directors in St. John's, Newfoundland, in the spring of 1981, was how the bank was going to handle the $250 million of fishery loans about to go sour on them.

The explosive years of expansion now quickly turned on H.B. Nickerson and Sons. Under the pressure of defaulting loan repayments, Jerry Nickerson approached Bill Morrow in a seemingly casual airport conversation offering to sell him some of the Nickerson assets. After some consideration, National Sea expressed an interest in only two of the assets, which Nickerson was offering at $65 million. This amount equaled three-quarters of Nickersons' debt load. Since the Morrow counter offer of $30 million was significantly lower than the asking price, Merrill Lynch was hired to come up with a "fairness of opinion." Their substantially lower assessment of $16.5 million further complicated the deal.

Morrow began to feel pressure on all sides, to the point that the pro-Jerry directors on the NatSea board were threatening him with being forced to resign or being fired if he did not help the Nickersons out by purchasing the assets at a higher price than the Merrill Lynch recommendation. All of these negotiations came to an abrupt halt when George Hitchman, former vice chairman of the Bank of Nova Scotia, was brought out of retirement to spearhead the bank's recovery of its loan money. Hitchman's first decision was to fire Merrill Lynch before they had submitted their final formal opinion on the worth of the Nickerson assets. This would be one of many aggressive moves made by the bank's chief negotiator, including the firing of the Clarkson Gordon consultant, who the bank itself had hired, when he recommended that the bank wash $49 million in loans in order for NatSea to take over the operations of a number of Newfoundland fish companies. While further negotiations of this nature were aborted, the open dislike between the negotiating parties – Jerry Nickerson, George Hitchman, and Bill Morrow – began to grow.

By the fall of 1981, the depression in the fishing industry had forced NatSea to lay off 1800 fish plant employees. By the time the rest of the industry had followed suit, a total of 4000 workers were unemployed.

Meanwhile, the bank's involvement was growing. On December 22, 1981, the Bank of Nova Scotia assumed the power of attorney for H.B. Nickerson and Sons, giving the bank the major shareholder position in NatSea. Taking control, Hitchman threatened to call in all outstanding industry loans. This was the trigger for the federal government to step in. Both the federal and provincial governments had to face the fact that the East Coast fishery was about to collapse, taking 44 000 jobs down with it. Immediate action was required.

In February 1982, Prime Minister Pierre Elliott Trudeau reacted with the appointment of one of his closest advisors, Michael Kirby, to head up a commission to investigate the fishing industry. While Kirby and his task force researched all angles of the fishery, troubled times did not stop for NatSea.

NatSea's problems at this point didn't arise from financial losses, but from the company's slim 1981 profits. In a year when all other East Coast fish companies experienced significant losses, the company had been able to keep its head above water. In June 1982, the Bank of Nova Scotia decided to take advantage of NatSea's performance. It instructed the company to lease two old fish processing plants from Nickersons and to follow through with a questionable marketing agreement. This arrangement required NatSea to sell not only their own product, but all of Nickersons as well. To add salt to the wound, NatSea was given no control over the types of species to be fished by Nickersons and was instructed to pay cash up front for all the product. This meant that the company had to come up with hard cash for product that NatSea already had inventoried. As might be expected, this angered Bill Morrow and his struggling company. "With our own heavy inventory in a sloppy market, we got a case of indigestion from trying to take on these extra responsibilities. The agreement didn't work out as expected due to not only the inventory, but the questionable quality of the Nickerson product. We wasted a lot of time arguing about fairness of pricing. We ended up being taken advantage of."

The battle heated up when Hitchman ordered a third party assessment of the quantity, quality, and market value of the inventoried fish. Out of an inventory valued at $122 million, NatSea's own estimate had only varied by $463 from the consultant's estimate. But it had cost the company close to a third of a million dollars to make the assessment.

In an effort to liquidate part of its debt, the bank decided to take action on the size of the inventories. "They hated seeing inventory in anyone's books," says Morrow. "They started to treat us as though we were bankrupt, and we weren't. In 1982, National Sea still had about $40 million in net equity. A lot of our Scandinavian friends were asking what we were doing selling our product so cheap when we should have been out there trying to get the market up. We were ordered by Hitchman to get rid of it [the inventory], no matter what the cost; after all it was his money. This is what escalated the spiral downward."

Throughout 1982, while NatSea and Nickersons were struggling to survive, Kirby and his task force were hard at work. In November 1982, they submitted their report, entitled "Navigating through Troubled Waters." Although the 57 recommendations appeared to address the critical problems, the report was unsuccessful in resolving the very deep-rooted issues about which it wrote. It didn't, for example, answer the fundamental question—does the fishing industry exist to support local employment or to achieve its own economic viability?

In early 1983, Kirby reconvened the brightest of the task force members—Peter John Nicholson, Jack Hart, and David

Mann. Their mandate was to deal with the most pressing issue—what to do to prevent the region's major fishing enterprises from collapsing. They were instructed to bring together all the critical participants—the major fishing companies, the banks, and the federal and provincial governments. Their task was to recommend a restructured fishing industry, designed to at least keep the fishery alive, if not the fish companies.

For months, newspapers had been filled with the prospects of government involvement in the fishery. One such recommendation came from Brian Peckford, then premier of Newfoundland. He advocated the creation of one super company combining all the offshore trawler fleets. It would be owned and controlled by the federal and provincial governments, the banks, and the 27 000 member Newfoundland Fishermen, Food, and Allied Workers Union. Peckford's self-acclaimed "revolutionary way of looking at the fishing industry" slapped current shareholders with the charge that they had not reinvested their profits in plant modernization and upgrading, and had tolerated poor management practices. As such, Peckford claimed that they "should not be rewarded for their failures."

The first official word on the restructuring of the East Coast fishery came on September 26, 1983, with the announcement of the establishment of Fishery Products International, a new Newfoundland super fish company, which included the assets of seven Newfoundland fish companies and the Nickersons' Nova Scotia-based scallop fleet. The federal government's injection of $75.3 million gave it 60% ownership, while the provincial government assumed 25% with its conversion of $31.5 million worth of debt to equity. The Bank of Nova Scotia claimed 15% with its conversion of debt to equity. Bill Morrow reviewed the restructuring with deep concern. The blatant absence of any of the existing owners of the Newfoundland fish companies in the agreement warned him of deals yet to come.

Less than a month later, the Kirby task force was ready to present its recommendations for National Sea Products. The future already looked bleak with the prospect of the Bank of Nova Scotia calling in more than $100 million in outstanding loans, and traditional suppliers asking for cash before or on delivery. On October 16, 1983, the day that Morrow remembers as the beginning of the turnaround, Michael Kirby brought all the necessary parties together to gain acceptance of NatSea's restructuring into a pseudo-nationalized rather than privately owned company. The task force knew that NatSea would not like the proposed resolution, which recommended that 75% of the newly restructured National Sea be owned by the federal government, the Nova Scotia government, and the Bank of Nova Scotia. As Morrow listened to the proposal, he realized it was even worse than he had expected. Unless he and the other private shareholders were able to come up with $22 million, their investment of 43.5% would be reduced to an insignificant 6.8%. As disastrous as the recommendation was for the private investors, Kirby and his task force did not expect the company to come up with any other alternative. After all, what private investor would be interested in such a bleak prospect?

Pulling the Rabbit out of the Hat

What the task force had not realized was that behind Bill Morrow's gentlemanly exterior lurked a tenacious man who was not about to be lumped in with the other executives being blamed for the demise of the fishing industry. Morrow had been doing his own digging for a private sector solution and had found one – David Hennigar, the head of a $3.5-billion family financial empire of far-ranging corporate activity. As grandson of the well-known Nova Scotia industrialist, Roy Jodrey, Hennigar was and still is one of eastern Canada's most important investors.

Hennigar's interest should not have come as a surprise to the bank. He had recommended a takeover when the Bank of Nova Scotia had initially become involved. Hitchman passed him off to Jerry Nickerson, who flatly refused any such maneuver. Hennigar continued to be rebuffed by McLeod Young Weir, professional advisors appointed by the federal government. During their search for financial alternatives, Hennigar was never approached, raising the question of whether the federal government was ever interested in a private sector solution.

Armed with the knowledge that Hennigar was ready to fight for his 12.5% shareholder position, Morrow requested some additional time to come up with a private sector alternative. Immediately after the October meeting, he called Hennigar to inform him of the disappointing recommendation, and the task force's approval for a short adjournment. The battle, at least for a short time, was still alive.

While the NatSea restructuring committee continued with the bank and government negotiations, Morrow and Hennigar moved into action. Meeting after meeting with private sector and government officials produced frustrating results. Finally Hennigar had to threaten Pierre DeBané, the federal fisheries minister, with legal action and press exposure unless a private investment deal was seriously sought. DeBané, who had been consistently denying to the press that any private investors were interested, was forced to listen. Hennigar contended that the government projections of financial recovery were based on false assumptions. He believed that the company would be able to regain profitability on a much faster basis than was being proposed. Although DeBané began to demonstrate some openness to a private sector alternative, he made it clear that Hennigar's proposed investment of $10 million was too low.

To add to NatSea's private investors' worries, in late November 1983 Ottawa shepherded a bill through Parliament authorizing it to spend $455 million—in the form of cash, loan guarantees, and conversion to debt equity—to finance the restructuring of the East Coast fishery into two super-companies in Newfoundland and Nova Scotia. The main shareholders were to be the federal and provincial governments and the Bank of Nova Scotia. The reality of the super-company structure became even more apparent when Hennigar and Morrow met with the Bank of Nova Scotia's chairman, Cedric Ritchie, and president, Gordon Bell, in December 1983. At this meeting, the bank refused to deal.

The Royal Bank of Canada was a different story. It had been National Sea's banker since 1920, when Bill Morrow's father had borrowed $250 for the purchase of five shares in a

Lunenburg fishing company. When the Bank of Nova Scotia assumed controlling interest of NatSea, the Royal had been pushed into the background. They had been left out of all the restructuring discussions with the other bank, much to their anger and that of NatSea's management. On January 4, 1984, the Royal decided to support the private investors. As Morrow remembers, "Dave Hennigar couldn't believe it when we walked into the Royal Bank and were told, 'You get rid of the Bank of Nova Scotia as your major shareholder, and you've got $100 million [in an operating line of credit].'" The Bank of Nova Scotia was not impressed. On January 6, 1984, they publicly refused to negotiate further with Hennigar.

As the war between private and public sector ownership raged in the newspapers, Hennigar worked tirelessly, zigzagging across Canada, trying to put together a deal. Finally, he approached Sobey's, whose buyout by the Nickersons had eventually led to the NatSea demise. The Jodrey-Sobey relationship was already well established through joint real estate ventures as well as by their mutual distaste of government intervention and their loyalty to the province of Nova Scotia. Together, the Hennigar-Sobey group decided to tackle the Bank of Nova Scotia. Again, hardball was the name of the game. The bank refused a 48-hour extension on their January 12 deadline. The bank was now in the position to foreclose if its $75-million loan was not repaid by January 26.

The only recourse for the private investors was to turn to a political solution. Meeting with Deputy Prime Minister Allan MacEachen, Premier John Buchanan, Nova Scotia Development Minister Roland Thornhill, and the private investors, David Hennigar outlined his proposal and emphasized that he would pursue legal action if his recommendation was refused. They now agreed to take his proposal seriously.

As the deal-making rounded the final corner, the private investors jacked up their offer by 100% to a total of $20 million. They then went after a bank that would be willing to buy the company's $75 million worth of difficulty-preferred shares. (These are term-preferred shares that are offered at approximately half prime, but their dividends are tax-free.) Since the Royal Bank was not in the position to accept further tax writeoffs, the Toronto Dominion Bank purchased the shares, to be paid back in three equal installments between 1987 and 1989. This was the same deal that the Bank of Nova Scotia had refused six weeks earlier.

On February 6, the financial package, already endorsed by the federal and provincial governments, was presented to National Sea's board of directors for their approval. The terms of the agreement were as follows:

1. The private investment group would provide $20 million in new investment in return for $15 million worth of the company's common shares and $5 million in preferred shares. This translated into 47% share ownership by Scotia Investments Limited (the Jodreys), Empire Company Limited (the Sobeys), and Isleview Investments Limited (the Morrows).
2. The Nova Scotia government would convert $25 million of its $34-million total debt in H.B. Nickerson and Sons Limited and National Sea debt into equity. Five million dollars would go into preferred shares in National Sea and $20 million into preferred shares in the Canso fish plant, a former Nickerson asset which stood with a $13-million defaulted loan.
3. The federal government would pay $80 million to the Bank of Nova Scotia to release from debt National Sea and F.P.I. (the new Newfoundland fish company). In addition, they would voluntarily place, without request, $10 million in non-voting preferred shares in NatSea. In return for their investment, they would receive 20% ownership.
4. The Toronto Dominion Bank would agree to buy $75 million of difficulty term-preferred shares, which would be used to pay off the company's debt to the Bank of Nova Scotia.
5. The Royal Bank would reassume its banking relationship with the company, and with it, a $100-million line of credit.

At the end of the day, the new ownership structure was 47% held by the private investment group, 20% by the federal government, 14% by the Bank of Nova Scotia, and a common float of 19%. The Bank of Nova Scotia was the obvious winner in this restructuring. The first turning point had finally been reached.

A collective sigh of relief spread through National Sea. For months employees had mechanically gone about their jobs not knowing whether the next day would be their last. As one employee recounted, "You'd come into work, sit at your desk, and wait for the phone to ring, telling you to go home because the company had folded." Fear of the unknown had been compounded by a lack of information and direction. While the war between Nickerson and Sons, the NatSea management, and the financial backers raged, little attention had been given to the company's operations or its people. "The biggest tension," recounts Gail Levangie, assistant manager of packaging, "was not hearing anything from senior management as to what was happening. There was never a feeling that there was somebody at the helm."

While Bill Morrow's paternalistic management style had created a strong sense of fairness and company loyalty, his over-delegation had allowed a lack of employee accountability to take place. "The problem was that people would really become irresponsible and screw up, but nobody was ever fired," says Henry Demone, currently executive vice president of international and trading. Jerry Nickerson operated at the other end of the spectrum. Demone continues, "Jerry was the other way round. He had this huge operation underneath him, yet he always had to know what was going on everywhere. He would find someone three levels down and say, 'What the hell is going on in Belgium, or what happened on the third line in the North Sydney plant last night?' He carried this to such an extreme that no one had any self-confidence. It was the sort of organization where you were noticed only if you screwed up."

As Nickerson and Sons fell into more and more financial difficulty, NatSea became a holding bin for their excess employees, as well as their fish. Ingrid Jangaard, who joined the company in 1981, recalls, "People would go into Jerry Nickerson's office and come out with either their pink slip or a job in NatSea." When the crunch came and people had to be laid off, both NatSea and Nickerson employees came under the gun. The atmosphere became increasingly competitive. "Everybody was looking out for themselves," recounts one NatSea employee. "The deadwood became even more visible, particularly at the senior ranks. These individuals, who had been with NatSea for their entire working lives, had been able to handle their jobs when everything was going well. As soon as the company began to get into trouble, they didn't know what to do. They didn't have the necessary business experience to make the right decisions. Some of the decisions they were making to save money were simply ridiculous." Decisions to significantly cut back research, product development, advertising, and sales had robbed NatSea of its positioning in the marketplace, let alone its future.

The underlying problem was that nobody felt responsible for anything that was going on, the suspension of strategic and operating decisions had stripped accountability from everyone. Several temporary plant shutdowns and the permanent closure of the Halifax division had left the production employees with a feeling of powerlessness and job insecurity. Concern about long-term employment opportunities was compounded by the lack of mobility of these workers, whose families had lived for generations in small fishing communities where the fish plants were the mainstay of employment. The warring years with the Nickersons and the Bank of Nova Scotia had taken their toll on the company and its employees.

Refitting the Ship

By early 1984, Bill Morrow was exhausted. Instead of managing the company, he had spent three strenuous years fighting to keep it alive. In June 1984, five months after the restructuring deal had gone through, the company was projecting a $5-million loss. Hennigar was furious. He turned to Rod McCulloch, his Clarkson Gordon advisor, and demanded to know what had happened to the projections McCulloch had used for the basis of the $20-million investment. McCulloch called in his Toronto-based colleague, Gordon Cummings, who had been providing him with advice throughout the restructuring negotiations. "He didn't want me to rush," recalls Cummings. "He just wanted me down that night." As Cummings, at the time a senior partner with Woods Gordon, suggests, "By 1984, Bill had already turned the company around two or three times during his tenure as president. Now that the focus had to be directed towards turning NatSea around, he really wasn't up to it. This next one would have to be done by somebody else, which is where I came into the picture."

After two days interviewing members of the management team, McCulloch and Cummings were ready. "We went over to see Hennigar, to give him the good news," recalls Cummings. "We told him that the company was about to exceed his fondest expectations. Instead of losing $5 million, we were projecting a $15-million loss. Hennigar has since retold the story by saying that night he went home and cried and slept like a baby. That is, he slept for an hour, woke up, and cried for an hour. The next question," Cummings remembers, "was one consultants never want to answer–'Will it turn around or not?' Ultimately, you say one thing or another and then you get sued." Taking the risk, they stated that NatSea had the ability to do a lot better. They contended the problem was that the company didn't know where it was going. The lack of leadership, drive, and focus had produced an operating committee that was sitting back waiting for things to change.

They cited the Enterprise Allocation System as one example. It was evident that NatSea was not taking advantage of this new quota system, introduced as a result of the Kirby report. Enterprise Allocation had replaced the traditional free-for-all with established quotas for each of the large offshore fishing companies. Instead of rushing out to haul in as much of a species quota as it could before its competitors, each company was given a specific quota for each fishing zone and species. In contrast to building large inventories or selling product off at fire sale prices, each organization was able to keep its inventory swimming until the market was ready to bear competitive prices. As a result, NatSea had the potential to replace its resource-driven adage of "Fish like hell, then try to sell" with a market-driven thrust. Cummings and McCulloch concluded that instead of taking advantage of the market opportunities, National Sea had used the new system as a reason to avoid competing against other fish companies.

Three weeks later, McCulloch phoned Cummings to offer him a three-month assignment with NatSea. It involved three tasks: (1) to help Sandy Roche, senior vice president of Canadian operations, with the growth in operations from four plants to twenty-one; (2) to make the operating committee work; and (3) to develop a strategic direction for the company. Cummings responded that he would be delighted to take on the assignment, but it wasn't in Woods Gordon's best interest to have him working exclusively on one client. After extensive discussions within the two consulting firms, a decision was made. "Rightly or wrongly," Cummings notes, "we decided that Hennigar was important enough for me to take on the assignment."

Cummings, unaware of how much the assignment would change his life, started in August 1984, spending four days a week in NatSea's East Coast operations. His first task was to interview, with Sandy Roche, the key people in each plant. Percy McDonald, who later replaced Roche, was a Newfoundland plant manager during that fall. He remembers Cummings as aggressive and in the know. "His knowledge of the facts made it clear that he'd obviously done his homework." These characteristics would become Cummings's trademark. "He wanted to find something out about you as a person. He wasn't interested in what you knew about the fishing industry; rather he wanted to see if your style would fit . . . if you could be a part of a changing organization." By the time Cummings and Roche had completed their tour, they had a good idea who was going to make it in the new regime and who wasn't.

Cummings then focused his attention on the operating committee. He knew that centralized control was critical for initiating a corporate turnaround. The problem lay in the committee's laissez faire manner of operating. Cummings soon realized that Morrow's approach to decision-making was to talk to members of senior management individually. "Bill's idea was to keep the meetings short, get through the agenda, and get yourself out of there. Whether decisions were made or not was irrelevant," recalls one participant. Cummings took on the responsibility of setting the agenda and facilitating consensus decisions. "I was always focused on the decision-making, asking questions like 'Are you sure that everyone around this table is comfortable with the decision?' Everyone would say yes, yes, yes, then I would say, 'Well, what about so-and-so sitting over there like a fly on the wall?' 'He must be in agreement,' they would tell me. 'Why don't you just ask him,' I would suggest. Of course they'd ask him and he'd say, 'No, I disagree.' The fact was that group had never worked together. They found all of this pretty uncomfortable at first."

In September 1984, the operating committee got a real workout when Cummings brought in a Woods Gordon associate to assist the group in its strategic planning. The exercise forced them to make two significant conclusions: one, that they didn't listen to one another, and two, that they were more interested in protecting their own interests than in searching for answers to their very real operating problems. The issue that highlighted these stumbling blocks was maximizing fish quality. Although the committee realized that fresh fish was their ticket to profitability, their fishing, storing, and unloading practices were not conducive to maintaining high-quality fresh products. The fleet, wishing to protect its turf, immediately rejected the idea of containerizing their vessels as the means to ensure onboard fish quality. By the end of the strategic planning meeting, the operating committee had been able to work through the issue sufficiently to make a decision to set up a separate company-wide task force to explore the containerization options. The meeting had made them aware that they needed to build decisions rather than approve them, and that they had a long way to go to become a team. The seeds, however, were now planted.

During this strategic planning exercise, Cummings confirmed his suspicion that he had become more than just a facilitator to the committee. They needed his input as much as his guidance. "It was early October," Cummings remembers, "I left a meeting for about 20 minutes. When I came back, they were still dealing with the same subject. When I asked them why they hadn't moved on, I was told that they wanted to check their decision with me before they made it. 'My God,' I thought, 'I've been here too long.' In a matter of weeks I would be gone and they'd be on their own."

Cummings didn't have to wait weeks to discover what the future had in store. Shortly following this meeting, the monthly financial report for August was published, five weeks after month end. In that one month, the company had lost $5 million. "Here we were in September doing this great strategic planning stuff," says Cummings, "when we should have been talking about survival."

Due to his lack of involvement in the day-to-day operations, the financial crisis took Cummings by surprise. Hennigar called him to attend an emergency operating meeting. As the meeting opened, it was obvious that Hennigar wanted immediate explanations and solutions. This was the moment when Cummings began to lead the company. He suggested that Hennigar leave them for six hours so that they could analyze the situation and come up with some solutions. "Rightly, or wrongly, I took charge of the meeting," Cummings recalls. "I knew I had to get Hennigar out of the room, otherwise several people would have irrevocably ruined their careers. They were going to make dumb statements that they couldn't live up to. They would have done this not because they were stupid, but because they didn't know what they were going to do."

A number of tough decisions were made that day. NatSea had to become market-driven to survive. Quality was no longer just a desirable characteristic; it had to become the driving force behind all operating decisions. Unprofitable plants had to be sold and some key people had to be replaced. One decision was not talked about, but was apparent to all in attendance; it was only a matter of time before Cummings would officially be running the show.

Within a week, Cummings received the offer from Hennigar. Although honored by the request, he wasn't sure he could do the job. "I'd never run more than 15 people in my life, let alone 8000," worried Cummings. But Hennigar was not to be put off. He discussed Cummings's ability to do the job with John

Wilson, chairman of Woods Gordon, at Cummings's own request. Wilson agreed with Hennigar's opinion of Cummings. Later that day Wilson phoned Cummings to support his decision to join NatSea. "Hennigar's a smooth guy," he told his associate. "Here he is, he steals a partner away from me, gets me to pay for lunch, and then borrows a subway token from me."

Cummings decided to give it a try. The one condition he made was that Bill Morrow had to remain in an executive capacity. "It would have been idiotic to say, 'Let's blame Bill and throw him out.' Wouldn't that have conveyed a lot of change?" Cummings states rhetorically. "Bill is tremendous with the fleet, our competitors, major customers, and our outside investment partners. The management style I bring to the company deals with things Bill doesn't like doing, so it isn't a matter of us running into conflict trying to do the same thing." Cummings took on the role of executive vice president and chief operating officer, while Bill Morrow retained the position of president and chief executive officer. David Hennigar became chairman of the board.

Taking Charge

Cummings's management style was as aggressive as the previous one had been passive. He knew his job was to turn the people, not the company, around. Cummings dismissed mass firings as a change strategy that would only last 24 hours. His task was to change losers into winners by helping them regain their self-confidence. "How do you change people's attitude?" asks Cummings. "You change it by having them succeed in something. When you're down, the temptation is to go after home runs so that you can get back in the game with one swing of the bat. When you're down, it's not very likely you can hit a home run. It's more likely you'll hit a single. The way to win is to hit a lot of singles to build confidence."

The 1984 net loss of $19 million gave Cummings plenty of opportunity to test his management philosophy. To make matters worse, he discovered that the company's 1985 budget was calling for a $10-million loss. At his first board meeting in December, he requested a one-month postponement to get the budget into shape. The tough side of the new leader emerged when he announced to the management of NatSea that the budget was simply unacceptable. The Christmas holidays turned into budget review meetings or, as they were better known, "the nasty Gord Cummings's inquisitions." Cummings explains, "Certainly there were a number of people who thought I was the most miserable, obstinate–whatever you want to use as an adjective." It soon became obvious that no one had given a great deal of thought to their departmental budgets. "They didn't know what was in their 1984 data, but they took it anyway and added 5%," recalls Cummings. The fact that there were no plans in place to back the budgets, confirmed the absence of any corporate accountability.

"I invented two categories of managers," clarifies Cummings, "the anxiety raisers and the problem solvers. I gave the anxiety types every chance to cross over to the other camp. After all, you are either part of the problem or part of the solution. Each person was told the same thing. 'I expect you to know your business, to run your business, and to make money. I don't expect you to make any more excuses. Are we clear?' They seemed to catch on to that last one pretty quickly. One of two things happens: they either live up to the expectation or they don't. If they do, that's great. We've got someone turned around. If they don't, they get dumped. The one thing I can never predict correctly is who will live up to the expectation and who won't."

The final 1985 budget that went to the board showed a profit, slight as it was, rather than the original $10-million loss. The profit motive was reinforced with rigorous follow-up. Monthly reviews were performed at each level of the company. Every aspect of the business was put under tight scrutiny. Managers knew they would be embarrassed if they didn't have the answers Cummings was looking for. Key indicator reports, produced every Wednesday, came next. Three months later, weekly income statements were introduced. Each one became yet another tool for members of NatSea to understand and control their business.

As managers started to demonstrate accountability, the

review periods changed from monthly to quarterly. "I kept telling them that I was going to get off their backs when they knew what the hell they were doing in running their business and meeting their targets," says Cummings, "and that's exactly what I started doing."

Throughout the budgeting process, a fundamental change in NatSea's operating strategy and internal powerbase had started to take shape. The market had replaced the fleet and the plants as the driving force behind the entire operation. Forecasts and weekly marketing analyses from the marketing divisions now determined the type and amount of fish that were required on a monthly basis by the various markets. The production planning department was able to take on the more powerful coordinating role of converting these forecasts into kilograms of fish, which, in turn, went to the fleet in the form of monthly fishing plans. The fleet could then respond with what they could match based on their allowable quotas within the Enterprise Allocation System. Maureen Yeadon explains, "I think that the turning point came when we started to fish to market rather than fish to fish. Before, when the vessels left the dock, they went out to fish what they wanted. As a result, we weren't in control of our planning and our responsiveness to the market was very poor. Now when vessels go to sea, they have established fishing plans, a 'shopping list' so to speak. They know exactly where they have to go and what they have to catch."

The fleet could no longer land whatever was in their hold, expecting the production plants to re-gear their production process at a moment's notice. The plants could no longer operate as separate businesses. The no longer viable Pictou and Digby plants were sold off to their existing management and employees. All of the remaining plants had to become part of a production network with specific production plans. The traditional prima donna thinking characteristic of the larger, more established production units disappeared when teamwork replaced empire building. Plants were divided into "off-shore" and "inshore" processing units. As filleting machines replaced people, plants had to specialize in the processing of specific species. The result was that when a vessel landed the wrong species of catch, certain machines would sit idle, while the stock waited to be filleted by the overworked species-specific machines. Positions such as the raw materials coordinator were created to assist in the wide-sweeping coordinating efforts that were now critical to moving fish from the water to the consumer's dinner plate quickly and effectively.

A significant shift in power had begun. The fleet captains, formally the "gods of the seas," had lost their entrepreneurial edge, as had the plant managers. It took a comprehensive education process and a clear statement of the consequence if the changes didn't take place, to help them understand the severity of the situation. "It was a real challenge to explain to the captains that their jobs were on the line if we couldn't make the shift," says Yeadon. "They were told that their long-term survival depended on it." The plants faced the same message, driven home by the Night of the Long Knives. This refers to the 24-hour period in which a number of longstanding plant managers were moved or replaced by the new breed of corporate market-driven thinkers. As decision-making became centralized, the people who had once autonomously run their businesses looked suspiciously at the corporate members who now held the strings. What they had to realize was that the tradeoff—giving up individual power for the larger corporate good—would mean the difference between being on a losing team or a winning one.

The critical messages started to take hold. Membership on the winning team meant that you had to (1) understand your business, (2) be market-driven, (3) have plans, (4) be a team-player, and (5) be a winner. Assuming the critical role of cheer-leader, Cummings says, "We are not here to play, we are here to win. Playing hard just isn't good enough."

In keeping with winning and hitting singles, the Three Percent Program was launched. Everyone in the company was asked to identify a 3% improvement in their business. "The magic of 3%," explains Cummings, "was that it was small enough that no one could say he or she couldn't do it. By the time you had a 3% decrease in fishing costs, and 3% in plant processing costs, added to getting selling prices up by 3%, pretty soon you had reached the multiplier effect of 9%." It wasn't long before the same people who had been sitting back waiting for things to change were aggressively competing with one another for budget approval of new ideas.

The next challenge was to limit the projects based on what the company could afford. "How do you indicate that the bank's open without having everyone walk off with the vault?" questions Cummings. "We decided to accept any idea that had a two-year payback. We were saying that the door is open, but the idea had better be good."

As momentum built in all areas of the business, quality became a corporate value rather than the latest buzzword. Fish is at its best when it comes out of the water. Everything that happens to it from then on has the potential to damage it, resulting in a lower market value. Dockside grading was installed to measure quality and to compensate the captains and crews accordingly. Now a crew could increase its income based on the quality of fish they landed in conjunction with their fishing plan. The more fish they brought in that could service the fresh fish market, the more money they could make. Fish that had been caught at the beginning of the voyage or had signs of handling earned less because it would be processed into lower-priced entrees, frozen fillets, or blocks. Likewise, the plants were compensated on the basis of quality and quantity of products as well as the relative market prices for the various species.

Next, everyone realized they could benefit from any technology that would improve the quality of the fish landings. Containerization, which started out as a contentious issue during the original strategic planning meeting, turned into a means for the warring parties to develop the technology that would best fit all their needs. Under the leadership of Percy McDonald, the task force reworked the original concept into one that involved plastic boxlike containers which stored the fish by species and catch date in the ships' holds. The ships' hulls were split in two and lengthened to accommodate the containers while maximizing holding capacity. Air unloaders, which vacuumed the fish out of the holds, were replaced with conveyer belts, which moved the containers from the vessels' holds, to dockside grading and into the plant for processing. All of this enabled NatSea to control and upgrade the quality of its product, resulting in significantly higher market prices.

Management had proven that consensus decision-making really did work. They also discovered that the company was committed to investing money in quality. "I guess I'll always remember going to the board in 1985 for their approval to spend $2 million on the initial containerization," recalls Cummings. "Having listened to my presentation, Tom MacQuarrie, a board member, asked me that if this made sense, how many ships should be containerized? I dreaded that question because I knew the answer was probably 21 and that would mean a $20-million expenditure. Tom then made the very salient observation that this was a $20-million decision rather than a $2-million one. As such we should decide to spend zero or $20 million. He continued with his recommendation that based on what he had heard, he was all for the $20-million expenditure. Well, I just about lost my false teeth then and there!"

With containerization under way, the management turned to another means of increasing the company's competitive edge by processing at sea. Factory freezer trawlers had long been used by other fishing nations, but the three available Canadian licenses had never been granted. The federal government had always viewed processing at sea as a threat to the volatile employment situation in the East Coast fish plants and the inshore fishery. By June 1985, NatSea felt the time had come to go after a license. After four months of heavy lobbying, together with a large-scale employee communication campaign, the license was secured, and NatSea purchased Canada's first factory freezer trawler (FFT), the *Cape North*, from West German interests. Her crew of 60 people stay out to sea for 40 to 60 days. The two 30-person shifts, working around the clock, catch and process 12 000 tonnes of fish a year, worth $15 million when sold in the international market. Under the leadership of Captain Larry Mossman and Relieving Captain Chris Morrow, Bill Morrow's son, each of the crew members can earn up to $2000 in bonuses, depending on the success of the trip.

As with the other innovations NatSea had introduced, the

process itself was as important as the end result. The video communication package and employee meetings expressed management's desire to involve its people in critical operating decisions. The company's success in securing the license also served to strengthen management's determination to use a corporate-wide team to become more competitive. As Cummings explains, "The FFT contract really allowed us to crystallize management and indeed the atmosphere of National Sea. We now knew we could change things and win. We could no longer go back to our old way of saying that we couldn't effect change, especially in terms of the government."

In one of the most remarkable turnarounds of 1985, National Sea managed to reverse a $19-million loss in 1984 to a $7-million profit in 1985. The outstanding results provoked a call from the Toronto Stock Exchange in January 1986. A worried TSE official wanted to know why there had been a run on NatSea's stock. The reason was simple and totally legal. The stock, which had traded for less than $5 before the Hennigar takeover, had suddenly jumped to $19.50 from $13 in less than a month. This was only the beginning for Cummings, who said at the time, "I would not hold out $7 million in profit on $450 million in sales as a big bag of money. It's only a 1½% return. We want to make 10 cents on every sales dollar."

In recognition of the role he had played in the turnaround, Cummings was appointed president and chief operating officer, while Bill Morrow moved to the position of vice chairman and chief executive officer. The blending of the old and new styles of management created problems at first, possibly due to Morrow's feeling that Cummings's arrival was six months to a year too soon. Their distinct leadership styles created obvious friction points. Cummings's aggressiveness and results orientation contrasted significantly with Morrow's "nice guy" approach, which placed concern for people's feelings over and above their performance. Cummings explains, "I didn't start off with everybody loving me. One out of four wasn't bad. When managers didn't perform, Bill's style was to say, 'God, don't upset him. We can't lose him.' My management style is a little different in that I have to give managers all sorts of rope so that I can understand what they can do. Then I make sure I find out what the hell they are doing." Cummings's professional management techniques demand accountability and flexibility from NatSea employees. His passion is still seen today by some as intimidating and arrogant, and at times unpredictable.

There is no question that Cummings brought control to the company, a fact which Morrow is quick to praise. "Gordon brought with him the types of internal controls needed to run the business. This was an area I was glad to give up because I had lost a lot of control for the two years I hadn't been around while dealing with the bank. Gordon was the ideal guy because he's a numbers man. Gordon and I don't always agree 100%, but we agree more than we disagree. I think we complement each other."

Members of the management concur with Morrow's perception. "It's just fascinating when we come to a major decision or problem," Robbie Shaw, executive vice president explains. "Gordon will stop the meeting and say, 'Okay, Bill, what do you think?' Sometimes I think he will take Bill's opinion over his own. Bill's the goodwill ambassador for the company with a fantastic network of industry contacts. He has so much knowledge in his head about the fishing business that when we have a problem with a major customer, more often that not, Bill will be the fireman who will solve it. Unlike most chairmen, he goes in and gets his hands dirty working alongside the other managers."

Management are also unanimous in their praise of Cummings's "infectious enthusiasm and ability to motivate people brought about by his incredible memory, analytical mind, and thorough understanding of every aspect of the business." His tell-it-like-it-is communication style, while jarring compared to Morrow's smooth diplomacy, has enabled NatSea employees to trust and believe in him as the leader who restored their confidence.

While Cummings's sensitivity may not always show in his demeanor, it does in his strategy. "Feelings are still hypersensitive in the early stages of a turnaround. In fact, even ordinary locker room banter is dangerous until the team returns to a winning position. It has to be remembered that tact is the art of making a point without making an enemy. In a turnaround case, you can prejudice the whole exercise by touching the wrong nerve at the wrong time."

Nineteen eighty-five had been the year of doing things differently and succeeding. The next year became the year of focus and direction. The problem was not finding exciting things to do, but cutting them back. "When I joined National Sea in 1984, I recorded my own personal target list," Cummings recalls. "It had 12 items on it. At the end of that first year, I had been successful in some of my directions, but by no means all. In fact, a few of my efforts had failed miserably. By the end of my second year, I had actually accomplished 11 out of my original 12 objectives. My honest conclusion was the list was twice as long as it should have been, because it took two years to accomplish. The message was clear—I wasn't in focus. I had too much in my sights."

In 1986 Cummings brought the same discipline to the rest of the company. He explains, "I asked each member of the operating committee to give me their objectives for 1986, and I insisted that they have no more than five. In fact, we decided that there would only be five targets for the entire company to accomplish in a year. This was a function of confidence. If you don't have confidence, you try to do everything to solve the problem. When you're confident, you know that you can drop things."

With growing confidence in the management of the company, David Hennigar resigned as chairman of the board in 1986. Bill Morrow assumed the role of chairman, while Cummings became president and chief executive officer.

Next Stop—The World

Onward and outward became the rallying cry as NatSea steadily progressed beyond its initial turnaround. Consumer health consciousness started to play into NatSea's hands. As information on the nutritional benefits of seafood was publicized, consumption rates took an upward swing. In the U.S. alone, consumption went from 5.6 kilograms per capita in

1983 to 6.8 kilograms in 1986. Product development, dormant since the downturn, started to pick up speed under Ron Whynacht, the newly appointed vice president of product development. NatSea launched five new entrees and lighter-batter frozen seafood into the Canadian retail market. As the seafood entree market began to grow, the High Liner brand name, with close to 80 retail products, maintained its prominent marketshare.

The company also branched out by introducing its first non-seafood frozen retail food, Captain's Chicken. Cummings proudly explains, "We took the Captain and Billy down to the farm and went into the chicken business. Within five months, we had won 25% of the entire Canadian market for frozen precooked chicken in Canada. In Ontario, we became the market leader."

However, High Liner was not doing as well in the highly competitive U.S. market. By 1986, National Sea Products Inc. (the U.S. subsidiary) had come to the conclusion that the High Liner brand name was not going to make it in the U.S. retail market. This brought about the purchase of the Booth brand label from Consolidated Foods to help NatSea break into the tough American market.

To meet the demands of the lucrative fresh fish market, the Louisbourg, Nova Scotia, plant underwent a $16-million renovation. In keeping with the company's new aggressiveness, not one day of operations was lost in the changeover from the old plant to the new.

The Finite Fruits of the Sea

The ocean that had always seemed so plentiful started to show signs of overfishing. The tremendous expansion of the inshore fishery, along with their misrecordings of true catch numbers, reversed the predictions that the resource was secure. Plant rationalization and closures throughout Nova Scotia apparently had little effect on the inshore fishermen who continued to build deeper and wider vessels to increase their catch capacity.

Still within the Olympic system of "catch-as-catch-can," the inshore fleets worked all the angles to keep up with their heavy bank payments. Reduced offshore quotas reflected the government's concern over depleting fish stock. Now government relations became increasingly important to NatSea.

In early January 1987, Gordon Cummings jumped into the political fray. The issue was the secret signing of a fishing treaty with France which allowed French fishermen to take 16 000 tonnes of fish and have continued access to the disputed territory near the French islands of St. Pierre and Miquelon. The federal government had gone ahead and signed the treaty without first consulting with the industry. Cummings called a news conference to denounce it on the grounds that the allowance, in addition to France's tendency to cheat, would significantly deplete Canada's cod stocks. As Cummings watched the news coverage on the CBC "National" broadcast that evening, he became infuriated by the reporter's slant. The story ended with the issue being a Newfoundland-Ottawa conflict rather than an international fisheries fiasco. "We realized that this story had to get away from Newfoundland. On Tuesday we got a hold of Nova Scotia's premier, John Buchanan, and asked him to go to the media. He refused on the basis that he didn't know enough about the situation and didn't want to be caught off guard. Dick Young of F.P.I. wouldn't do it, so that afternoon, I did. I went to the media and lambasted the government and had a great time. By Wednesday night, there was an emergency debate in the House of Commons on this issue. MPs O'Neil, Comeau, and Forrestal got up and lambasted me."

Cummings knew exactly what he was doing. He was trying to keep the story alive until a resolution was reached. "By Wednesday night, they had to have an emergency debate. By Friday, there still was no resolution. They were trying to ride the story. We kept the story going over the weekend and into the second week. During that week, there was an emergency conference of provincial first ministers. By the next Friday, they had appointed John Crosby, then Minister of Transportation, to look after it. Now that they'd done what we wanted, we wanted the story to die. No way! It was their turn to get me.

I spent the toughest three hours I've ever spent in front of the Senate committee as a whole. I was grilled by everybody and his uncle. By this time, I no longer wanted to take on the government, rather I was trying to compliment them on the way they had seen the light. Allan MacEachern, then leader of the Opposition in the Senate, was up for 45 minutes trying to get me to attack the government."

It took until March 1989 for the French territory issue to finally be resolved. The 1989 conflict, however, proved that the company was already strong and confident enough to take on the government and win — only three years after the dramatic fight to keep NatSea from nationalization.

The corporate philosophy of fishing to market brought with it a responsibility to meet the needs of the market whether NatSea vessels could land the catch or not. The company turned to other markets around the world for its supply. In 1986, it added a trading subsidiary, National Sea Products (Japan) Ltd., to its foreign investments in Australia (International Sea Products (Pty) Limited) and Uruguay (Astra Pesquerias Uruguayas S.A.). As the trading function took on increased responsibilities to deal with the shortages and surpluses of NatSea products, N.S.P. Int'l U.S.A. was revitalized under Ken Ritsey, the former president of National Sea Products in the States. With the addition of yet another trading company in Portugal, NatSea positioned itself in the international salt cod market. Because wheeling and dealing fish has as much to do with market prices and international exchange rates as it does with supply and demand, the growing trading network attempted to challenge these traditional uncontrollable variables that stood to make or break NatSea's success.

Throughout 1986 and 1987, all the variables that had cast a shadow on NatSea's operations started to work in their favor. "Every time you looked at a financial statement, it got getter and better, and that is where the luck came in," says Henry Demone, executive vice president of international and trading. "Improving quality, containerizing the vessels, modernizing the plants, focusing on fresh fish, adding more chain restaurant business were all conscious decisions that would have turned NatSea around anyway. But superimposed on top were rising fish prices, a falling Canadian dollar, falling oil prices. It was one of those times that everything seemed to go right." Whatever the combination between Lady Luck and strategic management, NatSea's income was a shareholder's dream. In 1986, the company declared an income of $22 million and in 1987, $27.5 million. Due to the rapid turnaround, the difficulty-term preferred shares had become expensive. As a result, the company paid off the Toronto Dominion Bank a full two years ahead of schedule. In keeping with their long-term interests, they reinvested close to $100 million in the new capital expenditures.

Buoyed by success, NatSea continued to go after alternatives to its traditional fishing operations. Its three-point plan included for 1987/88: (1) adding to its international trading and processing operations; (2) expanding its shrimp business; and (3) entering into salmon aquaculture. To meet its globilization plan, Hong Kong was added to its trading network in July 1987. The 1988 acquisition of the French trading company, Bretagne Export S.A., its processing subsidiary, La Surgelation Lorientaise S.A., and its 33% ownership of a factory freezer trawler, enabled the company to produce, harvest, process, and sell fish within the European East Bloc countries. The growing shrimp business resulted in NatSea's November 1988 purchase of Treasure Isle, Inc., the second largest shrimp processing operation in North America. Northern shrimp was added to NatSea's list of products through its joint venture with the Labrador Inuit Development Corporation. And the expanding science of aquaculture led the company to their 1987 purchase of Pacific Aqua Foods Ltd., one of the largest fish farming companies in British Columbia, specializing in salmon and oysters.

The company's steady progress was not accomplished by Gordon Cummings alone. A new aggressive set of strategic leaders—Henry Demone, John McNeil, Percy McDonald, Geoff Southwood, and Maureen Yeadon—had shown Cummings that they were ready to spread their wings and fly on their own. This group, along with Rod McCulloch, Cummings's old buddy who had joined the company in 1986 as vice president of finance and administration, and Robbie Shaw, executive vice president of government relations and strategic planning, had taken on their own business units.

Such a dramatic shift in power might seem uncharacteristic in a man who had taken charge back in 1984 with such a passion for control. But what really drives Gord Cummings is results. The centralized management style and functional organizational structure that had brought the company through its turnaround had started to show signs of wear. What had once served the purpose of teambuilding and control was now starting to slow down the operation. "When Cummings first came on board there was little communication and coordination between the functional units. It was necessary to have strong centralized control maintained through extremely low authority levels and once-a-week meetings that forced all the decision-makers to be together in the same room," says Demone.

Cummings maintained his promise to back off from his managers as they consistently met their targets. He now had the infrastructure of skilled managers necessary to diversify the business. The decision to diversify was made during the September 1987 strategic planning meeting. Two months later, the new structure, designed by Cummings, was implemented. The restructured organization broke the corporation into six business units: Fleet, Canadian Products, North American Retail, International Trading, U.S. Food Service, and Corporate.

The team of executive vice presidents make up the management committee, replacing the operating committee. True to Cummings's commitment to let go, the new committee's mandate is strictly one of policy-making. Operating decisions are the responsibility of the business leaders, as Cummings explains, "If U.S. Food Services can purchase its cod from sources cheaper than Canadian Products, then that's the decision that Geoff Southwood must take in order to achieve his profit target."

Not wanting to be left totally out of the picture, Cummings insists on centralized control for budgeting and reporting, capital expenditures, and head count. "The reason that I want to control these items," explains Cummings, "is that head count and capital are where you start changing strategy. I want to know when changes are happening."

The Bubble Bursts

The rising market price of cod throughout 1987 seemed too good to be true. And, in fact, it was. By the time the commodity price of cod blocks had reached their high of $2.05 at the very end of the year, consumers had started to turn to the cheaper alternatives of whiting and pollock. Within five months, the market price for cod blocks had crashed to $1.25. With cod blocks contributing 50% to NatSea's overall sales figures, the bubble burst with a bang. Without the necessary market intelligence in place, the company had been taken by surprise by the switch to other forms of whitefish.

NatSea was determined not to be shaken for long. With its now standard practice of facing problems with a multi-pronged solution, it went to work to meet the market's needs with cod alternatives; to reposition cod as a superior product to whitefish alternatives; and to put in place a strategic marketing function that would give advance warning of changing market trends.

If whiting and pollock were what the market wanted, then NatSea was going to give it to them. In August 1988, it acquired a 50% interest in the Argentinian company, Alpargatas S.A., a whiting harvesting and processing operation. This operation, along with the 15% interest already held in the company in Uruguay, gave NatSea a 25% or more share of the world's whiting market.

Pollock is now the next item on the acquisition list. "We will certainly be going into the Alaskan pollock business," confirms Robbie Shaw. "We are in the last stages of our economic analysis to determine which of three ways we should do it— through a shore-based processing facility on Ocean Island; a factory freezer trawler similar to the *Cape North*, only bigger; or a mothership processor."

An ad hoc task force was put together to determine a strategy for upgrading the consumer's perception of cod in the market-place. Having determined its flake and taste advantage, the committee decided to concentrate on promoting the advantages of this age-old species. The fish would now go to market under a new name, North Atlantic cod. Its new image is currently being reinforced by a wide advertising campaign directed at the food service industry.

To avoid being caught napping again by the competition, the company has established a strategic marketing function under Ron Whynacht. Strategic marketing officers work to compile information from many different sources to determine producer, consumer, and price trends of the various species around the world.

However, softening market prices and exchange rates came back to haunt NatSea throughout 1988. Although the company had rapidly responded to the cod price crisis, it was unable to control the sale of the whitefish alternatives into its most important market—the U.S. Taking advantage of the 320-kilometer limit restriction, Alaska forced out foreign vessels and began harvesting its own pollock. The influx of domestic pollock fillets and South American whiting into the American market contributed to an oversupply of groundfish during the year.

In addition, the increasing value of the Canadian dollar removed the price advantage of NatSea products in foreign markets, particularly the U.S. Hardest hit by market conditions and exchange rates were fresh fish and U.S. Food Service, both of which sell large quantities of Canadian fillets directly to U.S. customers. Sales prices on some commodity items dropped as much as 30% compared with 1987 prices, with exchange rates adding a further 8% to that decrease.

Sales revenue only increased by 2% over 1987 in spite of the added sales from the French and Treasure Isle acquisitions. These small gains were offset by not only the soft U.S. commodity markets and strong Canadian dollar, but also by the increased costs of catching fish brought on by the reduced quotas. The lower volumes harvested by the fleet had the effect of raising the per-unit cost of such species as perch, sole, and haddock. Globalization opened up the North American market to exotic species, such as Australia's orange roughee, resulting in a further reduction in sales of these traditional species.

A slight easing off had occurred during 1988. Trepidation replaced infectious enthusiasm as the 1988 quarterly financial statements came up for review. The third quarter's results showed NatSea's first loss since the turnaround in 1985. By year end, the accumulated damage of the war against the uncontrollables totaled an annual net loss of $6 million. This was a rude awakening compared to the company's $25-million profit the year before. Such a dramatic slide takes on new meaning when put into context. Lower margins on fillets alone reduced pre-tax income by approximately $30 million. The impact of foreign currency on U.S. dollar cash flows reduced profit by approximately $12 million. Media advertising and promotion efforts for the Booth label cost $7 million, while $3 million was incurred in the acquisition expenses of the new French subsidiaries and Treasure Isle. Total assets rose to $403 million in 1988 from $301 million in 1987, but common share-holders' equity was down about 9%.

Had management not been able to shift quickly by taking advantage of its business unit structure, the results would have been far worse. Cummings maintains that increased market sensitivity, biting the bullet on inventories rather than wishfully hoping the market price would go up, and shifting product out of U.S. Food Service into the salt cod and international markets were positive decisions that had helped stabilize the downward swing. Initiatives already in place, such as cost control, quality improvement, and diversification from the commodity ground fish markets, also reduced the slide.

Teamwork, coordination, and communication came to-gether in the first quarter of 1989 to bring sales up to $165 million in the first four months of '89 compared to sales of $142 million for the same period in '88. The company was able to reduce the downturn to a $1-million loss compared to the $8-million loss experienced in the fourth quarter of 1988. "These are not, by any stretch of the imagination, great numbers," Cummings told shareholders at the 1988 annual meeting. "But neither are they tragic numbers. That's because behind the balance sheet a lot of costly, and in the long term, very necessary diversification has been going on." In December 1988, NatSea was hit by a ten-week strike by its 1800 Newfoundland CAW members. It had been six years since any substantial contract negotiations had taken place. Wages, inequities between plants, and increased benefits were the focus of the negotiations, which reached agreement in early April.

The biggest challenge facing NatSea, and the entire East Coast fishing industry, is the ongoing reduction of quotas. Cummings explains the impact of the company's quota drop in groundfish of 180 000 tonnes to 152 000 tonnes for 1989. "Any arbitrary and unilateral change in enterprise allocations by the Department of Fisheries and Oceans, has the effect of altering the swimming and growing stock stored in our ocean inventory – the stock on the basis of which our fleet is configured, our capital expenditures undertaken, our marketing ventures planned, and our future as a company of 7000 people is determined. There's virtually not a perch or pollock that we produce that we make any money on. And it's because our overheads are too high for the amount of fish we are dealing with."

While members of the offshore fishery accuse inshore fishermen of overfishing and misrecording their catch, the former are likewise charged with dumping and the discarding of fish at sea. Regardless of who is to blame, scientists have recommended that the total catch of northern cod be cut to 125 000 tonnes in 1990 from 235 000 tonnes in 1989. Once again, this has resulted in the federal government looking at a special aid plan for the Atlantic fishery.

The 35% decrease in NatSea's quotas between the introduction of the Enterprise Allocation System in 1984 and its first permanent year in 1989 is having a dramatic impact on the fishing communities throughout Nova Scotia and Newfoundland. The Lockeport, Nova Scotia, plant was closed permanently, taking with it 220 of the 900 residents in the community. Eight other plants were closed over the summer of 1989.

Cummings is all too aware of the crippling effect the quota reductions are having on the industry and the communities it supports. He does, however, take exception to the media's role in the situation. "If you read the newspaper it looks as if we are about to catch our last two fish."

Aside from the reduction in quotas, NatSea is having to deal with the decline in US. per capita consumption of fish from 15.4 to 15.0 pounds. Much of this decrease in consumer demand has been attributed to many "nebulous" contaminants such as medical waste washing up on U.S. beaches, oil spills, and the East Coast mussel scare. "A thousand small stories are much more difficult to deal with than one large one," comments Cummings, "and they have even more impact on consumer eating habits."

A company-wide strategic planning exercise is rigorously underway to offset the damage. Its objective is to instill a market-driven orientation in the day to day thoughts and actions of every employee. NatSea's management recognizes that it takes years for people to put the customer truly in the driver's seat. Priorities for 1989 have been geared to value-added products, such as fresh fish and entrees, which have the best consumer and price advantage and are more stable in earnings. International and trading activity have also taken on a more prominent position as the five-year investment plan continues to unfold. "Our international strategy looks even better now than it did when we first developed it," says Cummings. "I'm remaining cautiously optimistic."

In a culture that employees call "benevolent ruthlessness," Gordon Cummings made his team accountable. He made them confident. He made them into a winning team which has now been hit by the harsh reality that each season brings new challenges no matter how many seasons it has won before.

Despite his many accomplishments, Gordon Cummings's words came back to haunt him. He had made it clear that playing wasn't good enough—you had to win. Truly unaware of how much this assignment would change his life, he fell victim to his own prognosis. On August 21, 1989, the board, citing mounting financial losses, reduced quotas and a rising Canadian dollar, forced Gordon Cummings to resign. Bill Morrow, the man who has witnessed his fair share of turning points, assumed the position of chief executive officer, while Henry Demone, executive vice president of international trading, was promoted to the position of president—at the age of 35.

Snapshot of National Sea Products

Crisis #1 (Year End 1983):

On the brink of nationalization, NatSea sits with $244 million in accumulated debt, $122 million worth of unsold fish, and a net loss of $17.3 million. This crisis followed the 1981 collapse of the East Coast fishery and, the bankruptcy of H.B. Nickersons, NatSea's controlling shareholder.

Turnaround Strategy:

- Re-establish NatSea as a private fishing corporation
- New leadership
- Establish centralized control and strategic direction
- Sell unprofitable plants and downsize other areas of company
- Set up stringent budget reviews
- Initiate a shift to a market orientation
- Introduce technological advances such as containerization, factory freezer trawler, and plant upgrading to enable shift to a market orientation
- Launch three percent program to identify and install business improvements
- Force divisions to identify no more than five objectives per year
- Take advantage of the health awareness by developing new products
- Establish five-year strategic plan, which emphasizes long-term investment orientation
- Decentralize into strategic business units

Crisis #2 (1988):

Commodity price crashes for cod blocks, affecting 50% of NatSea's overall sales figures. This dramatic market decline, along with reduced fish quotas, strengthening Canadian dollar, and increasing interest rates forces the company into a $6-million loss for 1988 compared to the $27.5-million profit the year before.

Turnaround Strategy:

- Reduce inventories
- Introduce strategic marketing function to analyze global factors and marketing trends
- Install corporate-wide strategic planning throughout organization
- Close some plants due to quota reductions
- Give production priorities to the products with best consumer and price advantage

Crisis #3 (1989):

- $2.95 million loss at the end of the second quarter comes as a result of reduced quotas, lower consumption and a rising Canadian dollar. Gordon Cummings is forced to resign

Result: NatSea's multi-prong approach to its latest crisis, along with its commitment to long-term strategy, are signs of a company positioned to weather the chronic problems facing the East Coast fishery and win.

Manufacturers Life Insurance:

How to Merge, Move and Cope

"Think of the worst scenario you can imagine – of all the things that could go wrong – and then multiply it by ten, and you may be in the ballpark."

This was the advice offered to Manufacturers Life Insurance Co. President and Chief Executive Officer Tom Di Giacomo by a member of his board of directors when told that the company had bought Dominion Life Assurance Co., a medium-sized Waterloo-based insurance company, and was planning to merge its Toronto-based Canadian operations with the new purchase.

"In hindsight," Di Giacomo adds, "that statement was probably close to the truth."

Manufacturers was an organization in transition. After a dozen years of steady growth under the guidance of Sydney Jackson, the company was taking a new direction. In September 1985, Jackson handed the reins of day-to-day decision-making to 44-year-old Di Giacomo, who had come up through the business side of the company. An MBA from the University of Chicago, Di Giacomo had been an effective manager of Manulife's investment division, and his appointment signaled a shift in management style to a leaner, more business-like orientation.

In 1984, Manufacturers was Canada's second largest life insurance company, with assets of more than $16 billion and business dealings in 15 countries. But the venerable life insurance institution started in 1887, whose first chairman was Sir John A. Macdonald, was losing its hold on the hearts and wallets of Canadians. Although headquartered in Canada, the majority of its business was conducted in the U.S., followed by Britain and the growing Far Eastern market. In Canada, it was struggling to remain among the top ten insurers, and its market-share was dropping. "In fact," Di Giacomo admits, at that time, "we were eleventh or twelfth in size."

The company's strategy to deal with both its increasing international business and its dwindling Canadian operation was twofold: decentralize and buy another insurance company to double its Canadian base. After its first attempt at a purchase (of Standard Life) failed, the company became even more anxious to succeed.

An internal debate on strategic planning took place within the executive ranks. One plan proposed a major infusion of money to expand, open new branches, hire more agents, and price products more aggressively. But, in the open-ended, consensus-building decision-making process that is the hallmark of Manufacturers' corporate culture, another point of view maintained that an acquisition was the only sensible way to increase growth without serious risk. So, when Dominion Life was put on the block in the summer of 1984, Manufacturers seized the opportunity. According to then Chief Actuary Robin Leckie, "When Dominion Life came up as a possibility, I thought it was the 'savior,' an instant, justifiable fix."

The Purchase of Dominion Life

At first glance, Dominion seemed an ideal fit for Manufacturers, at least from a strictly business point of view. The majority of Manufacturers' Canadian business was centered on pensions and annuities; Dominion's healthy group life business provided strength in a weak area. A subsidiary of Lincoln National Life Insurance Co., based in Fort Wayne, Indiana, Dominion was an efficiently run medium-sized business with 508 employees. Manufacturers paid $157.5 million to acquire the company.

Dominion also seemed to offer an attractive solution to another Manufacturers' problem: how to efficiently and speedily decentralize Canadian operations from the international business. Moving the whole Canadian division from Toronto to Waterloo, while merging operations with Dominion Life, seemed to provide the answer.

The announcement that Manufacturers had decided to buy Dominion Life, and proposed to move Canadian operations to Waterloo, electrified employees at the company's luxurious headquarters on Bloor Street in the heart of the city. Working as they did in the recently completed North Tower of the organization's office complex, which overlooked a ravine, was surrounded by beautiful gardens, and had a new fitness center in the basement, employees could be justified for liking their country club environment. The thought of upheaval, moving to Waterloo, and/or losing one's job, created enormous stress. And the situation was hardly improved when Di Giacomo called an employee meeting and stated bluntly, in the hardnosed manner that marks his style, that the company was not concerned with moving people below the senior level to Waterloo.

Down in Waterloo, Dominion Lifers were equally anxious. They had been aware of the impending sale for the last six months, a period which they lived through, from day to day unsure whether they would have jobs the next morning. Unreliable rumors about the potential purchaser ran through the company with disturbing regularity. At one stage, "things got so bad," one long-time Dominion Life employee stated, "that the story went round that a construction group ... from Vancouver had purchased the company. They were supposedly a money laundering front for the Mafia." News of their purchase by Manufacturers reached employees through the newspapers, not through a company announcement. News was scarce, rumors ran riot, and morale was poor.

Over the years, Manufacturers had developed a reputation as an excellent employer, concerned for the welfare of its people. It prided itself on maintaining a caring, sensitive approach to its employees, and although the new climate under Di Giacomo heralded a leaner, less luxurious organization, the company set out to uphold that tradition within its newly decentralized Canadian division.

The new management team, ten entrepreneurial and aggressive young managers in their late thirties and early forties, enthusiastically headed down to Waterloo in early 1985 to oversee the move and merger, under the guidance of Senior Vice President John Clark. "I came to Waterloo mainly because of the excitement of the merger," says Individual Insurance Vice President Bill MacLean. "I really wanted to see what starting afresh, going through a massive amount of change was like. I wanted to be involved. It turned out to be exciting, that's for sure. It certainly fulfilled my fantasies."

Manufacturers' team went into high gear to facilitate the merger. A number of task forces were established to deal with the logistics of the move. Some of the senior group remained in Toronto to oversee events at that end, while John Clark and Vice President Finance Dave Allen moved to Waterloo to take charge at Dominion Life. Many executives commuted back and forth between Waterloo and Toronto, a 130-kilometer drive.

What they didn't realize at first was how significant a cultural chasm divided the two groups, and how crucial that difference would be in the initial attempts to merge the two organizations. "Dominion was operationally driven, but hadn't been very successful in a marketing or sales sense," explains former Dominion Life executive Bryce Walker, now vice president, group, in Manufacturers' Canadian division. "It was a very expense-driven type of company." According to Walker, the culture was "top-down driven and far less participative than Manufacturers'. Decision-making was clear – get the president onside with a decision you wanted and you were on your way. At Manufacturers, by contrast, there's more emphasis on cross-boundary management, getting a number of people who have a stake in the issue onside. It's getting a mass of support developing that creates the success of something."

Manufacturers' culture was aggressive, entrepreneurial, and marketing- and sales-oriented. Dominion, by contrast, was bureaucratic, formal, and more patriarchal, with its eyes tightly focused on financial controls and bottom-line numbers. The differences can partly be explained in small-town versus big-city terms. John Clark recalls an incident that summed up the difference for him: "It was in the early days of 1985. I had gone to the dentist, and was sitting in the dentist's chair, my mouth full of instruments, when the receptionist interrupted us with the message that I had to take a call from the president. My mind raced through possible emergencies. 'It must be something really serious for Tom [Di Giacomo] to interrupt me at the dentist.' But when I picked up the phone, it turned out to be John Acheson, the president of Dominion Life, calling me for some reason. That was how he was always referred to—as the president."

One of Clark's first tasks was making assessments about duplications in personnel, and terminations. The company brought in consultants from McKinsey & Co. to do evaluations of the Dominion Life management team. Within the first six months, 70 of the 508 Dominion Lifers either resigned, took early retirement, or were fired, including the majority of the senior management. Only two of the senior group found jobs within Manufacturers. The rest were let go because of "poor fit." Although Manufacturers tried to handle the departures fairly, with sensitivity and a generous termination package, resentments and bitterness ran high in the tight-knit community for many months.

One of the two senior Dominion Life survivors, Bryce Walker, explains his feelings: "My first reaction was one of pure concern about what was going to happen, and fear of the unknown. I was moved to part of the organization that was predominantly Manufacturers. Right away I was virtually out of Dominion. What helped me personally a great deal was that there was a lot of turmoil surrounding the move—and that brought me closer to my superiors in Toronto, and we got off to a good start. . . . Being taken out of the old and put into the new, that was a key factor that enabled me to work through the merger."

Not everyone was as fortunate. Many Dominion Life employees didn't know how to cope with the new and unfamiliar culture. As one branch representative says: "At Manufacturers, decision-making was pushed down into the organization. But for us at the branch level, that was very confusing. We didn't know where to go to get answers when we needed a decision." Another Dominion Life person adds: "We saw the Manufacturer's culture as a real opportunity, not a threat. But we also saw it as power without control or restraint. It was freedom, but we were frightened by it."

Back at international headquarters in Toronto, the mood was one of uncertainty. The company had backtracked on its initial statement that only senior people would be moved to Waterloo, and was in fact actively wooing people to make the switch. Although there were almost no actual layoffs, major job changes occurred for the majority of the Canadian division's 546 workers. Most job functions moved to Waterloo, but only 160 workers actually made the move, while, of the remainder, 183 elected to leave the company and 203 were moved, gradually, into other positions elsewhere in the organization.

To facilitate the move to Waterloo, a number of communications strategies were implemented. Regular bus tours of Waterloo were set up and Manufacturers' employees were put up in the homes of Dominion Life workers for orientation sessions. A get-to-know Waterloo information center was established at Manufacturers' main Toronto building. Efforts were made to explain the reasons behind the move to all employees.

Gradually, one by one, the individual business groups moved their operations to Waterloo. The move shocked many who had grown accustomed to the spacious and ergonomically efficient Toronto offices. Dominion Life was located in two different locations, and the pressure of added staff meant that two additional office locations had to be rented; even so, accommodation was crowded and uncomfortable. "I must say I did have second thoughts about the move when I saw the Dominion Life building in Waterloo," says one Manufacturers' employee who made the move.

New staff was hired to cope with the burdensome workload caused by the merging of the two organizations. In the annuity area, to give one example of the difficulty caused by the merger, five different computer systems were in use.

By the end of 1985, the physical move was largely complete, but the real merger had hardly begun.

1986: Into the Trough

Dave Allen, vice president finance, had joined Manufacturers in April 1984, just after finishing his MBA degree, which had included a course on mergers and acquisitions. So when the purchase of Dominion Life was announced and he realized that he would be closely involved, he went back to the textbooks and reviewed "all the horror stories of how bad things could be." As time went on, "I sat there waiting for things to happen, and nothing went wrong. . . . We wrote some stuff at the end of 1985 that said, 'Sales are up, we don't have any problems.' And then, the floor fell in! Everything that could go wrong went wrong at that time."

The first indication that something was seriously amiss came early in the summer of 1986. Allen suddenly realized that the budgeting process was out of control. Spending was far exceeding estimates. Once the dust cleared at the end of 1986, and number crunching was complete, it became clear that new business sales were 17% below projections, and that actual expenditures were $11.5 million higher than anticipated on a total earnings budget of $114 million.

During that summer, although the full extent of the budget problem was not known, the senior management group realized they needed to tackle some serious difficulties. Allen explains that the problem was in large measure a result of the swift merging of the two organizations, which had different financial accounting systems. "Nobody really knew how much money they should be spending because there was no trend line, and people didn't know how to control things. Dominion had been excessively focused on monthly budgeting, whereas Manufacturers grew successful by focusing on things like marketing, innovative selling, and maintaining a stable working environment." Budget estimates had been put together without any real knowledge of how they would be achieved.

Just before the crisis broke, Clark had decided that one of the division's weaknesses lay in the area of human resources. The Dominion Life human resources manager proved unequal to the task and was soon let go. In April 1986, Clark hired Keith Beveridge, a veteran of several previous mergers, including the Petro-Canada/Gulf merger, as vice president of human resources.

"Manufacturers' people had been used to loose management and budgetary controls. Planning budgeting, and managing the budgets were not strengths I observed when I arrived. Things were out of control.

"We went into the proverbial trough in '86 ... at that point the only issue was 'how deep is the trough and how long are you going to be in it.' Every company in an acquisition has one."

Dave Allen took on the job of getting the numbers right. His straightforward solution to clearing up the financial confusion was: "I cared about the problem, and I got everybody else to care about it, too." After making some management changes, a new budgeting system was worked out. "We hunkered down and went through a multi-year process of grinding the budget out.... We've done that and the results are showing. We've improved our financial position every year, and now are well under budget."

John Clark believes that in looking at an overview of the merger, the budget crisis was largely academic: "It wasn't as if we were throwing money around ... it was just that we didn't know what figures to use. In another way it was an accounting problem, because when you put two sets of books together, and say, 'there's your budget,' but the figures are wrong, where's the reality? It was a technical, academic crisis. The real crisis issue was our annuity service."

The annuity crisis was a real and intractable problem. Manufacturers had built up a substantial annuity business over the years, and the operation worked very smoothly. Dominion managed some annuities as well. When the two groups were merged, service suddenly declined sharply. Policies weren't issued on time, inaccuracies multiplied, and worst of all, payment schedules were not being met on time.

John Clark explains that the crisis occurred quite suddenly: "We lost nearly every experienced annuity person over a period of two to three months. . . . We were administering around 120 000 payments a month, but they were run by only six or seven key people. We lost every one of them . . . there were people in Toronto who didn't want to move to Waterloo, and at Dominion Life, there were only three people running annuities, and all of them left. Suddenly there was nobody who knew how to do things and about five different computer systems. The combination left us with a situation that just got worse and worse and worse."

Manufacturers had underestimated the importance and value of retaining experienced clerical workers. Many of the junior clerical workers in Toronto were simply taken for granted, and were not moved to Waterloo on the assumption that new clerical workers could be hired there. What actually happened is that systems that had run smoothly for years suddenly didn't function any longer when those clerical employees, who had made their operation seem automatic, weren't around to run them.

As Marketing and Agency Vice President John Neilson sees it, the problem stemmed from a number of causes: "Both companies had inadequate systems, then there was the lack of experienced clerical staff." And on top of that, an incomplete decentralization of functions between the Toronto head office and the Waterloo operation meant that essential annuity information, such as changes of address or bank account, were simply not being communicated to the correct department. "We weren't aware of the problems in time . . . we were three months behind in annuity payments. We weren't monitoring things closely enough," says Neilson. As a result, management had to bring some experienced workers down from Toronto on weekends to help sort out the mess, new managers were hired, and part-time workers brought in to clear service backlogs.

"That was a real problem," John Clark exclaims. "It was the single worst thing that happened during the merger."

The next problem to strike the already beleaguered management team was a tremendous backlog in processing group health and life claims. "At one point we had 20 000 claims backed up, and that was tough," says Clark. To sort things out, he brought in an experienced data processing manager from corporate headquarters. Put in charge of Group Life and Health, Vice President Tom Dunlop shouldered the Herculean task of clearing the claims backlog. "When I came down here, we had some pretty horrendous service problems, a shortage of people, and we were not doing very well even on routine service functions like paying claims," he says. "People expect claims to be paid quickly. We had tremendous backlogs and lots of complaints."

Dunlop tackled the backlog problems through a combination of overtime, hiring part-time workers, and trying, gradually, to revamp the claims processing systems. "You're always torn, in those kinds of situations, beween trying to tough it out and process the business, and being able to step back from it and look at things from the longer term view." Dunlop's approach was to get basic service back on track before concentrating "on putting management controls and practices back in place."

The pressure on the work force during this period was intense. Most employees had to work long overtime hours, trying to clear the backlog. As well, they were housed in cramped and inadequate work locations, many of them squeezed into a basement originally built for storage. At the same time, these two very different groups of workers from the two organizations were having to try and adjust to each other and work as one company.

Strains caused by the quick merger soon came to the surface. According to Human Resources Vice President Keith Beveridge, "People began to feel like secondhand goods – 'I've been bought.' And then you met arrogance on the part of the acquiring company's employees – 'We must be better; we bought you.' People felt they were really stressed. We imposed high performance expectations, and yet there was a lack of strategic direction."

The Larger Picture

When Keith Beveridge first arrived at Manufacturers in the spring of 1986, he met a management group who "were in the trees, instead of surveying the forest at large.

"Management simply thought, having moved and merged, that was it . . . there was no acknowledgment of how people felt—the anger and the shock. There were no warning systems set up to catch problems when they did occur. They tended all to be reacting to events."

Bill MacLean, individual insurance vice president, says, "We trivialized the whole thing. We underestimated the magnitude of just about the whole thing—the systems side, the administrative side, the new problems we had, and the cultural change, too."

Bryce Walker adds, "When you get into a merger situation, people don't realize that they're no longer managing a business, but managing a merger."

Neville Henderson, the vice president in charge of marketing, says, "This company is very dynamic. As a result, they put tremendous work pressure on the organization . . . there was a sense that they could not let something like the merger and acquisition slow them down in terms of progress, and yet the level of work in the merger was so great that it created a lot of frustrations. The good thing is that eventually the organization did recognize this and try and alleviate some of that pressure, although, quite frankly, some of it is still there."

Too many pressures and changes on all sides, all at once, summarize the human side of this merger. Characteristically, these human strains and stresses in a merger always seem to come down to a lack of communication. As John Clark admits, "Communications were really critical—and we really tried—but there should have been a lot more of it in the beginning."

Although Manufacturers spent a great deal of time and effort communicating to its own employees about the move to Waterloo and the purchase of the new company, Dominion Life workers felt more isolated. Their early, and mistaken, understanding of the merger, which Manufacturers did not dispel at first, was that this was a merging of two organizations, with the best of each remaining largely intact. They simply were not aware of the fact that this was an acquisition, with Manufacturers' management clearly in the driver's seat. It took time for that realization to sink in.

Bill MacLean believes that a firm gesture at the beginning might have set the tone. "If we had presented it to Dominion Life as a takeover, they would have been able to deal with it in a much neater way." One of MacLean's employees suggested that "Tom Di Giacomo should have come down in a Cadillac, gotten out of the car, smoking a big cigar, and looked over the premises he had just bought. That would have put the message across."

Long-time Dominion Life employees recall feeling a need for more information right at the beginning of the merger, particularly about Manufacturers and its culture. "We needed to give the enemy a face," is how one worker remembers it. They also had to go through the process of grieving, of "saying goodbye to the old organization before embracing the new one."

When Keith Beveridge analyzed the merger process for a presentation to a U.S. group in 1988, he described the effects on employees as creating "a high level of ambiguity, weakened trust, an urge of self-preservation, coupled with anxiety and stress." In organizational terms, this produced conflicting values and policies, poor communications, lost commitment, and reduced productivity. To counter these negative effects, the organization reacted on a variety of levels: communications programs were improved, focus groups and counseling were provided to cope with stress, training programs were implemented to try and create "one company," and temporary staff were kept on, to try and reduce the workload. Gradually, through a combination of sheer hard work, tighter management controls, better communications, implementation of new computer systems, and attention to "people" concerns, the organization began to come out of the trough and move forward again.

But the single most important plan to improve the culture and communications problems, came in the form of a new building.

In July of 1988, 1200 employees of Manufacturers' Canadian division moved from their four cramped locations spread around Kitchener/Waterloo to a gleaming new flagship building in Waterloo. The chrome and glass building stands out as one of the most innovative and striking architectural designs in this prosperous southern Ontario city. And the interior upholds Manufacturers' tradition of quality and concern for its employees. Its bright and comfortable offices look out onto landscaped gardens and parkland.

Employees are unanimous in agreeing that the turnaround occurred with the move into the new building. Bryce Walker explains, "We went through a period of time after the merger when there was a lot of chaos . . . the building helped to bring people together." Dave Allen says that the move has "already done a lot to consolidate culture, making it possible to manage by walking around, function as a team, and much easier to communicate." Although it certainly wouldn't have had the desired effect without all the other efforts to pull the organization together, the physical move to one attractive location was the catalyst to turn the organization around.

Was the Merger a Success?

"It was the right strategic decision to come to Waterloo, but we underestimated what was involved. We fought our way out of it, and by any objective factors you care to name, we got a turnaround," say Keith Beveridge. John Clark backs up this assessment: "I thought we did really well, to be quite honest . . . look at what we had in 1984, and then look at what we have in 1989. . . . We've ended up with an organization that is, by and large, a new organization. There are 1200 people in Waterloo who think they are part of a really good company. Out of all this has come one of the top organizations in this country. Today we are regarded as the competition. We were not the competition five years ago."

There's no doubt that in strict business terms, the answer has to be yes. Five years ago Manufacturers had a declining presence in the Canadian life insurance industry, with a 3.5% share of the individual life market. Today, the company's share has increased to 5.1% and is growing. Sales credits for 1988 are 12.6% higher than for 1985.

But can you measure the success of a series of events as traumatic as a merger in straight dollars and cents? Although Manufacturers appears to have achieved their business objectives, surely the human cost must be taken into account as well. Couldn't some of the stress and upheaval have been minimized through more effective analysis, better communications, and tighter management of the merger process? Having survived what is often referred to in the company as "a time of chaos," managers and workers alike have some thoughtful views on what could have been done differently or better.

One Manufacturers' worker who made the move from Toronto to Waterloo believes the company could have "done further research into the administrative aspects of the two organizations, to overcome some of the problems brought about by the merger." She believes the merger was accomplished too quickly, and that with more thought and planning, the ensuing administrative problems could have been lessened. Dave Allen agrees, "If we'd thought of it dispassionately, and been very analytical, we might have been able to see things, anticipate problems before they occurred." Other workers believe programs should have been established much sooner to deal with merger-related issues of stress and workload.

John Neilson presents the most detailed action plan. If he had it to do over again, he would "set up a training unit for each of the four major business units in the organization, creating four work simplification teams, to facilitate the merger of the business groups." He would also "create a small organizational development unit for each group, whose task would be simply to communicate with people, to find out what problems are developing." Neilson explains that the managers were simply too busy trying to manage the business, instead of communicating. Hiring some extra staff to deal with the communications issue would have saved money in the long run, he believes.

Tom Di Giacomo muses: "I look back on it and I ask myself, 'Would you go through that again?' 'No thanks, once is enough!' But I can unequivocally say yes, in business terms, it accomplished what we set out to do." However, Di Giacomo adds that "major challenges still remain out of the merger: a sense of urgency of service is still missing."

Lessons Learned

Going through a merger is not always a positive experience, and, in fact, business school studies prove that the majority of mergers are failures, in terms of the objectives set out before the acquisition occurred. Nevertheless, Manufacturers has tried to take a few positive lessons from the experience. Keith Beveridge sums up the experience as providing an opportunity to create a "new" organization. He believes the following steps need to be taken in order to achieve a successful merger:

- Need to develop a vision
- Need a "hands-on" approach
- Need a balance between "too much" and "too little" action
- Need to involve employees
- Need to acknowledge what has been lost before moving on to what might be

Beveridge believes it takes a minimum of three to four years after a merger for an organization to regain its momentum and move forward as a unified group again. Four years after the merger of Manufacturers and Dominion Life, the merged company is the largest life insurer in Canada.

Snapshot of Manufacturers

Crisis:

Manufacturers is Canada's second largest life insurance company with assets of more than $16 billion, but the majority of its profits come from its business in 15 other countries. Its Canadian marketshare has dropped to eleventh or twelfth position. Its share of the individual life market is 3.5%. In 1985, Manufacturers buys Dominion Life Assurance Co. and initiates Canadian division move to Waterloo, Ontario, and merger of the two companies. In 1986, company experiences budget overruns, a decline in service, a backlog of claims, low employee morale.

Turnaround Strategy:

- Implement new budget system
- Hire new full-time and part-time personnel in problem areas
- Improve human resources function
- Add more communications programs
- Tighten management controls
- Monitor business more closely
- Consolidate employees from four different sites into new building
- Institute productivity improvement programs.

Result: Today Manufacturers Life is the largest life insurer in Canada, with assets close to $24 billion. Its Canadian division has 1200 employees in Waterloo. Its share of the individual life insurance market has grown to 5.1%, and sales credits are 12.6% higher than in 1985.

Symphony Nova Scotia:

Rising Out of the Ashes

Imagine yourself going to a city's major shopping center Saturday. You open the large glass doors leading into the mall and find yourself engulfed in the sweet sound of live symphonic music. Your curiosity piqued, you follow the musical melody down the mall to find a dozen musicians seated on a temporary stage. They are playing to a packed audience, from babes in arms to senior citizens. Some are comfortably seated at tables in the elegant makeshift tea room, while others are standing around the stage and in the more precarious positions offered by the upper balcony. You notice the CBC broadcasting booth and realize that other listeners are present in spirit, if not in body.

If the location is the Halifax Shopping Centre, this is not a dream. By chance, or by intent, you have become part of the budding romance between Symphony Nova Scotia (SNS) and its enthusiastic public. At first glance, this Saturday adventure in music might appear as an unorthodox scenario for the only professional symphony in Canada to sell more tickets to its main stage celebrity series (the classics) than to its pops (popular music) concerts. But as one begins to uncover the essence of this orchestra, this afternoon sojourn with its public represents a clever and strategic step in bringing to life one of the symphony's key philosophies—"bring the music to the people."

SNS is indeed an unqualified artistic success not only in its native province, but throughout Canada. It has made this journey with a balanced budget in four of its six years in operation. This extraordinary rise in acclaim is even more compelling given the fact that SNS rose from the ashes of the dead and buried Atlantic Symphony Orchestra (ASO). In September 1982, the ASO became the first million-dollar arts organization to declare bankruptcy in Canada. The unheard of and controversial move by the ASO board and then president, Hector McInnes, a well-known east coast lawyer, sent shock waves through the arts communities across Canada. It was the sign of the times as orchestras, theaters, and dance companies faced having to close their doors under the pressures of reduced government funding, shrinking corporate sponsorship, and the changing habits of arts subscribers.

The ASO was not an ordinary business that had declared bankruptcy. It was a deep-rooted component of the Canadian cultural scene and its demise indicated that centuries of music could not be sustained in the Atlantic provinces in the form of a professional symphonic orchestra. This was a devastating slap in the face for the Canada Council (the major funding organization for the arts in Canada), the provincial governments, the corporate sponsors, the lovers of music who had subscribed to the symphony, and the orchestra's 52 musicians — all of whom had struggled to keep symphonic music alive and well in the East.

The journey back would take much more than the standard turnaround practices used in business and industry. The traditional reasons for rebuilding a dying organization would not be found in this largely volunteer, non-profit organization. The bank indebtedness was not sufficient to demand innovative restructuring, the government shareholders had many more viable opportunities in which to invest public funds, corporate sponsors would have one less "charity" in which to donate their "good corporate citizen" monies, the public had other options for their interest and subscription dollars, the musicians had other orchestras to play in, and the volunteer board of directors had other headaches to deal with in other community activities, let alone their own businesses. All those involved were forced to face the fact that the symphony had become the playground of the elite who themselves had turned their attention and financial support to other endeavors. Nothing less than a total transformation of the community's attitude towards symphonic music was necessary.

The major problem with the ASO lay in the very reason the symphony had been granted its initial large chunk of funding — regional development. Symphony orchestras had sprung up across the country in the early sixties. To justify a professional orchestra for the population base offered by the Atlantic provinces, a regional orchestra seemed to be the ticket. It would represent all four provinces — Nova Scotia, Newfoundland, Prince Edward Island, and New Brunswick — and, as such, would attract the Canada Council's attention. One of the individuals who was very much involved in the establishment of the ASO was Brian Flemming, a Halifax lawyer, who would later become acting chairman of the Canada Council from 1974 to 1975. "In 1967, I chaired the interprovincial committee that founded the ASO. As treasurer, I negotiated the largest grant from the Canada Council they had ever given to a regional arts program," Flemming proudly recalls. Canada Council's motive was to encourage a higher standard of excellence within the Atlantic region by preventing the proliferation of mediocre community orchestras. In keeping with the regional mandate, each Atlantic province appointed directors to the board, and assigned their respective communities with the responsibilities of sponsorship and ticket sales in their areas.

All went well in the first few years when ASO's success was fostered through lavish grants and government support. But by the mid-1970s the cost of taking 52 musicians on tour around the Atlantic provinces could no longer be offset by ticket sales and government grants. To make things worse, diminishing government grants reflected the cutbacks that were being faced by all federal and provincial programs as they struggled with increasing deficits.

Gradually, the ASO became a Nova Scotia orchestra with a New Brunswick tour. Having lost touch with the many communities it served, it was seen as an organization of the elite. Provincial rivalries started to take hold, and soon the various communities were no longer working towards the same goal. Dwindling audiences throughout the region gave ample evidence that the scattered accountability for the symphony's success wasn't working. Peggy Forshner, the former administrative assistant for the ASO, now public relations manager for Symphony Nova Scotia, explains, "A community such as Moncton was responsible for getting the audience into the concert hall, and yet all their budgeting and financing, including accounts payable, were being handled in the quasi-head office in Halifax. When the orchestra went to play in Moncton, they would find less people in the hall than on the stage. The response from the Moncton organizers would be 'Well, we didn't make any money, so we have nothing to give you for the concert.' In reality, nobody was really in control."

This problem of control extended to quality in the music-making arm. No performance standard had been used in recruiting the musicians. Management's hands were tied due to the musicians' collective agreement, which provided tenure for players regardless of their performance quality. Musician-management conflicts escalated to the point that neither side was talking to the other. As a result, the musicians had no idea that bankruptcy loomed.

Poor orchestra quality, decreasing audience appeal, and incidents of community rivalry were only some of the problems facing the ASO. The $700 000 projected deficit seemed overwhelming to a board that was struggling with its own involvement and commitment. By September 1982, the board had reached the conclusion that they could only bandage the deep-rooted problems. Paralyzed, they could not arrive at a solution that would ensure the long-term viability of the symphony. In a move they felt was their only recourse, the board of directors shut down the ASO.

The Halifax cocktail circuit had been buzzing for months

with rumors about the growing problems facing the symphony. No one had ever thought that the community, along with the provincial and federal governments, would let this organization go under. Brian Flemming received a "mystery call" from an individual the night before the announcement, telling him that a couple of senior people associated with the symphony had decided to pull the plug. He was outraged. "The technique for saving orchestras, whether it be in Vancouver, Montreal, Winnipeg, or wherever, is to cry for help. You embarrass the governments and local communities into giving you more money. You get everyone you can get your hands on to talk up the symphony. Bankruptcy means the end. In the case of the ASO, the irreplaceable music library would go on the auction block along with everything else, just like if your local pizzaria went belly up. The board and the management should have had the good sense to cry for help. They should have realized that you never let an arts organization go bankrupt."

On that Monday morning in September when the news broke, the phone lines around the Atlantic provinces lit up. The reaction ranged from "gutless, nonsensical decision" to "the only thing they could do under the circumstances." Dollars and cents weren't at the center of the outrage; the loss of faith in the ethics and integrity of the symphony was.

One subscriber who was up in arms over the bankruptcy decision was Norman Newman, a well-established Halifax entrepreneur. "I was burning," he declares. "I woke up one morning to read in the newspaper that the symphony had gone down the tubes. As a subscriber, my cheque had already been cashed for the following season's tickets. I was livid that the contract had been broken, demonstrating a total breech of faith. This was no way to do business." Explaining to anyone that the 1982/83 season would bring the ASO's existing $400 000 accumulated debt to $700 000 was tough enough. Trying to rationalize that this state of indebtedness had come as a complete surprise was almost impossible, even for the most eloquent of advocates.

The real tragedy, however, far surpassed the mere loss of a $150 subscription. The bankruptcy decision shattered the lives of the musicians and office staff who, without warning, were unemployed overnight. If the players had been aware of the pending decision, many would not have waited around all summer, trying to make ends meet with temporary employment until their incomes resumed again with the beginning of the new season. The office staff were shocked to hear about their loss of employment on the local newscast. The only individual who had any idea of what was in store was Peggy Forshner, who had become increasingly concerned about the confidential information she was typing in the minutes of the board meetings. "I started to feel really scared. To add to this, I was told by the general manager not to discuss any of it with the other office staff or musicians. We carried on as usual ordering the year's brochures, selling tickets, and doing all the things we normally would. Then the weekend came when I typed the board agenda that spelled out the decision to kill the orchestra, or try to save it. I was getting ready on Monday morning when there it was on the radio – bang, ASO had been folded."

A Cry for Help

A cry for help was sent throughout Halifax. Brian Flemming was asked to help by several symphony supporters, including Chris Wilcox, then an ASO musician and now the head of the Scotia Festival of Music. "I refused," says Flemming. "I kept pushing the requests away, explaining that I didn't want to take this kind of challenge on. It was only a matter of days before I found myself involved in organizing and incorporating a temporary orchestra, named the Symphony Musicians' Trust Fund."

The Symphony Musicians' Trust Fund was a type of pick-up orchestra, established to provide the out-of-work musicians with desperately needed income and an incentive to remain in Halifax. Under the artistic direction of Boris Brott, the Hamilton Philharmonic conductor, the orchestra played a 20-concert season, starting in January 1983, which enabled the musicians to later qualify for unemployment insurance benefits. Their efforts were augmented by many well-known entertainers, such as Harry Belafonte, Anne Mortifee, Skitch Henderson, and Toller Cranston, who performed with them in fundraising concerts. Former ASO subscribers, who were willing to overlook their outrage to cautiously support the Musicians' Trust Fund, were appeased with discount tickets. Other financial support came in the form of small grants that Flemming and others were able to squeeze from government and business sponsors.

Luck finally started to play a role when the orchestra's assets were won back in an auction bid. "Our biggest concern was the music library," recalls Flemming. "A group of us put together our money to register a bid against Moosehead Breweries and some other companies for the library, furniture, bandshell, music stands. We were the lucky ones because we paid $10 000 for a quarter of a million dollars worth of assets."

Since it was never the intention to create a full-time orchestra out of the Symphony Musicians' Trust Fund, efforts to build a permanent replacement for the ASO were started. The difficulty, however, was that the entire community was split into many camps. From the moment the ASO went down, factions began to form, not only in the Halifax arts community, but throughout the Atlantic provinces. Realizing that split camps were only impeding the possibility of resurrecting the symphony, Louis Steven, Nova Scotia Deputy Minister of Culture, Fitness and Recreation, and Brian Flemming decided an old-fashioned town meeting would provide the only vehicle possible to vent all the views and get something moving. To accomplish this, they needed a non-partisan to chair the meeting. Lloyd Newman (no relation to Norman) seemed to fit the bill. An active and outspoken individual, Newman had volunteered much of the previous 18 years of his free time to the theater arts community. He had held key positions, such as the president of the Neptune Theatre Foundation (Halifax's professional theater company), and had been the provincial representative to the National Theatre School of Canada. He spent increasing amounts of time away from Arcade Ladies Shoppe Ltd., the retail fashion chain he owns and operates. What made Newman perfect for chairing the meeting was that the sole extent of his involvement with the symphony had been as a subscriber. Nova Scotia Director of Culture, Alison Bishop, contacted Newman to see if he would be interested.

"Why me?" Newman asked.

"Because you're clean," Bishop replied.

Newman accepted the task, not quite realizing the hornet's nest he was about to put his hand into. "All I knew was that I was supposed to show up and chair this meeting in November '82 in the Nova Scotia Hotel. I asked the province to give me all the material they had, since I was quite aware that a number of factions had axes to grind. From the numbers they gave me, it was obvious that some communities were doing better than others. Halifax was clearly doing the poorest financially, Fredericton was doing pretty well, and Sydney was in a fair position."

The town meeting indeed turned into a venting session for all. Lloyd Newman recalls the various positions that were presented from 7:30 p.m. to 11:30 p.m. that November evening:

"We did the best we could under the circumstances," declared Hector McInnes, ASO president, and Mark Warren, the former general manager.

"We're all good, underpaid guys that did everything possible. What's happened is obviously management's fault," responded the musicians' union.

"We're giving you all the money we possibly can. To add to your problem, you don't have an audience. This is obviously management's fault," said Franz Kramer, representing the Canada Council.

"We've been the senior partner giving more than anybody else—paying out the biggest bucks, taking the most heat, and getting the least benefits. We can't go on picking up all the deficit," replied the Nova Scotia government representative.

"We're giving more than our fair share of dollars for the least amount of service from the orchestra. It just doesn't make any sense for us as it currently stands," countered the New Brunswick government spokesperson.

"We don't really care," was implied by the absence of any P.E.I. representation.

"Of course, we support having a symphony, but we just

don't know how to organize one," the Halifax Board of Trade weakly added.

"Everybody vented their feelings, and the summation when it was all done was that another meeting was necessary, that's all," concludes Newman. What did result from this meeting was an ad hoc steering committee, which put together a "tentative" board for a new symphony orchestra. No permanent decision could be reached until all the disparate parties could come to a workable compromise as to if and how a new symphony could get off the ground. A handful of businessmen, including Flemming, Lloyd Newman, and Peter Andrews, another Halifax entrepreneur, came together to form this unofficial board. Others were asked to participate, but they declined to be involved. "Many of the people I approached said they simply could not afford being associated with another arts community failure," recalls Flemming. "I couldn't give them any guarantees that, after donating 400 odd hours of their lives, we would achieve a success."

By now it was evident that the various factions had divided into two camps. Lloyd Newman further explains: "The new board that came from the steering committee represented the right wing solution. The left wing path involved a group of musicians and others who thought having a symphony in the Atlantic provinces was very important and that success would be reached if the government simply spent more money on it. They were headed up by Peter Alapin, who worked at the time for the N.S. Department of Development. As a private citizen, he kept putting together plans, papers, and proposals on how the symphony and its organization should be put together."

The Nova Scotia government made no attempt to bridge the two groups. It believed that any concerned citizen had the right to propose an alternative solution and be heard. Eventually all the recommendations were handed to the steering committee, who in turn passed them on to the new board at their first meeting. Just before this meeting began, Lloyd Newman and Brian Flemming, the only two members with any arts board experience, had a brief side-line huddle to determine their playing positions. Newman recalls, "Prior to the meeting, Brian and I talked to some of the provincial officials who would ultimately be putting up the money for the symphony. We asked them who they wanted to see as president and vice president. They replied that it could be either myself or Brian, as long as whoever was going to carry the ball would be around and not out of town on a regular basis. So Brian and I met in the corner of the room while the other members were forming. I told him that his strong connections with the Canada Council and other government bodies meant he should take the presidency and I would be the V.P. He said fine as long as I would become the chairman of the executive. These quick and informal decisions carved out the roles we would play in the critical rebuilding years. Brian became our ambassadorlike chairman, wheeling and dealing on the outside, while I was the chief operating officer, involved with the dirtier side – the difficult, nitty gritty, day-to-day stuff. This didn't mean his job was any easier than mine; we simply had different jobs to do. I was the lightning rod that got things going, and he was the gentleman who straightened everything up neat as pie."

It would take more than this interplay to get the ad hoc board through their torturously long and difficult meetings, sponsored and held in provincial government offices. The individuals struggling to keep symphonic music alive in the province had realized how overwhelming the odds were in dealing with interprovincial organizations, especially those that are labor intensive with volunteers and require centralized management control. So, this group of concerned citizens went to bat trying to get something going for Nova Scotia alone.

Some of these board members, including Norman Newman for one, thought that a simple injection of "good business sense" was all the new organization needed. He soon realized that an arts board was unique. "I found myself involved with a very complex not-for-profit organization that operates differently from any business I've worked in. In my unschooled way, I realized that I had been used to mandating what I wanted, instead of consulting with a wide network of key players. The profile staggered me. I was now accountable to my fellow board members (20), some of whom I had disagreed with in the past. It was no longer just a club. We had to resolve our differences to pull together in the same direction."

The new board had no time to waste on personality differences. They had a tough mandate before them. One of their first tasks was to understand the critical path document that Peter Alapin had prepared for his group and then offered to the new board. "It stretched across three walls of the room," remembers Lloyd Newman. "But in actual fact, the big problems involved in putting a symphony orchestra on stage are really quite simple on paper, if not in practice. You need a band, an audience, and somebody to pay for both."

Next the board began their search for an artistic director. "Now conductors don't grow on trees," continues Lloyd, "unless you put an ad in the paper announcing that you have a certain amount of money. You'd be astonished by those who reply. Around the world, everybody wants to be a conductor, but the good ones are booked years in advance. The point is that you need a guy to show up on Thursday, not three years from Thursday."

Their next step was to assemble an orchestra, an extremely complicated undertaking. The ad hoc board commissioned Boris Brott and Mark Warren, the former ASO general manager, to recommend what the new orchestra should look like and how to get it to that point. Lloyd Newman recalls the highlights of the report: "Most of the ideas were a rehash of what Brott did in Hamilton, which Warren put into shape. It recommended that we put together a core orchestra, made up of a string quartet, a brass quintet, and a few other key musicians. Theoretically, this gives you the flexibility to split them up and have your string quartet playing in Yarmouth and the brass quintet performing in Truro. Then when you wanted to play a bigger piece of music, you could contract additional musicians."

The Brott-Warren report also recommended programing, which revolves around the pivotal question "how many different kinds of music will our population pay for—classical, opera, baroque, chamber, and pops?" A total transformation of the community's attitude towards symphonic music was necessary. This was accomplished by reversing the age-old adage of bringing the people to the music. Symphony Nova Scotia would bring its music to the people.

By their fourth meeting, the board had gathered sufficient momentum and credibility to incorporate itself, demonstrating its victory over the other divergent camps. As vice president, Lloyd Newman's first big job was to do a "back of an envelope" budget. "It wasn't a six-week exercise to figure out how much it was going to cost to play poker," explains Newman. "The most complicated version took about 40 minutes. It didn't take long to recognize the extent of the shortfall and what we would need from the obvious sources – the Canada Council, N.S. provincial government, and fundraising efforts."

The courtship for funds began again. The Canada Council and the province of Nova Scotia were approached. "We told them that the price of poker was $300 000 from both the federal and provincial agencies," recalls Lloyd Newman. They replied that the price was too high. Both governments were obviously nervous about funding a second failure. They agreed to put together a financial package they could afford.

Undaunted, Lloyd Newman went off to lobby with some members of the provincial cabinet. Edmund Morris, chairman of the Management Board, responded: "At $250 000 we can breathe; at $300 000 the air gets thin; and at $350 000 it gets rarified, and here is who you should see." With list in hand, Newman went off to seek the necessary financial backing. By the time the dust settled, both the Canada Council and the Nova Scotia government had agreed to jointly grant $450 000 to Symphony Nova Scotia for its first season of operation, on a $1.2-million annual budget. Additional fundraising drew $150 000 from the private sector. The Flemming-Newman team had indeed shown they could call the game.

Putting Talent in the Pit

One of the key lessons Flemming had learned from his ASO experience was the importance of being recognized, something he and the other organizers had failed to do. "As an orchestra grows, you can get some pretty poor players. In retrospect, the biggest mistake I made in the creation of the ASO was not to audition every single individual. We were determined never to let that happen again, so we got the SNS board to agree that everyone would get an audition—bar none," recounts Flemming. Boris Brott was appointed as a one-man audition committee to select 13 musicians to form the core orchestra.

The musicians were outraged. They had lost their jobs without warning. They had been only temporarily employed by the Musicians' Trust Fund. Now, adding insult to injury, they had to audition for a place they believed was rightfully theirs. To make matters worse, less than a quarter of the original musicians would be able to play. On principle, many refused to audition. Of those that did, only seven positions were filled. Angry letters and phone calls poured in. But the worst was yet to come. The blast came at the first union meeting. Lloyd Newman recalls the event: "The first thing I told the union was, 'We are a brand new orchestra, we want a brand new contract; we want to pay the musicians the right amount of money; and we want the best we possibly can for everybody concerned.' Those were the last words I said for 45 minutes to an hour. I was subjected to a tirade on the basis of the old contract and everything that had happened in the past." Lloyd was lucky that he had brought the right man to help him out later on— Norman Newman.

During his tenure as owner and president of a mid-size grocery chain, Norman Newman had been involved with a fair share of negotiations, including the reorganization of his 700 employees into a non-union work force. He was just the man to sit at the table with the handful of angry musicians. "Norman has an enormous capacity for detail," remarks Lloyd Newman. "He is the perfect negotiator. He is dogged, careful, consistent, unfailing, with an excellent memory and enormous patience. He is the antithesis of me in that sense. I lose patience in the first minute and a half. If I had negotiated with them, they would never have gotten on stage today."

Norman Newman's talent lay in his appreciation of how the musicians were feeling. "The musicians were hungry and insecure," recalls Norman. "They had to put bread on the table, so they knew that they had to keep their mouths shut and go along with us the best they could." This was a tall order for a group of musicians who were feeling extreme pressure from their unsuccessful peers. Even the musicians' board representative had to be replaced when he failed to pass his audition. It was going to take more than dogged determination and empathy to get a contract signed.

On the day of Symphony Nova Scotia's first concert, the contract was still up in the air. Underestimating the toughness and conviction of the new board, the musicians felt they were now in the power position. They were aghast when the out-of-town soloist took to the stage without them. The audience was given a free recital and raincheck for a future concert. The musicians came back to the table the next day, ready to sign a one-year contract.

During this time, the search continued for a conductor. Boris Brott, a talented artistic director and entrepreneur, had become increasingly involved in the orchestra through his work on the board's strategy report and subsequently his auditioning of the new orchestra. As such, he was a prime candidate for the position of SNS's artistic director for its 1983/84 season. He was not, however, going to be a shoo-in. The board was split between Brott and Simon Streatfeild, another well-known conductor. The Streatfeild supporters felt that what was needed was an artistic director who placed his personal goals second to the orchestra's needs in contrast to Brott's self-promoting style. They also felt Brott's dual role as the artistic director of the Hamilton Philharmonic would pull him in too many directions. Brott's politicking among board members irritated those who saw the resulting decline in interpersonal relationships as disastrous in an organization as fragile as the new symphony. The Brott backers argued that his talent and already established rapport with the Halifax audience would bring security at a time when the symphony was struggling with its tenuous future.

The board painfully went after a consensus. By the time an offer was made to Streatfeild, he had already accepted a position with the Quebec Symphony. The decision had been taken out of their hands—Boris Brott would be SNS's first artistic director.

Putting SNS on the Map

The new orchestra worked hard to rebuild its integrity and credibility, by including two free concerts for past subscribers and instituting a policy that held all subscription money in trust until the first concert of each season. The first season's program was heavily laced with popular music to draw a wide audience. By the end of this first season, the new orchestra had contracted a full complement of talented musicians. The second season was virtually sold out. The CBC broadcast a few concerts and the sponsors were happy with the results. Everything seemed to be coming up roses, until the musicians' contract had to be renegotiated for the second season.

"The union would not come to the table," recalls Flemming. The SNS musicians were still waging a two-year-old battle, which had started with the closing of the ASO and had resurfaced with the decision to audition all players for the limited number of positions in the core orchestra. They were demanding security, a key component demanded by the American Federation of Musicians Union, of which they all were members. The Federation's contractual agreement protected musicians from outside competition by forcing orchestras to hire players from their local area. The agreement also prevented the orchestra from being split up, thereby allowing some players to play a different schedule than others. It also secured the employment of musicians through tenure without any role for quality standards. Since the federation was not an official bargaining unit, it lacked a conciliation process and therefore allowed direct strike action.

Brian Flemming refused to be "blackmailed" into a substandard orchestra which could strike, as it had previously done on the symphony's opening night. He decided to sue the senior officers of the federation on the basis that their association was restricting people's freedom of rights—the freedom to work anywhere they wanted to. "On the same day, within a two-hour period, bailiffs were busy serving writs to all the senior officers of the music associations in eastern North America," recalls Flemming with obvious pleasure. "It was a fight over rights more than money," he contends. "Under the Canadian Charter of Rights and Freedom we were able to remove the restrictions. A lot of these and related rulings have subsequently been changed." With Norman Newman's help, a three-year contract running from 1984 to 1987 was finally established. The ink was dry on the agreement, but antagonisms ran deep, as evidenced in subsequent negotiations.

At this point, however, the show had to go on. Growth targets had been set for the number of musicians in the orchestra; but, they were limited by the cash flow. Not the least of their problems was the fact that no bank would touch them. "I actually went back to the Bank of Montreal and offered them the account for the new orchestra," recalls Brian Flemming. "They thought that was pretty gutsy, given the fact that they had taken a bath of a quarter of a million dollars with the ASO. Their answer was, 'We appreciate your coming to see us, but no thanks. We wouldn't touch you with a ten-foot barge pole.' So I went to my bank, the Bank of Nova Scotia, and convinced them to do our banking as long as we would never have one dollar of overdraft. We would never have a loan and would run solely on our cash flow. If you think running a million-dollar arts organization on its cash flow isn't exciting, you have another think coming. It's been just about the best business training I have ever had." To heighten the challenge, subscription monies were, and still are, locked away during the toughest period of the year – the end of the season. Managing the final quarter, before the new season's funding is made available, requires an innovative approach to financing.

During the first two seasons, stringent controls helped the orchestra remain within its annual $1.2-million budget. "One of the keys to the turnaround involved determining our means and then living within them," Flemming recalls. "We had to stop thinking that one sunny day, somebody would come along with a bag of money and make everything better. The first board met every Monday for the entire day. Everything was done at the board level, including if you wanted to buy ten dollars worth of postage stamps. From proposals to pencils; everyone had to be in on it."

By the end of the second season, Brian Flemming believed he had done the job he had started. The interim Musicians' Trust

Fund had wound down in year two of Symphony Nova Scotia, once it had been proven that Halifax could support a permanent orchestra. It finished in style, with a $30 000 surplus which was rolled into SNS. It became evident that the symphony was achieving its financial obligations when the board meetings dropped to three hours once a month. Much of this had to do with the disappearance of the suspicion and doubt that had plagued initial board meetings. By now, divergent factions that lingered from the original days of the board had assimilated into one hard-working team —not, however, without the type of conflict and challenge that keeps an organization healthy.

Handing over the Baton

The finale of SNS's last concert of the 1985/86 season marked the end of Boris Brott's tenure as artistic director. For a variety of reasons the board had decided not to renew his contract. Brott's dual conducting responsibilities had turned him into a "parachute conductor." Norman Newman explains the damage factor this created: "Brott would fly in and pick up the pieces cold. The musicians would have three rehearsals, at the most, before a concert and then they were expected to roll. Right after the concert, he would parachute back out. He was always in a rush. On a couple of occasions, he missed the rehearsals completely. This really blew the musicians away, since they take their music-making very seriously. Every time they go on stage, their skills and reputation are on the line. The lack of continuity between the concerts meant that there was no one around to keep the interpersonal relationships going amongst the musicians. They need all the care and nurturing they can get. It certainly became apparent to us that having someone fly in and out was not the answer to building a long-term symphony orchestra."

Brott's part-time conducting role wasn't the only issue behind the board's decision. The symphony's management had become concerned about mixed reviews from the audience and the growing number of non-renewals of subscriptions. The symphony's revitalization depended on an accurate understanding of the market, and the orchestra's ability to play to it. They couldn't afford to miss the mark—not even once. "We realized that the really hard core music lovers could go out and buy a wonderful recording on a compact disc without the bother of attending a live performance," explains Peggy Forshner. It was clear that the quality of the orchestra was not increasing sufficiently to expand its audience base. The board put together a search committee to hunt for potential conductors, who would then be tested in live concerts throughout the 1986/87 season. This recruitment strategy was critical in a business where the chemistry between the leader and his followers is one of the main determinants of success.

It was in the midst of the decision-making for the 1986/87 season that Luc Charlebois came on the scene as the new general manager. The symphony had outgrown its previous general manager and was in need of a more professional approach to management. This was especially the case in an organization whose board of directors was turning over every two to three years. As such, continuity was a necessity in its management ranks as well as in its artistic direction.

Charlebois had spent the bulk of his career in an assortment of symphony management positions. He came to SNS from the Vancouver Symphony, which was experiencing the same economic difficulties that had destroyed the ASO in 1982. Having replaced a general manager who was a former ASO musician, Charlebois wanted to offset any potential feelings of alienation by the orchestra. This was especially important, since the Brott years had left the musicians feeling particularly vulnerable. Charlebois immediately started working with them to gain their trust.

Another individual interested in maintaining his level of trust with the musicians was Norman Newman, coming in as president in September 1986. In only six months, the three-year contract he had negotiated with the musicians would be up for renegotiation. Based on the events surrounding the last two negotiations, Newman decided to start the process early, this time with another skilled negotiator, Kevin McNamara.

With his excellent track record in health care negotiations, McNamara was asked to join the board for a three-year term, although he only saw himself being involved for the duration of the negotiations. "The challenge presented by the situation appealed to me," recalls McNamara.

When McNamara first met with the musicians, it became evident that they were still struggling with the same issues that were outstanding in previous negotiations. A new provision that musicians would be let go if and when their performance deteriorated, or if they did not grow with the orchestra, added more fuel to the fire. After a series of discussions that stretched over the season, the musicians and McNamara were able to mutually agree that their main focus was the long-term viability of the orchestra. "The key to negotiations is sitting down with the expectations and dealing with the realities. We didn't change the size of the orchestra or the length of the season, because we were able to convince the musicians that economically, we were not in the position to afford that type of growth in the short term. We finished up in jubilation, since we had reached a three-year agreement without any animosity," concludes McNamara.

The one thing everyone agreed on was the type of artistic director the orchestra needed. As McNamara explains, "With an average age of 30, SNS is made up of young musicians, many of whom want to use this experience as a springboard into other career opportunities. Even the musicians who see themselves permanently planted in this community want to grow. They all wanted an artistic director who was going to help them develop."

In the fall of 1986, SNS met the man who would lead these young musicians to greater musical heights—Austrian conductor Georg Tintner. Ironically, when Tintner came to Halifax as a guest conductor for an evening of Viennese music, he had no idea the orchestra was looking for a new full-time artistic director. But having spent the last 30 years in Australia, he was looking for a change.

From the moment Tintner raised his arms in rehearsal, a rare musical bond was forged. The SNS musicians were drawn out of themselves, captivated by the maestro's talent. During the intermission, an ex-student of Tintner's, who was also an orchestra member, excitedly approached board members to express the conductor's interest in the position. Later that evening, recognizing that such an opportunity might never come again, a decision was taken to approach Tintner about the job. The artistic turnaround of the orchestra was launched that night.

Why would a 69-year-old, internationally known conductor be interested in moving halfway round the world to lead a struggling provincial orchestra? The answer can only be found in the intriguing contrasts that define Georg Tintner. He views himself as a simple man, yet his frail frame and white flowing hair hide a vast reservoir of energy and drive. His attitude to the members of the orchestra is unorthodox: "I see the musicians as collaborators, not as slaves or students. They are my fellow workers." His goal is simple—"to be the best."

His conducting technique is equally intriguing. In rehearsal, he never raises his voice, never scolds a musician. Yet he conducts with passion. He does not use a baton, since he claims nothing should come between himself and the music. "It doesn't matter whether you lift your left finger or your right; whether you stand on your head or not," says Tintner. "What matters is that you have definite and pronounced feelings about the music you love, and somehow communicate that. Some people have this, and some do not. I have seen great conductors standing in front of brilliant musicians and not be able to do that. And I have seen a leader stand in front of not-so-good musicians with a belief that they can do so much better, and I have watched them rise to the heights."

Tintner's leadership of the orchestra is best summed up in his own words: "I have no ambition . . . nothing. I want to make great music . . . that's all!"

Not a Moment Too Soon

Tintner's arrival in December 1987 was expedient, coming as it did on the heels of Symphony Nova Scotia's first real deficit—

$84 000. Ironically, it occurred in Norman Newman's first year as president. This was particularly hard for Newman to swallow, because it had been he who had chastised ASO's former management for its poor financial management. With his characteristic sense of humor, Newman describes the deficit as "the blot in my career." At the time, however, he saw nothing funny in the financial situation that he knew was developing, but had no way of stopping. Government grants were on the decrease and expenses were on the rise. With a $1.5-million budget, the shortfall had to be met through the fundraising activities of the board and its volunteers. They were assigned the tall order of pursuing every possible avenue. Unfortunately, their efforts also fell short.

As a result the board gave Kevin McNamara the fundraising job for the 1987/88 season. Aside from his prowess as a negotiator, McNamara's national reputation as a fundraiser made him the ideal candidate for this vice president's role. McNamara soon found that the fundraising function was in an embryonic phase, involving only cataloging and record keeping of sponsors and donors. Nowhere did he see the type of thinking that produced capital campaigns or special events sponsorship.

Realizing that the job was too large for one man alone, McNamara convinced the board to hire a full-time professional fundraiser. The board had barely begun its search when Lana Robinson unexpectedly arrived on the scene.

In June 1987, Robinson was in Halifax to arrange the Canadian Opera Company's gala launch of the *Tales of Hoffmann*. As the special events coordinator for the opera company, she had to meet with the symphony to discuss the performance schedule for the fall. Robinson was intrigued by the symphony's board, its musicians, and Tintner's imminent arrival. "I am what you call an intuitive opportunist," Robinson explains. "I knew from Mr. Tintner's face that he was going to be something very special. I believed that something very unusual was going to happen with SNS. And I wanted to be there." She asked if the symphony would be interested in hiring her. If her credentials and experience hadn't been enough, the success of the opera gala sent out the message loud and clear that this woman knew what she was doing. Now schooled in the art of grabbing opportunity wherever it knocked, the symphony took her up on her offer. In January 1988, Robinson started her job as director of development.

If Robinson had any doubts, they were soon erased by her discovery that she and Tintner shared the same goal – to serve the music. They also shouldered the repair work needed to resurrect the symphony from its ASO demise. While Tintner's mandate was to rebuild the orchestra's quality, Robinson's challenge was to reconstruct the image of the symphony as a worthwhile investment for donors and sponsors.

Fundraising requires a complex combination of concurrent activities from special events to what Robinson calls "marketing marriages." The first special event designed to attract attention was already underway when Robinson arrived. A Black Tie Bingo, which combined the elegance of formal attire with the lively fun of bingo, brought in $18 000 from a crowd in which 80% were non-subscribers. When Shell Canada approached the symphony in early 1988, it discovered that the school program it wanted to sponsor was already spoken for. To meet their needs, the symphony developed the Shell Family Series, targeted at families with eight- to twelve-year-olds – the subscribers of the future. These six Saturday concerts were held in halls limited to 300 people so that the children could be close to the musicians and the instruments. With Shell lending their name to the programs, Robinson was able to interest other sponsors to back each concert at less cost than the main stage or Pops performances required. Yet another marketing marriage was put together when the *Chronicle-Herald* newspaper provided free advertising for the concerts. Under the artistic direction of guest conductor Mario Duschenes, the series was such a success that the symphony will be offering an additional series for five- to eight-year-olds in its 1989/90 season.

When Robinson arrived in Halifax, the principal flute was the only orchestra "chair" being sponsored. Realizing that $1200 might be too steep for some donors, she decided to sell the chair's legs, enabling donors to translate their funding into sponsorship. In Robinson's words: "When dealing with donors and sponsors, there's no such thing as no. No amount is too small." The underlying premise to all this activity is to make the community believe SNS is their symphony.

The initial success of the fundraising function became immediately apparent at the end of the 1987/88 season when the corporate sponsorship total alone jumped from the previous season's tally of $35 000 to $84 000. The total budget shortfall was still $5000 until Norman Newman decided that he wasn't about to have another deficit on his hands. He appealed to each board member to help make up the balance. That season SNS made 37 cents profit.

Norman Newman now felt he had all the pieces in place. He had secured two brilliant directors to lead the symphony both artistically and financially; as well, he had established a professional approach to management. All this had enabled him to turn the board into a policy-making committee, replacing the operational orientation the leadership of the board needed during the initial turnaround years. They were ready to be transferred once again. This time it was to Kevin McNamara.

The Irony of Success

When McNamara took over as president in the fall of 1988, he knew he had artistic success on his side. Along with hundreds of others he had witnessed a growing fascination with symphonic music. "Unlike my namesake, I'm not musical at all," McNamara concedes. "I can't sing, dance, play an instrument, or tell when they've changed tunes if it's at the same speed. Now I'm hooked. In my first year with the board, I went to one token concert. You couldn't keep me away this past year. My daughter has even helped me learn the names of the instruments." Dry wit is characteristic of this man who softly sells himself and the orchestra. But there is nothing soft in McNamara's drive to push through the many barricades still hindering the symphony from achieving financial security. Ironically, he has discovered that one of the thorns in the symphony's side is its artistic success. Many sponsors now feel that the orchestra has "made it" and no longer requires their help.

The financial statements tell another story: SNS is projecting a $75 000 loss for its 1988/89 season. Plagued by the chronic problems of decreasing grants and increasing expenses, McNamara and his board are in the constant process of making ends meet. The budget rose to $1.7 million due to the increase in salaries that make up 70% of the expenses. Limited by the size of the Rebecca Cohn Concert Hall and subscriptions that are close to a sell-out, few additional funds can be raised from ticket sales on the existing program series.

To meet these challenges, SNS has taken on a three-pronged development strategy. The first goal is to maximize the utilization of the orchestra. Regardless of the amount of playing time, musicians are paid for a 31-week contract. The challenge now is to program as much playing time as possible. Translated into action, this means finding ways to broaden the audience base with an exciting and attractive repertoire of additional concert series.

In addition to its Baroque, Mozart, Celebrity, Pops, and Shell Family concerts, SNS has begun to bring the music to people outside Halifax. Its 1988/89 season included a Cole Harbor Series for the outlying community close to Dartmouth and a Christmas concert in Glace Bay, Cape Breton. The symphony will continue to spread its magic throughout the Atlantic region in its 1989/90 season, bringing its history full cycle. This time, however, stringent cost control and playing already rehearsed pieces will ensure these tours are financially viable. An Encore Series will also be added, which will offer a repeat of four concerts in the main concert hall.

The second goal is to continue to improve the fundraising function. In spite of the fact that 1988/89 corporate sponsorship is up 40% to $140 000, and overall fundraising revenue is $270 000, the symphony is competing for contributions in a city that is saturated with other professional fundraising campaigns. In addition to Robinson's innovative search for new and different ways to secure sponsorship, board member Gillian King is aggressively recruiting board members whose specific mandate is to raise money. Although individuals are asked to join the board because of their unique skills, each one must fulfill a demanding role in fundraising.

This brings SNS to its third goal—to ensure cost effectiveness in everything it does. It's one thing to have the musicians working; it's another to ensure a profitable return on investment. For example, its 1988 *Merry Widow* gala was a flamboyant and artistic success. Yet the costs in time and dollars were so high that the SNS only realized a small profit margin. A special task force of board members has been put together, who will be completing a trend analysis on all symphony activities. Their objective is to ensure that every marketing, business, and artistic decision is contributing to the symphony's profit. Other sources of income will be generated by maximizing ad sales in the concert programs. These have already shown a phenomenal jump in annual income to $25 000 compared to one-fifth of that figure three years before. Another avenue for revenue will consist of a gradual restructuring of seat sales in the Rebecca Cohn, to charge higher prices.

The Fundamental Dream

Where does all of this leave the 38 musicians who are key to the success of the symphony? They see the administrative structure as necessary, yet secondary to the force that binds them to their profession—the desire to play great music. To make ends meet, many are forced to supplement their salary with additional jobs, such as teaching music or selling real estate. "It is a very hard and insecure life," explains Tintner, speaking from experience. "You never know from one day to the next where the money will come from. It is not right that they are forced to sell real estate. What is right is for them to teach their instrument, but this is not easy with a demanding rehearsal and performance schedule. They come together and play with joy and enthusiasm, but all of the rest isn't fair. They should not have such worries."

Georg Tintner will do anything in his power to provide a better life for his musicians. His first aim is to extend the season so that they have more paid time to tide them over the lean months. His second goal is to put opera on a more important footing with his audience, thereby increasing the size of the orchestra. With the planned tour of the *Marriage of Figaro* he will take this dream on the road during the 1989/90 season.

Tintner's dreams, and those of the many other SNS supporters, made it possible to raise this orchestra from the ashes. From shopping malls and factories to churches and the main stage, they have brought the music to the people. Like other turnarounds, no one individual or group can be singled out. The symphony today bears little resemblance to either the ASO or the initial Symphony Nova Scotia that struggled for recognition back in 1983. Most of the individuals that make up the board, as well as the staff and the orchestra, are new. Rebuilding an organization using the same players is one thing. Doing it with a constantly changing roster is another. This was a turnaround that nobody had to do. It was done by a group of prominent businessmen and -women who put aside their own entrepreneurial endeavors to rebuild an organization for the benefit of their community. Brian Flemming, Lloyd Newman, and Norman Newman, and scores of other dedicated arts lovers, came to realize that resurrecting a dead symphony takes a great deal more ingenuity and hard work than starting one from scratch. The new band of leaders want to make sure that history does not repeat itself. Their struggles are far from over, but there is no doubt that none of them will give up until the phoenix is in full and unshakable flight.

Snapshot of Symphony Nova Scotia

Crisis (September 1982):

Atlantic Symphony Orchestra declares bankruptcy.

Turnaround Strategy:

- Establish interim orchestra
- Appoint new board
- Secure provincial and federal government funding
- Implement strategy to recover audience
- Hire Boris Brott as artistic director for three seasons commencing the fall of 1983
- Place stringent controls on all aspects of the orchestra from musician auditions to budgeting
- Introduce professional approach to management by hiring new general manager
- Appoint skilled negotiator to handle contract negotiations
- Upgrade musical quality of symphony with the addition of maestro Georg Tintner
- Hire professional fundraiser
- Add concert series and tours to attract new audiences and increase box office draw
- Put special task force in place to initiate and implement cost effectiveness initiatives

Result: Symphony Nova Scotia is one of Canada's most respected orchestras. Although it has had a balanced budget in four of its six years of operation, it is now struggling to combat its accumulated deficit due to shrinking government grants and its inability to gain financial support from any lending institution.

Fruehauf:

Where Cash Is King

Turning a failing business around by a combination of team-work, hard work, and local know-how is the story of how Ed Van Doorn and Andy Tarrant made a success of a failing trailer manufacturer in just four short years. It's a tale of two completely different personalities – the one a prairie boy from Flin Flon, Manitoba, and the other a city boy from Burlington, Ontario – whose success is a clear testimonial to the veracity of that old adage that "two minds work better than one."

The first member of the duo is Van Doorn. Nicknamed "Bumper" by union members for his aggressive tactics on the picket line, he is six foot one and 110 kilograms of only just repressed tension and energy. Known for his innovative and driving sales and marketing ability, he's a shrewd negotiator and a tough bargainer. Van Doorn is also impatient, both with details and with failure. His operating style has been described as "Shoot, ready, aim." He has to be in constant touch with events, so he's never out of reach of a phone.

Then, there's the soft-spoken Tarrant, the thinker and

numbers man. A high school drop-out whose 18 months as a steelworker sent him rushing back to school for his accountant's degree, Tarrant has staying power and quiet determination. Patient and persevering, he works the numbers until they come out right.

The two met in 1975 when they both went to work for Brantford, Ontario-based Trailmobile, a manufacturer of truck vans and trailers. U.S.-owned, Trailmobile went through a series of owners during the '70s and early 1980s. During this period, both Van Doorn and Tarrant moved up the promotional ladder to increasingly senior positions within the Canadian company. By 1982, Tarrant was vice president, finance, while Van Doorn, after a stint as vice president, marketing, was named president.

However, 1982 was not an auspicious time to assume top jobs in the truck trailer industry. It was a period of recession, leading to ever-decreasing sales, downsizing, and strikes. At Trailmobile alone in 1982, some 16 040 trailers had to be repossessed due to bankruptcy or failure to meet payment schedules. For Tarrant, 1982 stands out in his memory as the year "in which I spent six months of my time with lawyers dealing with bankruptcies."

The next year wasn't much better, because that was the year of the "big strike," which nearly caused the collapse of the company. The majority of the plant workers—approximately 130 members—went on a protracted strike, called by the United Auto Workers Union, demanding parity with U.S. auto workers. Two months into the strike, with no end in sight, Van Doorn and Tarrant were called to head office and bluntly told to calculate the costs to shut down the whole operation. Allied Signal Inc., the U.S. conglomerate that owned the money-losing Canadian operation, gave strict orders about the closure. Tarrant and Van Doorn were to head back to Brantford and run a skeleton staff until the company either sold or closed the operation. "You can retain 12 people in head office, including yourselves, if you so desire," they were told. This meant immediate layoffs of 100 office staff.

Tarrant and Van Doorn flew back to Brantford and proceeded with the shutdown, including themselves in the dozen workers kept on the payroll. After completing their calculations of what a total shutdown would cost, they flew back to Chicago to present their estimates to the U.S. owners. "We were at 35 000 feet when I said to Andy, 'This is dumb. We could buy it from them for a buck and save them all this money [the money the shutdown would cost],' " says Van Doorn. That's when the idea first surfaced that they might be able to salvage the company by buying it themselves. The two managers were convinced there was nothing wrong with the company that a few months' careful management wouldn't put right.

However, Allied Signal's top brass didn't immediately grasp the brilliance of Tarrant and Van Doorn's proposal and told them to proceed with the shutdown. Back in Brantford, events were turning nasty. The strike was particularly violent, with Molotov cocktails being thrown, transformers being shot out, and strong-arm tactics being used on the picket lines. After a couple of unpleasant incidents, "Bumper" Van Doorn (who tried to drive through an unrelenting, unmoving picket line) was transferred to the Chicago head office. Having planted the seed of the idea of selling Trailmobile to the local management, Van Doorn continued to promote the concept whenever he could.

In Brantford in the meantime, after a bitter nine-month-long dispute, the strike was finally settled and work resumed at the plant. (The strike had ended in a draw, since neither side had achieved its aims.) But Allied Signal continued its efforts to find a buyer for the company, in spite of the fact that Trailmobile actually started to make money in the spring of 1984. By January 1985, the U.S. management started to come round to the idea of selling the company to the local managers. Van Doorn and Tarrant were delighted but apprehensive. "We didn't know how to do it, and we didn't have any money," Tarrant recalls.

The two men sat around Ed Van Doorn's kitchen table, armed with a real estate house purchase form as their only guide, in their first attempt to iron out the details of what the deal would eventually look like. "Strangely enough, what we worked out on New Year's Day, 1984, was pretty close to what we eventually did when the sale finally closed," says

Van Doorn. Allied Signal's board decided to help them out, at least with the question of "how to do it." They sent a New York consultant to Brantford to guide them through the buyout process.

According to Van Doorn, there were two keys to their success in achieving their dream of a management buyout. "First, you have to believe really strongly that you can do it. And secondly, your sales/marketing and financial team have to be well organized." Tarrant also attributes part of their success to Van Doorn's persuasive sales technique in bringing the American owners round to the idea of a management buyout.

After months of work developing a professional prospectus with their N.Y. consultant, Van Doorn and Tarrant were ready to attack the second part of the equation necessary for a successful sale – the financing. Up to this point they still hadn't been given a final sale price by the U.S. management. Now they were told to find $15.9 million in order to complete the sale. They approached four banks with their now-polished prospectus: Toronto Dominion, the Royal Bank of Canada, the Continental Bank of Canada, and the National Bank of Detroit. Only one of the banks, T-D, turned them down. "That's the point at which Andy became a believer," chuckles Van Doorn. Van Doorn himself, as the quintessential salesman, had always believed it could be done and simply took minor setbacks in his stride. "Every time I got turned down, I looked upon it as an opportunity. Now I know better; now the next guy I go to, I won't make that same mistake again."

After a lot of negotiation, the complex financing was arranged, drawn from four groups: the Royal Bank, Penfund (an association of some of Ontario's largest pension funds), the Ontario Development Corp. (ODC, an Ontario government-sponsored venture capital scheme), and the management group. Van Doorn and Tarrant persuaded ten other senior managers in Trailmobile to come in with them on the buyout. The majority of the managers mortgaged their homes in order to find the cash for the buyout. The ODC matched the amount the managers were able to raise personally in the form of an interest-free loan, to be paid back within three years.

The deal was finally completed on November 26, 1985.

Although Van Doorn says he remained positive throughout the year-long buyout process, convinced that it should work, there were moments when he thought the deal would never close. "There were too many lawyers, too many accountants, far too many complications and roadblocks along the way." The day the deal was completed, Tarrant stayed in Brantford, while Van Doorn raced around Toronto all day delivering the cheques that would close the deal. "Up and down elevators, all day, and when the last cheque had finally been delivered, the lawyers all disappeared and it was done. There I was, alone, and there was no one to celebrate with. So I drove home, but I stopped along the way in a little hamburger joint. That was my celebration."

Now that they owned the company, a turnaround was needed to make their investment in the company grow. The senior management group held a strategy session in a local hotel and debated about the future of the trailer industry and the company itself—"where we were at the present, and where we wanted to go in the future," says Mike Hand, vice president, manufacturing. In addition to keeping track of all expenses and initiating a just-in-time inventory control system, the group made a conscious decision to run a more open and less reactive management style. "It's very hands-on, management by walking around," says Tarrant. New incentive programs, tied both to performance and to profit margins, were implemented. The new owner-managers wanted to create a sense of stability and permanence within the organization. They believed that workers have more faith in a company that was owned by the people who managed it. "It's our bread and butter as well as theirs," says Hand.

Stringent financial controls had already been imposed during 1984 to keep costs down, and these continued. As Hand explains, "When you're spending your own money, you're much more conscious of how it's spent." Van Doorn attributes much of the company's continued success to the tough training imposed in the days when they were a branch plant. "That training by the multinationals provided us with the financial discipline we needed." That discipline includes the necessity to prepare annual reports outlining objectives, and backing them up with solid detail and research. Without the discipline imposed by such a process, "it would be all too easy to short circuit the process and make mistakes along the way," explains Van Doorn.

Probably the single most important management lesson learned by Tarrant and Van Doorn came from their contact with Allied Signal senior management. The two men had become accustomed to presenting revenue projections for the coming year to their U.S. bosses. But one year, Allied Signal executive Rich Russell threw their revenue projections out the window and bluntly demanded, "How much cash are you generating?" Van Doorn and Tarrant didn't know—they'd never been asked that question before. But they found out very quickly. "That philosophy was instilled in us at that time, and it's remained our most important principle," explains Tarrant. "Quite simply put, cash is king." That motto, of watching and generating cash flow, has guided the company through a period of dramatic growth.

The company also significantly improved their labor relations by successfully negotiating a new three-year deal with the Canadian Auto Workers without a strike.

Tarrant and Van Doorn then knuckled down to deal with some of the broader business problems: new product development, getting inventory levels down, and improving cash flow. "We knew what had to be done, so we went out and did it," explains Van Doorn. Although the two men had an extensive background in strategic planning, they rejected this method as "too slow and not action-oriented." Instead, they aggressively pursued opportunities whenever and wherever they appeared. The fact that the economy went into an upswing, and that the trailer market took off again, certainly helped Trailmobile to expand rapidly.

One year after purchasing Trailmobile for $15.9 million, this private company posted revenues of $130 million. In September 1987, less than two years after the initial buyout, Trailmobile went on the acquisition trail. Having streamlined the Brantford operation and cut costs wherever feasible, Trailmobile's internal house was in order. However, the external environment was worrying. Although the company ranked second in sales in Canada, the owners were concerned. "It became apparent to us that the company would not survive if free trade occurred. Trailmobile was simply too small and didn't have access to the U.S. market," says Tarrant. It became clear that they had to buy a company which would give them access to the larger market to the south.

After reading a small newspaper notice announcing that their number one competitor in Canada, Fruehauf Canada Inc., was up for sale by its U.S. parent, Trailmobile moved quickly to eat up its major competitor. Although slightly larger than Trailmobile, with sales of $141 million, its two plants, including one in Ingersoll, Ontario, were just what Trailmobile needed to expand its capacity and give it the ability to sell into the U.S. The initial agreement to purchase was settled very quickly less than two months later, with Trailmobile agreeing to pay $105.5 million for Fruehauf in a leveraged buyout deal. But then the federal government's competition watchdog reviewed the sale, voicing fears about the lack of competition that would occur if the two rivals were allowed to merge. The Bureau of Competition Policy initially blocked the merger, and then revised its decision by posting certain restrictions before allowing the sale to proceed. Trailmobile was allowed to purchase the larger company as long as it ran the two organizations completely autonomously until it had sold both the Trailmobile name and toolings. (In fact, the company was unable to find a buyer for the toolings, so eventually the Bureau dropped this requirement.)

This decision was the start of the most difficult period Andy Tarrant and Ed Van Doorn had experienced in their partnership. The two men had become accustomed to, and even depended upon, their ability to function as a team. Suddenly they were forced to operate independently, without even the opportunity to contact each other. The easy camaraderie they enjoyed, the ability to rely on the other partner's strengths, the opportunity to discuss all major decisions—suddenly that all vanished. Ed Van Doorn retained the title of president of Trailmobile, while Andy Tarrant took over as president of Fruehauf. For the nine months it took them to sell the Trailmobile name, the two men operated what were in effect separate companies, in competition to each other. "It was most unnerving," admits Van Doorn. "I missed the other half. 'Where's my sounding board?' I kept asking." Tarrant remembers the isolation most keenly. He had to move into a new company as the new boss, who had just taken over the business. "It was tough to break the ice at Fruehauf, where I didn't have any friends." The two men admit that it really hit home afterwards how important the team approach had been in creating and maintaining their success. "The Ed and Andy Show" remains the cornerstone of their success.

In October 1988, with the sale of the Trailmobile name and van designs complete, the show was allowed to resume, and the two men set about consolidating the gains from their acquisition. They were finally allowed to merge the two operations.

The nine months that Tarrant spent running Fruehauf were real eye-openers for him. This was an organization frozen in the past. Computers were almost unknown, even accounts were posted manually. The management style was secretive and old-fashioned. There was no sense of urgency and very little accountability. No one seemed to understand that the decisions they made had an impact on the organization's bottom line. And, almost worst of all in business terms, there was a two-year inventory of trailers stacked up in the parking lots. In March of 1988, Fruehauf had $58 million in inventory.

Major changes were quickly made to shrink Fruehauf down to an economical and cost-effective size. Tarrant and Van Doorn closed down and sold the Fruehauf's Mississauga plant for $20 million, while retaining a 25% ownership in the acquiring company. Unprofitable dealerships were sold, and inventory was disposed of. Inventory stocks were cut almost in half, bringing the number down to $28 million. As occurs all too often in the majority of turnaround situations, there were layoffs and terminations. In early 1988, the merged companies had approximately 1800 employees. By mid-1989, that number was down to 1100 with the terminations coming from both the Trailmobile and Fruehauf employee groups. Some retraining occurred to avoid even greater numbers of dismissals.

Van Doorn and Tarrant instituted many of the methods they had already used at Trailmobile to energize and motivate the remaining Fruehauf work force. Communications strategies, including a newsletter, and quarterly employee meetings were put in place. Lateral job switches became common, to broaden and stimulate some stagnant workers. Pay for performance and bonuses were instituted. And everyone throughout the expanded organization became aware of the importance of positive cash flow. "Cash is king" remains the motto of this aggressive firm.

New business strategies were evolved, centering on new product development. Lighter vans and trailers are being developed, as well as a lighter refrigerated trailer.

This paring down and cost-cutting did not have an immediate effect on the bottom line. Sales for 1988 were $225 million, but profits were low. Van Doorn and Tarrant hope their long-term business strategy will pay off in increased profitability in the 1990s.

But despite all their efforts to become cost-effective and efficient, the two men still remain somewhat pessimistic about long-term chances for success. Free trade remains a nagging worry. Can a Canadian trailer manufacturer of medium size compete effectively against the U.S. giants? Another issue complicating their capacity to compete are new, stringent trailer design rules, which stipulate that Canadian trailers be of a heavier weight than American ones, thus giving U.S. trailers an immediate advantage in the Canadian marketplace. Add to that the time-consuming and costly WHIMIS program, as well as new environmental regulations, and you end up with a much more tightly regulated industry. Van Doorn, the concept man, isn't sure that they can pull it off, and Tarrant, the numbers man, says they may be able to compete, but will they make any money?

Being able to achieve cost reductions, and still work on development of new products, while at the same time operating the company is taxing the capabilities of this medium-sized and medium-capitalized company. The business environment in which Fruehauf must work has changed significantly from when Van Doorn and Tarrant bought Trailmobile in 1985. A whole variety of new factors have complicated the trailer business. With free trade, the ability to compete effectively in the larger U.S. markets remains a question mark.

The uncertainty created by these factors eventually resulted in Fruehauf seeking better financial backing. Under a financial restructuring concluded on July 26, 1989, Fruehauf Canada was sold to a group of investors led by an Indonesian diversified conglomerate. The Wanandi Group of Jakarta, a privately held family firm with international interests in the auto parts industry, bought the controlling 60% interest in Fruehauf. A financial investment group from New York bought 20%, while Penfund retains a 10% interest. The present Fruehauf management group retains a 10% ownership position and will continue to run the company.

"What we'll be able to do now," explains Van Doorn, "is implement our strategy much faster. Our focus will change from sales and marketing to manufacturing. We're looking for increased manufacturing efficiencies, and deliveries, together with higher-quality products. Our secondary thrust will be to sell more effectively to the whole North American transportation market."

The Ed and Andy show effectively turned around a sick organization with a combination of teamwork, hard work, and tight management control. Starting in 1984 with just a few ideas, they borrowed their way to success. In just five short years, they have parlayed their ideas into hard cash, now owning (together with their senior managers) 10% of a new well-financed company with sales in the region of $225 million, and good opportunities for growth.

Snapshot of Fruehauf Canada

Crisis (1984):

Nine-month-long strike brings Trailmobile to verge of closure; U.S. parent decides to sell company to senior managers. Managers acquire struggling company for $15.9 million.

Turnaround Strategy:

- Cash is king—keep close track of expenses and cash flow
- Implement new incentive programs, tied to performance
- Manage by walking around
- Improve labor relations
- Improve communications
- New product development
- Implement "just-in-time" inventory control system
- Growth through acquisitions—buy your major competitor
- Close unproductive divisions and lay off unnecessary staff
- Search for cheaper suppliers

Result: Today Fruehauf is the largest truck trailer and van manufacturer in Canada, with sales of more than $225 million.

Royal Trust:

From Country Club to Global Competitor

During the mid-1980s, Royal Trust transformed itself from a paternalistic, simple trust company, with a country club atmosphere, into a dynamic, multi-faceted financial institution, selling a much broader range of goods and services on a global scale. This reborn company bore little resemblance to the organization whose first motto outlined its purpose as "executing trusts and administering estates, and as a safety deposit company and general financial agents."

Incorporated in 1892 as the Royal Trust and Fidelity Co., the name was shortened to Royal Trust Co. in 1895; however, it wasn't until 1899 that the company opened its doors to the public. Donald Smith, immortalized in Canadian history as the man who drove in the last spike to complete the Canadian Pacific Railway, was the company's first president. Growth was rapid, and by 1914, Royal Trust had branches in every major Canadian city. Expansion into Britain in 1929 was followed by the establishment of additional offices in a variety of overseas locations.

By 1982, Royal Trust was one of Canada's largest trust companies—a staid, old-school-tie firm, which although profitable (a 1980 net income of $37 million), was seeing its market-share declining in most areas. "The word that comes to mind to describe the company back then is very *paternal*. The trust business was a gentleman's game—you didn't go for market-share, and you didn't take a kick at the other guy," says Charles MacFarlane, senior vice president, personal financial services, marketing and sales. This was a traditional retail mortgage company, with very little corporate business. In its eyes, other trust companies were the only real competition, and banking was a whole other business.

Its size, combined with its strong financial performance, steady asset growth (at the end of 1983, assets were up more than 8% from the previous year at $10.6 billion, half of that being held in mortgage loans), and an aging management team, made the company an inviting target. Robert Campeau recognized this as early as 1980 when he tried to take over the company in one of the most spectacular takeover attempts this country has ever seen. His unsuccessful bid for Royal Trust unwittingly set the stage for the successful bidder. After the failure of his attempt, Campeau sold off his block of 8% of Royal Trustco shares, allowing Olympia & York to increase their holdings in Royal Trust to 23%. Meanwhile, Brascan upped its holdings to 17%. But it was Trilon Financial Corp., another of the Bronfman family of companies, that successfully took control of the company in July 1983 when it bought out both the Brascan and Olympia & York blocks, ending up with 42% of the shares. This percentage was eventually increased to more than 50%.

This wasn't the first time that these two heavyweight business families, the Bronfmans and the Reichmanns, had collaborated in a business venture. The two groups had earlier cooperated in the joint ownership of Calgary-based real estate company Trizec Corp. Ltd. The partnership in Trizec, and their rescue of the firm from near bankruptcy, set the pattern for their working relationship with Royal Trust. In May 1981, Albert Reichmann and lawyer James Tory were appointed to the Royal Trust board, together with Michael Cornelissen and one other Bronfman nominee. That number was upped to six with the appointment of Mel Hawkrigg, senior vice president of Brascan, and Earl Orser, chief executive officer of London Life. Brascan President Trevor Eyton took over the chairmanship of the board in September 1983, publicly cementing Brascan control of the venerable trust company.

In what has now become a trademark pattern with Bronfman takeovers, after acquiring a solid company with a steady if uninspiring financial balance sheet, the Bronfman board members moved quietly but firmly to take control and change the direction of the firm.

In early 1983, John Scholes, president of the company, resigned due to ill health. There was no obvious successor in the wings, so the long arm of Brascan flexed its muscles and appointed Michael Cornelissen to the new position of vice president of the company. Cornelissen had already acquired something of a reputation as a turnaround specialist from his part in the revitalization of Trizec.

A chartered accountant with a degree from the University of Natal and an MBA from the University of Capetown, the native of South Africa had been audit supervisor with Touche Ross & Co. and then vice president, finance, for Rennies Consolidated Holdings Ltd. before moving to Canada in 1976. After a short period as VP for Edper Investments Ltd., Cornelissen joined Trizec in 1977 at a moment when the firm didn't even have enough money to meet its payroll. Trizec had been a good proving ground for Cornelissen, a conservative yet innovative financial manager. He took much of the responsibility for diversifying Trizec's debt away from floating bank loans and into fixed long-term debt and Euro-market syndicated loans.

At the beginning of 1983, Cornelissen was executive vice president and chief operating officer at Trizec. In March, he moved to the vice chairman's job at Royal Trust. He spent six months examining the company from all angles, assessing both strengths and weaknesses. At the end of August, he took over as president.

The Turning Point Had Been Reached

"At that time I guess we thought we were pretty good. The press said we were one of the best managed companies . . . our performance was relatively good. But looking back now I see it much differently. Our turning point was certainly Mike Cornelissen," recalls William Gordon, vice president, central Ontario region.

"When I first joined Royal Trust, I saw huge opportunities everywhere," says Cornelissen. "It was a wonderful 85-year-old company. But it had been allowed to go to seed over the past ten years. It was over-institutionalized and out of touch with reality. Senior management had no clear vision of where to take the company." Cornelissen took it all in hand and decided to turn it around to achieve the potential he could see lying dormant everywhere.

Charles MacFarlane, senior vice president, sales and marketing, personal financial services, says: "For 19 years I've been very proud of working for Royal Trust. I still am. We were not a poor company earlier. We were just not as dynamic as we could have been. During the first year of the turning point, I went home really tired, really excited, because I knew I was getting an education that I hadn't had in my previous years. I felt like part of the team that was going to win the ball game, because we had a game plan."

Implementation

What was so fundamentally missing at RT was a sense of mission and purpose. When Cornelissen was named president, he set out to create that mission. One of the senior vice presidents describes the process: "The genesis came early in 1984, when Mike Cornelissen said, 'I'm president of this company and we don't have a focus. We don't have a direction, and I don't have a vision. Well, 35 to 40 of us are going to go away for two days, and we're not going to come out of the room until we have a vision.' "

Even the skeptics were dragged along: "And we all went. We all said to ourselves, 'Sure we are, we're going to change the culture.' Well, we went away for two days and came away with that mouthful. The culture did change – it was the most incredible thing I've seen, ever ... We came out with that document signed in blood. . . ."

"That mouthful" was the new company mission statement: "Royal Trust will be the acclaimed provider of modular financial personal lifetime services for middle and upper income Canadians, and profits will double by 1990." Not exactly a household slogan, but that somewhat tortured and clumsy summary was a major step forward. For many of these executives, it presented the first time they had ever focused on the company's specific business goal. And as their grasp of the new focus evolved and grew, they clarified it to a much more precise and zippier slogan: "Make a million people wealthier every day."

The company's new strategic plan was embodied in a document called "Vision 1990," which outlined the following policy thrusts:

- Design the company around the client
- Create a new sales orientation and culture
- Institute a commitment to quality
- Aggressively establish a diverse set of new products that are the best in the business
- Invest in management information and electronic communication systems

The next stage was a structural reorganization: all job titles, positions and perks were done away with until a new structure could be put in place. "All of a sudden you didn't have a job, per se, although you were employed," says one senior manager who lived through it all. Cornelissen appointed three chairmen who in turn appointed their own teams. No jobs were sacred or guaranteed, no territory protected. It took three months before the organization chart was completely redrawn.

The challenge was to define the nature of the work to be done, and then to create job functions to get them done. Then the right people were appointed to fill the newly created jobs. The basic ground rules were simple: fewer layers, while those that remained were to be market- and client-oriented.

Cornelissen also imposed a new set of corporate values on his managers and, through them, to the rest of the company: a sense of urgency, combined with hard work and a results orientation. Gentlemanly banker's hours were replaced by 7:00 a.m. meetings, as well as late night and weekend sessions. The proof of his success in transforming the culture is the description current senior managers give of the present Royal Trust ethos: "aggressive, dedicated, focused, not risk averse, and not worrying about the bottom line."

Charlie MacFarlane remembers very clearly the immediate impact Cornelissen had on the way he viewed the trust business: "He made me look at my business differently . . . because he was asking for data that I'd never asked for before. 'How much do you make off your average customer? How many customers do you have? How many products does your client have? What's the profit margin on that product?' I was able to say my business made money. I wasn't able to say which of my products made most of that money, and which of my products lost money. And I began to ask myself, 'Why didn't I ever ask for that data before? It's relevant data — I should know that if I'm running the business.' "

Although there's no doubt that Cornelissen put his own special stamp on the culture he imposed on the company, the values clearly belong to a broader framework shared by the senior managerial group in all Bronfman-controlled companies. This group company philosophy is put into play, in a variety of versions, in all the companies that the Bronfmans control.

As Brascan Ltd. President Trevor Eyton explains it, "When we became acquisitors, we quickly realized that if we were going to be good at this, and achieve profitable returns from the companies we were buying, we had to develop a clear philosophy. We had to establish a level of trust and cooperation. At Brascan we believe in public companies and in establishing objectives acceptable to other stakeholders. We needed to gain their support."

The genesis of this philosophy goes right back to Peter and Edward Bronfman, according to Eyton. "Early in the 1970s, Peter and Edward gave this charge to us: if we were going to do business in their name, they wanted to do things that could stand public scrutiny and exposure." The philosophy has been developed, refined, and honed over the years behind the scenes by Brascan financial guru, Jack Cockwell, who prefers to remain out of the limelight. According to another member of the Bronfman team, Managing Partner Bill l'Heureux at Hees International Bancorp Ltd., Cockwell is the driving force behind the business philosophy. A master of the one-page memo on the topic of values, Cockwell's literary style has evolved from his early days at Mico (a precursor to Trizec Ltd.) when the philosophy used to be printed in verse form.

The result of Cornelissen's new broom approach created an uncomfortable atmosphere within Royal Trust. A number of senior people, unhappy with the new direction and culture, left. Others were dismissed. Seven of the senior managerial group were gone within a year of Cornelissen's arrival. So the inevitable second stage was to hire new people to fill out the senior ranks. Cornelissen went out of his way to hire multi-disciplinary staff—not just trust experts. The majority of the new people came to the company, not through head hunters, but drawn by RT's new ideas and culture. David Dunlop, senior vice president, corporate financial services, elaborates: "There was a clear recognition by Mike Cornelissen that essentially financial services is a people business. I don't think anybody in Canada had seen it quite as clearly as they had. So he went out and got that team together." The reorganization of the management team also included eliminating layers, simplifying the chain of command to leave only four layers between customer and president. Bureaucracy was ruthlessly stamped out.

After the new team was hired, a different compensation scheme was put into place. Following the Bronfman group policy, salary levels were fixed below market levels. But generous incentives were offered in terms of share ownership. The thrust of this philosophy is to encourage employees to share the risk and responsibility with the owners and shareholders. As

Trevor Eyton sums it up, "Basically we tell our managers, 'Take the shares, work hard and forget about the salary, and in three years you'll be rich.'" Mel Hawkrigg, chairman of Trilon Financial Corp., elaborates: "This salary philosophy is crucial to the success of our group of companies. It avoids turf wars, politics, and backstabbing from building up. We don't argue amongst ourselves. Instead, we work together to figure out how we can create more wealth. We try to take more risk." All senior employees at RT in effect put their own money on the line by taking a portion of their salaries in the form of loans to buy RT shares. As a result of this system, in 1989 more than 60% of RT employees actually owned shares in the company. Senior executives alone owned more than $65 million worth of company stock.

Having put a keen and motivated new team in place, the third stage was to change the focus and orientation of the business. As Murray Wallace, a former senior manager with RT, now president of Wellington Insurance Co. (another Bronfman-controlled company), explains, "Basically the vision was to target all your efforts to specific clients; to create the best products, targeted at the best people." That cumbersome mission which the senior people had struggled to articulate in that two-day marathon session shortly after Cornelissen's arrival was honed down and refined into something much more specific and easy to grasp. By 1988, it had been reduced to a graphically simple wealth triangle: clients, shareholders, and employees. "Royal Trust's mission is to create wealth for our shareholders, employees, and clients. We use a triangle to symbolize the mutuality of interests of these three groups."

Six years after the turnaround was initiated, Royal Trust is enthusiastically healthy. Although its financial performance never suffered significantly, even in its "resting on its laurels" days before Cornelissen's arrival, its current performance has improved dramatically. Net income for 1982, just prior to the turnaround, was $44 million. Figures for 1988 are well over four times that at $212 million.

Royal Trust is not only one of the country's two largest trust firms, it is also recognized as the most innovative. It has initiated a number of new financial instruments, such as the Guaranteed Market Investment Index, the Stock Price Adjusted Rate Certificates, and some unusual mortgage schemes.

It has also looked beyond traditional national boundaries to position itself as a global competitor. According to the firm's own projections, they expect international operations to account for 40% of their net income by 1992, almost doubling the current percentage. They have been aggressively pursuing that goal with a string of international acquisitions. The 1986 purchase of international firm Dow Financial Services gave RT immediate access to market interests in Hong Kong, Singapore, the Caribbean, Switzerland, and Britain. Cornelissen's drive to give RT a presence in the majority of the world's financial centers increased with the announcement of the purchase of Pacific First Financial Corp. of Tacoma, Washington, in the spring of 1989. This "super regional bank" fills in a glaring gap in the organization's American coverage and presages a major presence in the U.S. market in the future, bringing RT even closer to full international status.

Writing in *Maclean's*, Peter Newman states, "Royal Trust has been growing so fast that its non-fiduciary functions threaten to turn it into a giant money supermarket, instead of the stuffy trust company it was only four years ago." Six years ago, its major competition was other trust companies. Today, its challenge is directed at the banks themselves.

Why It Worked

The transformation from a stuffy trust company to a dynamic entrepreneurial success, in just six years, is a significant achievement. Credit for this transformation must certainly be attributed to the tough tactics of Mike Cornelissen. But the key to his success lies in the underlying philosophy that permeates the whole Bronfman group of companies. What makes this particular brand of philosophy work? Perhaps it is a canny combination of elements: trust, teamwork, accountability, and risk-taking, all resting on a foundation of hard work. In addition, this culture is aggressive, entrepreneurial, and people-oriented. It recognizes the fact that properly motivated and re-warded employees work harder and achieve superior results.

As Cornelissen explains, "The majority of the new people came to us because they were attracted by our ideas. They were well trained, well educated, well motivated." Once they had been indoctrinated with the company's mission, they were encouraged to take charge of different tasks, to build up their commitment to the corporate vision.

Excellent communication techniques were another essential requirement, to build that groundswell of commitment right through the ranks. That's how the Employee Annual Meeting came about. Instead of just having an annual meeting for shareholders, it was decided to bring employees up-to-date in a similar fashion. This annual meeting is now held at Royal Trust locations across the country. "All the senior managers attend," says Cornelissen. "It gives us an opportunity to talk to our employees in groups of 200 to 300. It's also a chance to personally evangelize our mission. It's worth gold to us. We all meet 75% of our employees each year."

In addition to publishing their regular annual report for shareholders, Royal Trust now also publishes a status report for their workers. The employee annual report summarizes the past year, highlighting achievements and outlining the company's objectives for the future in simpler, less financial terms than an annual report.

The turnaround was initiated by Michael Cornelissen. His hard-driving, aggressive, no-nonsense management style started the process. However, as one of his senior team said: "This was a team turnaround. Mike was the catalyst. But he couldn't have done it himself. The team fit together so well that the team concept goes right through the whole company." Cornelissen himself agrees with this assessment: "This was not a one-man process—it was a team turnaround. My biggest accomplishment was in assembling the team."

Chairman of the board Hart MacDougall says force-fully, "The bloody team works." Having spent many years on the senior levels at the Bank of Montreal, watching that organization trying less successfully to transform itself, he's more sanguine about RT's success: "It was a mixture of luck, the right contacts, being careful to hire people compatible in every respect."

MacDougall also attributes Royal Trust's success to the simple but effective concept of accountability. According to him, "Banks aren't accountable. But if you have a significant shareholder, they remind you how accountable you are. They remind you of the smaller shareholders, and so you act differently. I am more accountable than Bill Mulholland [chairman of the Bank of Montreal], for example."

Employees were all given quantifiable objectives to achieve. As Cornelissen succinctly put it, "If an objective is not quantifiable, it's not achievable." This fundamental, results-oriented approach soon became accepted as the norm in the company. "This results business will pass" was replaced by "I'd better take my objectives seriously." The rewards for achievement are high, but so is the toll. Hard work, long hours, and stress are taken for granted. And so is adherence to the company philosophy. Dissenters and doubters are not tolerated—they soon leave the company.

Michael Cornelissen forced the company to create a focus for itself. A new mission was articulated. That process started a reorganization. All jobs and functions in the company were re-examined and restructured in the light of the new focus. Incompatible employees, or those unwilling to adapt to the new focus, were let go. More senior managers, with similar ideas, were encouraged to join the team. The new management team then set about transforming the company to correspond to their new aims. A variety of management tools were used: communications programs, training and indoctrination sessions, motivational schemes such as incentive salary programs. The whole company philosophy was reoriented outward towards the client. Change and transformation were institutionalized to try and make them constant.

Trevor Eyton acknowledges the turnaround at Royal Trust as the jewel in the Brascan crown: "It was sensational because the company was so bad, and it is now so good. And being in the financial services sector, it's under enormous public scrutiny, and in spite of this scrutiny, it accomplished such an excellent turnaround. It's really the greatest success in our group of companies."

Snapshot of Royal Trust

Crisis:

Although still profitable, Royal Trust sees its marketshare eroding in most areas. In 1983, Trilon, one of the Bronfman companies, takes control of RT.

Turnaround Strategy:

- Install strong leadership
- Identify new corporate vision
- Put new management team into place
- Set up objective-setting program
- Implement pay-for-performance program
- Establish regular employee communications meetings
- Emphasize teamwork

Result: Today Royal Trust is not only Canada's largest trust company, managing assets exceeding $106 billion, but it is also the leading innovator in the financial services industry. In addition, it is the only Canadian trust company with an established international network.

Turbo Resources:

The Western Engine That Could

Every morning in Africa, a gazelle wakes up,
It knows that it must run faster than the fastest lion
or it will be killed.

Every morning a lion wakes up,
It knows it must run faster than the slowest gazelle
or it will starve to death.

It doesn't matter whether you're a lion or a gazelle,
When the sun comes up, you had better be running.

These words hang not on the wall of an African big game hunter, but in the office of Gerald Sioui, vice president, supply and distribution, of Turbo Resources, headquartered in Calgary, Alberta. The hunt refers not to the pursuit of wild animals, but to the largest game in western Canada – the oil and gas business. While the outcome of the lion and gazelle's game plan is always predictable, the oil patch is a different matter. In less than 18 months in the early 1980s, the oil industry's boom collapsed and Turbo, the lion, was transformed into a fleeing gazelle.

Falling oil prices; escalating royalty payments, petroleum taxes, and interest rates; overcapitalization; and Turbo's miscalculated takeover bid of Merland Exploration Limited combined to produce financial disaster. By 1982, Turbo's long-term debt had soared to just under $1 billion—a dramatic increase from the $128 million the company had incurred at its peak in 1980. The first net loss in 1981 of $20.5 million would seem insignificant when compared to the 1983 figure of $278 million.

What kept the receiver from closing the company's doors can best be described by the adage of the day, "If you want to get the bank on your side, get into them hard." Ironically, the very debt load that was bringing the company down was its protection from Chapter 22. The truth of the matter was that the Canadian Imperial Bank of Commerce and the 12 other lenders could not afford to shut the company down.

Turbo, along with its competitors, had ridden the waves of the boom and bust economy in style. Although the numbers may not be as dramatic as the infamous Dome Petroleum debt of $6 billion, their stories are similar. The vision and egos of Dome's Jack Gallager and Bill Richards were matched in style, if not proportion, by Bob Brawn and Ken Travis, co-founders of Turbo Resources Limited. And the CIBC was the primary banker for both companies.

Starting in 1981, the industry and the province of Alberta were forced into a slow and painful rebuilding process, which would require a very different type of thinking and set of skills than the original industry builders had used during the 1970s. The heroes who had created the industry would be replaced with new leaders who could work through the financial mess left behind. The financial institutions themselves would have to accept innovative equity arrangements rather than be forced to write off the burdensome debt load.

One component that would not change is the spirit that drives the industry. It was there at Leduc, Alberta, Canada's first significant oil discovery in 1939, and it will be there for as long as there are hydrocarbons below the earth's surface that beg to be discovered. It is often difficult to decipher whether the thrill is in the hunt for hydrocarbons or the economic riches they bring. As one begins to understand the egos behind the quest, it becomes easier to realize how the hunt transcends the dollars and cents practicalities.

The Thrill of the Hunt

The very nature of the oil industry is that of a high stakes poker game. It begins with the "elephant hunt" for large reserves and ends with the price wars between the local service stations. What makes the quest so intriguing is that geological and engineering sciences often play second fiddle to the egos of the hunters. In a business that involves intuition as much as it does science, those with a proven track record of successful discoveries assume herolike status in their own industry as well as in the financial, investment, and government communities that back them. Millions of dollars roll off the tongues of explorers, who themselves operate in such mind-boggling numbers as trillions of cubic meters. When one realizes that Canada's oil and gas supply is based on only five successful exploration strategies, it becomes easier to understand the types of odds that exist for success or failure, and thus the blinding challenge that stimulates the hunt.

Each exploration decision, costing millions of dollars, is seen as the one that could produce the next elephant discovery. Instead of being seen as a loss, dry holes are viewed as invaluable information sources for the ongoing search. Gerald Sioui, a 20-year oil and gas veteran, has worked for three oil and gas companies. He cites one such example with a pre-Turbo employer. "I remember a particular series of management meetings that went on throughout one summer. The main focus of our discussions was our multi-million-dollar offshore drilling program. At every Monday morning management meeting, the individual in charge of drilling would come into town to go over the well's progress. Timing was important because we had to be out of the drilling site by October before the ice formed. In October, this individual came into the meeting and said, 'Great, we pulled out today and got everything out in good order.' Everybody was enthusiastic about how well we'd been able to pull out. Nobody in that room asked if he had found any oil. It was a dry hole, but throughout the whole summer, the question had never been raised as to whether or not they were getting any good signs. There was just a different attitude. In the long run, they believed they just couldn't miss."

The potential wealth at the end of the drilling shaft, financed in part by the cash flow from the "peanuts" (the small producing reserves), captures the imagination of even the most practical of people, whether they be in exploration, production, or marketing. It is little wonder that the odds of the game, set in the context of depleting resource economics, would force financial accountability to take a back seat to the self-serving competitive spirit that drives the oil patch. "The years leading up to the turbulent '80s were the good years," recalls Sioui. "The thing I remember the most now when I look back is that never in my 20 years did we talk cash flow, or profit and loss. These figures simply did not enter our discussions. If we had to buy crude, well then, we went and bought it. If we needed a new refinery, then we went and built one. The motto of the day was, 'Don't fix it, buy a new one.' We made money in spite of ourselves. It was a continuous climb up. Nobody ever thought it was going to go the other way."

The members of the Organization of Petroleum Exporting Countries (OPEC) appeared equally oblivious to the potential for falling off the cliff. In 1973 the Arab-Israeli conflict caused Arab members of OPEC to impose an oil embargo on the United States and to cut back their production to other countries by 25%. The direct result was a jump in oil prices from $3.00 a barrel in September 1973 to $11.65 a barrel the following January. For the next ten years, the world economy would feel this sudden price shock. The resulting accelerated rate of inflation brought with it a worldwide recession, which hit North America particularly hard.

Countries that were experiencing balance of payment problems due to heavy oil importing costs were forced to cut back on their demand. Those nations that refused to be held ransom started promoting investments in oil conservation and alternate energy sources. The higher prices stimulated exploration and production in locations such as Alaska, the North Sea, and Mexico. The trend to reduce dependence on OPEC oil caused world oil demand to fall more than 20% between 1978 and 1983.

In hindsight, the mistake that OPEC had made was all too clear. It had caused the price of oil to jump too high too rapidly. The oil cartel went into action with a price freeze on oil in the late 1970s. By 1978, the recovering demand for oil was hit again by a 50% cut in Iranian oil production. The war between Iran and Iraq immediately followed in 1979, which dropped OPEC oil production even further. Oil prices abruptly doubled from $15 (U.S.) a barrel to $30 (U.S.), bringing with them a second shock wave to the world's economy. The call of the day was whether oil would peak at $70, $80 or $90 a barrel.

"How could so many people inside and outside the industry have been sucked in so completely?" asks Norm Gish, who came to Turbo in 1980 as corporate secretary and vice president of administration. "The only comfort we had was that the financial community, the investment community, and governments were right there with us. I can be harsh on the herd instinct because I was right up there in the pack. At the height of the so-called 'energy crisis,' I went all around British Columbia as chairman of the B.C. Energy Commission, telling business and community groups that everyone better be serious about energy conservation and substitute fuels because we wouldn't be able to afford oil, even at $60 a barrel."

What everyone was ignoring was history repeating itself. Cartels, whether they have dealt in tea, coffee, copper, tin, or uranium, have had a very poor track record. The only one that has worked is the diamond cartel controlled by the De Beers through the subsidiary, The Central Selling Agency. Gish explains, "Cartels fail because people, companies, and countries are greedy. The temptation is just too great not to quietly slip the price up a little, or slightly increase production above quota limits to improve revenues. Trouble is that there are no secrets in this world and soon others follow suit. Then the whole thing collapses. The De Beers control the sale of the majority of the world's diamonds only because they have not been greedy. They have increased the price of diamonds a little ahead of inflation.

"In the case of OPEC it was bound to fail," continues Gish. "They didn't control the majority of the world's crude supply, and the political and economic needs of their members were too diverse. To make our collective stupidity even worse, we were all aware the price of crude oil was being artificially raised and could not be supported on purely economic grounds. Crude oil is an international commodity, easily transportable by pipeline and tanker. A large portion of the world's proven reserves are held by low-cost producers who probably have enough supply to meet the world's needs for the next hundred years. We should have known better, but if you were in exploration and production, smoking the OPEC pipe sure felt good."

The euphoria produced by the OPEC pipe was contagious. "The banks were falling all over us trying to lend us money," recalls Gerry Sioui. "The federal government was pushing Canadian companies to purchase foreign corporations, particularly in the U.S. Turbo was no exception, running all around looking to snap up any business interests that had a foreign flair to them."

From the company's inception in 1970 to its peak in 1980, Turbo Resources carried out an aggressive set of acquisition activities. Expansion and diversification had long been the business strategy of its co-founders—Bob Brawn and Ken Travis. Brawn explains, "In 1960, I left Mobil Oil to work for the company that Ken had just taken out of receivership called International Drilling Fluids. In 1963, we formed Liberty Holdings Industries in which we each had 50% ownership. Together we went into the acquisition of small businesses, generally in the manufacturing and service industries. In 1965, I left Liberty Holdings and sold my interests back to Ken Travis. I then went into the oil recycling business, which I expanded into a small marketing and manufacturing operation by 1969. Meanwhile, Ken had bought an oil corporate shell called Newcalmer. We sold all of our individual interests back into the company for controlling shares. We then changed the name to

Turbo Resources Limited." Travis ended up owning 27% of the new company and Brawn, 20%.

It is easy to see how, under the direction of these two entrepreneurs, the Turbo group of companies acquired 22 subsidiaries by 1980. They were into everything, from exploration and development, resource services, manufacturing and refining, marketing, and transportation to real estate and development. In 1980, a partial list of their acquisition and expansion activities included doubling well servicing operations, tripling net land reserves, and acquiring Spur Oil Limited and its 79 service stations. Aside from purchasing land holdings in Austin, Texas, and downtown Calgary, the company also entered into numerous joint real estate ventures, ranging from the development of a Calgary industrial park to a luxury condominium complex in British Columbia. "Turbo was the darling of the stock market along with Dome and a couple of others," recalls Norm Gish. "The share price was moving up rapidly and there were new opportunities knocking at the door every day."

Bob Brawn was just the man for this time of entrepreneurial expansion. Gerry Sioui explains, "Boy, if you ever want to meet a guy that can fill your head in an hour, it is Bob Brawn. Every time I went out to lunch with him, I would come back with at least 40 ideas." This aura of excitement was both Brawn's trademark and the attraction that brought Turbo's current senior management team on the scene in 1980. All were looking for the type of opportunity and freedom their previous employers could not provide.

Norm Gish was lured from Vancouver in July 1980 by the excitement and challenge of a rapidly growing company and the compensation package heavily weighted towards share ownership.

Paul Core, vice president of refining, was in Chicago, about to accept an 18-month contract as a consultant in Saudi Arabia, when the call came asking him to look at a Turbo job opportunity. What hooked him? Core responds, "The impossible task." The challenge was the modular construction of Turbo's Balzac refinery on the outskirts of Calgary. Although the modular technique had been practiced in South America and Canada's north, where the weather, remoteness, and lack of skilled labor hindered standard stick construction, it was a new construction method for this type of refinery. The opportunity to participate in this type of innovation was simply too good for Core to turn down.

Robert McClinton, currently Turbo's vice president of finance and chief financial officer, joined as the assistant treasurer to gain a range of different experiences and learning opportunities.

David James, currently vice president and corporate secretary, was attracted by the varied and exciting opportunities within Turbo. "They weren't just talking about exciting opportunities. They were acting on them. When Brawn talked about a service station on the moon, you couldn't simply dismiss the idea. It was as if the sky really was the limit," says James.

Gerry Sioui, frustrated by the sluggish, non-entrepreneurial environment of the multinational oil and gas companies, was looking for fast-paced action when he landed on Turbo's doorstep. "I was used to a lot of people working for me, and there just wasn't a whole lot of fun in it. The large companies are so well regulated that most of the boo-boos have been screened out years ago. Their well-designed systems move the business smoothly along. In comparison, Turbo appeared disorganized, but I knew at the same time it would be a whole lot of fun. I thought if I was ever going to make a move like this, 1980 was the time. The other reason was that Bob Brawn really fascinated me."

Bob Brawn fascinated a lot of people, including his financial backers, who were more than willing to bankroll his vision of the future. This smart and tireless entrepreneur was driven by his overpowering vision and his inner sense of confidence. "The trouble was that when he started to succeed, he began to believe everything he heard himself saying," comments Bruce Millar, vice president of marketing.

Like any builder , he understood his strong sense of purpose and direction. The problem was that no one else did. "Brawn was too busy chasing rainbows in the sky to get involved with the more down-to-earth practices of his various operations," remarks a Turbo executive. Even his partner, Ken Travis, at the time chairman of the board, had difficulty persuading Brawn to commit to long-range plans. Such a request was the target of heated management meetings. "The meetings where we discussed long-term plans always turned into shouting matches," says Millar. "Bob always wanted to make everything a surprise. He simply would not disclose his direction. Getting a sense of where the company was going was like trying to read the weather."

The lack of a common clear vision was reflected by the diverse, totally decentralized enterprises Brawn had built around him. Each divisional vice president ran his own autonomous profit center. When Brawn did try to get involved, he was either given full reign to execute his ideas without challenge, or told to stop dabbling. "I think he got into a lot of trouble because of the yes men around him," comments Gerry Sioui. "I mean Bob came in with some pretty wild ideas. I remember arriving at the Vancouver airport to find that I was being paged. It was Bob on the phone wanting me to buy some Nigerian crude oil."

"Why do you want to do a crazy thing like that?" Sioui asked.

"I just got this flash of an idea. We could do a number of exciting things with it," Brawn replied.

"You are out of your mind, Bob," Sioui responded. "We are just not going to do it." "The problem," Sioui continues, "was that there were a lot of guys who wouldn't stop him. They would just go ahead blindly and do what he wanted."

But those were heady days for the oil patch. Between 1977 and 1981, the lives of thousands of Albertans were changed forever as the province wrestled the limelight away from central Canada. The booming oil industry transformed Calgary from a prairie hicktown into a thriving business center almost overnight. Housing prices more than doubled in a matter of months. Newly graduated engineers who had once been pleased with an annual salary in the high teens, snubbed any job offer under $27 000. Old serviceable pickup trucks were quickly traded in for fancy rigs with all the options. The West was reborn, or as Bruce Millar, a 20-year Turbo veteran, comments, "the joint went Hollywood."

The rocket ride into a world of power and affluence was further fueled by the East-West rivalry within Canada and the competition between the upstream (exploration and production) and downstream (refining and marketing) sides of the oil and gas business. For years Alberta had played second fiddle to the whims, ways, and snobbery of central Canada. Exploration and production departments had long been treated as regional arms of the more influential corporate head offices located in Montreal and Toronto. Downstream systems were routinely imposed on upstream operations. It felt like just reward when the shoe was placed on the other foot. Corporate executives that had once made "regional visits" to the West were now having to leave their homes in central Canada and set up shop and residency in the most expensive city in the country at that time.

While many members of the Albertan oil patch were able to cope with the heady experience of growth and success, some felt that Bob Brawn was not. "Bob was always trying to make a mark for himself," comments one of Brawn's former executives. "He was a western boy who liked to be lorded around Bay Street, having bankers and the investment community carry his bags for him." In an industry that is not always characterized as a gentleman's game, Brawn made no bones about jabbing his competitors, both privately and publicly. Brawn's own perception of that time is different. "We certainly rose in the West, which is where we had our political affiliation. I don't think we wanted to rub anybody's nose in the fact that we were a totally western company until we came head-to-head with the Ontario Securities Commission over the Merland takeover bid. This is where we were made victims of circumstance, poor media coverage, and certainly some very poor legal advice."

The Merland Fiasco

In early 1981, the final pieces in Turbo's expansion strategy were ready to come together. In May 1981, the company completed a successful $50-million equity issue, priced at $11¾. The offering was to help finance the construction of the company's $200-million refinery. At the same time, Brawn was keenly aware that the company's extensive list of developments did not yet include the one area that would make Turbo a fully integrated oil and gas company – exploration. Up to this point, the exploration and production division had only contributed about 2% annually to total operating revenue.

Brawn had had his eye on Merland Exploration Ltd. for some time. Starting in 1974, Turbo had been involved in Canadian and U.S. joint ventures with Merland, as well as with Jack and Walter Adams, the controlling shareholders of Merland. This upstream company's impressive exploration track record made it an ideal addition to Turbo's growing group of enterprises. In late June 1981, Brawn along with Ron Maxwell, V.P. of finance, and Turbo's legal counsel, left for Bermuda to purchase the 27% block of Merland shares owned by the two Adams. Turbo paid $13⅛ for these shares, which at the time were trading in the $9 range, financed totally by debt with the Canadian Imperial Bank of Commerce.

There is some controversy as to the extent of prior involvement by Turbo's board of directors in the takeover bid. Brawn insists that the deal was approved in a Calgary board meeting prior to his departure. Others recall that the board was both surprised and furious when Brawn returned to Calgary with the Merland shares. There is no question that one key player was not informed of the pending deal – Bob Dixon, president of Merland. Because this was not an Ontario deal, Brawn also felt it unnecessary to confer with any Ontario legal counsel before the deal was closed.

"We left Bermuda, where Jack Adams was residing, in two planes," explains Brawn. "I took one plane back to Calgary to convince Bob Dixon that this was a friendly takeover and we wanted his support. Dixon's response was shock that we had gone ahead with the deal without telling him, since he saw the purchase as a raid on his company. This certainly was not our intention. We wanted to form a senior producing company that we hoped Dixon would head up.

"The other plane," continues Brawn, "took our solicitor and Jack Adams to Toronto to tell the Ontario Securities Commission (OSC) about the deal. At this point we had received Ontario legal advice to appear before the OSC as a 'good corporate citizen.' This is where we fell victim to some very poor legal counsel. Since we were not in Ontario, we had absolutely no legal obligation to appear before the OSC. If we hadn't, they might have suspended Turbo stock on the exchange for a period of time. Nova had chosen not to respond in a similar situation involving a New York deal. Nothing had happened to them. It certainly was not a clear-cut situation by any stretch of the imagination."

By now Dixon had contacted the OSC and insisted on a hearing. It was set for July. As Brawn recalls, "That's when the real battle started." Robert McClinton adds, "Bob Dixon had been trying to put a deal together to buy the Adams's block himself. When Brawn got his 27% at top price, that set Dixon and Merland off to find a white knight." Dixon was not about to fight Turbo alone. He rallied with Dominique de Louis, a prinicipal in the Montreal investment firm, Maison Placement, to gain the support of the institutional investors. "Dominique went out to the institutions to try and get someone to make an offer significantly more than the Turbo offer," Brawn explains.

The OSC took the position that the characteristics of Turbo's initial block purchase were such that the company was obliged by law to make a follow-up offer of equal value; i.e., $13\frac{1}{8} a share, to the remaining minority shareholders. (This Securities Act ruling, put in place to protect the small shareholder, stipulates that if a company acquires more than 20% of another company's shares at a price 15% or more above the average market price, the company in the purchasing position must make the same offer to all the shareholders.) The point of contention was the location of the purchase–Bermuda. McClinton explains, "Brawn argued that it was bought offshore, so it involved repatriation of control. This meant that under one of OSC's policies, we should have received an exemption from the follow-up provisions."

The OSC fiasco was not about to stop Brawn from using

Turbo shares to gain controlling interest of Merland. Timing, however, was not going to be on his side. "We had an offer of Turbo stock ready to go to all the other shareholders of Merland. Dixon refused to supply us with a shareholders' list. Then our prospectus stale-dated since our accounting records were about to go out of date. At this point, we ran into the hearings. We had run out of time."

McClinton further explains, "The exchange bid was made in reaction to two things. The market started to fall, and along with it, so did Turbo's prices. The underwriters for the May equity issue were very concerned about a follow-up or an offer for the other 73% of Merland with Turbo shares. I think they still had an inventory of Turbo shares from the last issue. Then the rumors came out about Merland looking for a white knight. All this, coupled with the tarnished image Turbo was getting from the public fight with the OSC, caused Brawn to go back to the bank to get more money to make an exchange bid." Brawn agrees that Turbo was being hit hard in the media over the Merland deal. "I would say that the press releases regarding the Merland controversy were inaccurate at best and vicious at worst and likewise didn't help our share value and our corporate image."

Turbo acquired an additional 25% with a pro rata exchange bid at the same price as the initial block, bringing the ownership up to 52% and the debt to the CIBC to $133 million. But Turbo was a long way from being out of the woods. Meetings and hearings with Merland's minority shareholders and the OSC continued to plague the company. After a great deal of arguing and legal wrangling, the OSC issued a compliance order in July 1981. It stated that Turbo had to make its follow-up offer to the minority shareholders within 180 days. By now Turbo's shares had fallen so low that alternate financing for the follow-up offer would have been impossible. As Brawn explains, "We felt we couldn't offer our shares, yet we didn't have sufficient capital to weather the storm."

In February 1982, the OSC issued a court order demanding action on the follow-up offer. In response, Turbo proposed that Bankeno Mines Ltd., in which it had a 90% interest, purchase Merland's minority shares with Bankeno shares. Brawn's strategy was to have Merland and Bankeno form a major upstream company. Merland's minority shareholders did not share Brawn's enthusiasm. Few chose to respond. The OSC agreed that this offering did not comply with the compliance order.

On March 2, Turbo announced its intentions to sell its interest in Bankeno to reduce its bank debt. Bankeno now held approximately 55% of Merland. This was heralded as a positive move by Merland's minority, as they believed a separation from Turbo would be to their advantage. However, on March 22, the OSC froze the sale of both Bankeno and Merland shares until the Merland minority problem was resolved. By now, Turbo and the OSC were at loggerheads.

Reality Strikes

Turbo was ricocheting from one problem to another. No matter which way the company turned, it found itself trapped in an onslaught of uncontrollable forces. Not the least of these was the federal government's National Energy Program (NEP), or as many have come to call it, "the program that financed Petro-Canada." (Many Albertan cars at the time sported bumper stickers that read, "I'd rather walk 10 miles than pump my gas at a Petro-Canada station.") The program's monies did indeed go to fund Canadian ownership as well as to general revenue. The NEP had been announced earlier in 1981, but the National Pricing Agreement wasn't struck between Alberta and Ottawa until September. "As a result of that agreement, both the Alberta and federal governments took a huge chunk out of the profits in the upstream," says McClinton. "It was the final nail in our coffin."

When the dreaded 20% Petroleum Gas Revenue Tax (PGRT) was levied, the combined impact of the taxes and the drop in world oil prices had a severe impact on the cash flow of most of the producers. This, added to the sizable royalty payments, brought Canadian drilling to a halt. Since drilling and its related services, under the Challenger subsidiaries, had been the mainstay of Turbo's operating profit, cash flow dried up very quickly.

While the NEP was causing several major exploration companies to cancel or buy out long-term drilling contracts in Canada, moves to deregulate the petroleum industry in the U.S. were still providing considerable impetus to drilling operations. Challenger, like many of its Canadian competitors, decided to offset its losses by moving south. In addition to the 12 rigs the company purchased in 1980, Challenger spent close to $100 million (U.S.) in 1981 on rigs to be used in the States. By the end of 1981, this market too had crashed.

Even the strongest of senior management teams would have had difficulty battling the heat. Brawn clarifies, "All the senior management were involved with the OSC hearing. The Alberta-Ottawa Accord was dramatically impacting our psyche. The stories with regard to OSC were damaging our confidence. All in all, we certainly felt we were under attack."

The problem was that Turbo did not have a senior management team to stave off the attack. The autonomy that had allowed the various vice presidents to build their empires now backfired on Brawn as it became increasingly clear that the company was in grave trouble. The relationship between Travis and Brawn started to show signs of wear. Bruce Millar remarks, "Socially they were polite, while behind the scene, things were tense."

The lack of a committed and cohesive senior team was further exacerbated by the lack of integrated management systems. The company had grown so quickly that the administration systems hadn't been able to keep up. Each profit center had its own comptroller, accounting department, support functions, and policies. Each major subsidiary, such as Challenger, had its own banking relationships. Insufficient time had prevented Norm Gish from installing the corporate infrastructure required by Turbo's high-speed growth. Management information was moving at a snail's pace.

Early in 1982, Robert McClinton, treasurer, and Ian Mills, the corporate comptroller, began to realize that the financial situation was reaching a crisis point. "Cash was going out," McClinton recalls, "and no cash was coming in." McClinton reported to his boss, Ron Maxwell, that Turbo's lines of credit were becoming fully drawn. When asked what Maxwell did with this information, McClinton replied, "I have no idea."

The crisis came in April 1982. Turbo was on the verge of bankruptcy. McClinton phoned Brawn to tell him that he didn't think Turbo was going to make payroll the following week. At last he had the president's attention. "He came right over to my office," remembers McClinton.

"Tell me that again," demanded Brawn.

"We're not going to make payroll next week," McClinton replied.

"So what you are telling me is that we have a potential liquidity crisis," Brawn suggested.

"No, we have a real liquidity crisis," responded McClinton.

"Well then, you'd better tell me what we have to do," said Brawn.

McClinton's first recommendation was to issue an immediate bulletin to all vice presidents and managers informing them that any expenditures being contemplated or incurred over $25 000 had to be approved by Brawn himself. This was a significant blow to the vice presidents whose signing authority ranged from half a million to a million dollars. Its message was clear – the company was in the midst of a financial crisis. Expense restriction became the cornerstone of Turbo's economic restraint program. Other forms of debt reduction included a halt to all capital spending, salary cuts, and employee layoffs. "The problem was," remarks McClinton, "all of this was a little bit like putting your finger in the dyke when the bulk of the water has already gone through."

The really tough news, however, had to be given to Turbo's lenders. "We realized we had to get together very quickly with our bankers, particularly the CIBC, to advise them of the situation. The message was clear – because the company had no money, the interest payments would be stopped on all lines of credit. They were very happy," McClinton adds sarcastically. The CIBC responded with an immediate freeze to all lines of credit and lending.

Anyone who has been in the unfortunate position of reneging on a loan knows that a scared cat looks positively laid back next to a nervous banker. The foremost question on each of the lenders' minds was how were they going to get their money out of Turbo? The last thing they wanted was a classified loan. In the case of the CIBC, their $500-million unsecured loan to Turbo represented 25% of the oil company's capital base. Aside from Turbo, the CIBC was involved with many other oil patch companies, the largest of which was Dome Petroleum. Turbo's other lenders, the Royal Bank of Canada, Canada Trust, and Guarantee Trust, for example, had the same problem, but their necks were not as much on the line. The foreign banks were another story.

The booming economy in Canada had attracted many foreign banks, which came to compete against the major chartered banks for the large oil and gas accounts. "Foreign banks such as Barclays Bank of Canada, Bank of America, Banque Nationale de Paris, Continental Bank of Illinois, Credit E & A of Paris, and the Chemical Bank of New York had come into Canada between 1979 and 1980 to set up shop," McClinton explains. "They were licensed as Schedule 'B' banks. Their marketing approach was to offer low-cost, short-term lines of credit in the hope of competing with the major chartered banks for the term lending business. This meant that they were lending money to us at their cost of funds plus a half a percent. In many cases, this was 2% to 3% lower than prime on a 30-, 60-, and 90-day basis."

Their strategy, however, didn't consider the competitive drive of the chartered banks. "The Schedule 'B' banks were never able to get into term as a business," continues McClinton, "because the Schedule 'A' banks (the majors) really sharpened their pencils, leaving too small a margin for a borrower to switch. They were in a sense blowing their brains out on the short-term side in their attempts to secure business. As a result, they got caught in Dome, then Ocelot, Nuwest, and finally Turbo. In two or three cases, we had loans with those banks that were equal to their entire capital base."

Ron Maxwell had arranged $105 million in floating interest loans with these Schedule 'B' banks in denominations of five, ten and fifteen million dollars, all of which were totally unsecured. The risk was that if and when these loans went bad, they could take any one of these banks with them. Meanwhile, Turbo had $25 million (U.S.) outstanding in European debentures, and escalating debt owed to the federal government in terms of unpaid taxes and the Albertan government for the company's crude oil supply.

"If we knew then what we do now, this wouldn't have happened," comments Steve Savidant, assistant to the president of Dome Petroleum during and after its heyday. Savidant, currently the vice president of finance with Canadian Hunter Exploration Ltd., questions the amount of blame that can be placed on the banks. As he sees it, the banks were doing their job in stimulating Canada's economic growth. "When the oil patch went down, neither the financial institutions, companies, nor governments, knew what to do. They had to become pioneers trying to find the way. Since that time, there have been many paths blazed in the search for creative financial solutions."

Norm Gish isn't so kind. "I think the banking community needs to take some responsibility for what happened. They prefer not to, but in fact they were just throwing money at anybody. I can tell you all kinds of stories about hundreds of millions of dollars that were arranged in a matter of hours on the phone. All this may appear a little harsh. Since I am an old-fashioned person, I believe that when you borrow money, you have an obligation to your lenders. I am not as such blaming the banks. I am simply saying that they had some measure of responsibility to have carried out better analyses before they handed out all that money."

The End of the Brawn Era

Blame wasn't going to help anyone now. What was needed was a total restructuring of Turbo's debt. In Brawn's mind, two things had to happen. "First and most prominently, one lending institution had to take the lead and work it out. Secondly, while it was not a popular decision, these banks had to consider their loans as equity as opposed to debt. These were the keys to the restructuring."

The CIBC took the lead and offered 5% equity to the individual shareholders, excluding the employees. This was totally unacceptable to Brawn, whose loyalties sided with the shareholders rather than with Turbo's management. "I took the position of trying to protect the shareholders," Brawn explains. "This is what really created the adversarial relationship with the bank and with other members of Turbo's management." Brawn went head-to-head with the CIBC and eventually forced them up to a 23% equity position on the residual common shares. This further irritated the already strained relationship between the CIBC and Brawn. "If you've made a proposal of 5% and somebody forces you up to 23%, what do you think the attitude of the bank would be?" Brawn asks.

It was obvious by now that Brawn could no longer represent Turbo with its lenders. In the late spring of '82, Brawn moved over to become the chief executive officer of Bankeno/Merland. "A trait of financial institutions," says Brawn, "is that you can't be identified with the problem, but only with the solution. My strengths lie in being intuitive and creative. To sit around fighting about financial numbers and then be forced to take orders would be to destroy the creativity that is needed for other opportunities. The sooner I came to that conclusion, the easier it was to move on."

Brawn remained on Turbo's board of directors until he resigned in December 1982 over a controversy regarding the interest-free loans given to employees for the purchase of Turbo stock. "A number of the senior people had quite sizable loans, including Norm Gish and other members of management," recalls Brawn. "When the stock slid and we had difficulty servicing our loans, the decision was made to forgive all the employee loans in order to allow them to remain with the corporation. I didn't notice us relieving any of the other share-holders, so if we couldn't benefit them, then we couldn't benefit the employees. When the decision was made, I knew I had to resign from the board as well."

Ken Travis briefly tried to pick up the reins in May 1982 when Brawn left to run Bankeno/Merland, but he too was painted with the same brush as Brawn, at least as far as the lenders were concerned. The man the company turned to in the late spring of '82 was Norm Gish, the individual who would take Turbo through its first restructuring. The process would take close to three and a half years. "The trouble with all artificially induced euphoria is that when you take it away, the withdrawal symptoms are very painful," says Gish, "which is why we didn't get into a serious mode of restructuring until mid '82. This was not to put any particular blame on Ken Travis or Bob Brawn; it's just a fact of life that if you are at the head of an organization when things go wrong, it's very difficult to gain the confidence of your lenders and the rest of the management who are trying to lead the company.

"Ordering the two men who had worked so hard to build the company to dispose of some major assets was like asking them to cut off their left arms," continues Gish. "The time came when both Ken and Bob had to realize that it was time to step back and let someone else take charge. Only then could everyone get it into their minds that we could manage a restructuring and survive."

Bob Brawn had chosen to solicit his backers with dreams and then bulldoze them when reality hit. Gish chose a substantially different approach. "To regain the confidence of our lenders and shareholders," he explains, "we had to ensure that our financial statements and information flow were very frank, accurate, and regular. Our backers had to believe that we were telling them the complete truth, as difficult as it might be and as much as it might hurt."

Gish had to work hard and fast to convince the lenders there was another alternative to selling the assets and writing off their losses. "This was particularly difficult for the financial institutions, which had also gone into their bunkers. Never before in Canadian corporate or financial life had so many companies gone off the cliff at the same time, including the Depression. There were several times when the CIBC had to stop to go through a brainstorming session as to whether they were going to continue backing us or not. They had to be sure they were not investing in a black hole with no chance of success. I give them credit that they always concluded to continue backing us, even though I'm sure they received a lot of professional advice that said, 'Shut it down, cut your losses, and get out.' "

The key to survival lay in rebuilding credibility. This was a particularly difficult mandate given the fact that in June 1982, all the outside board of directors resigned. They were unwilling to assume personal liability for the Petroleum Marketing Tax (which totaled approximately $10 million at the time) without the assurance of the bank. A number of employee appointments were made to the board starting with Norm Gish, Ian Mills, the comptroller, and Robert McClinton, followed by Bruce Millar and Gerry Sioui. Millar candidly describes the honor as, "This is when our asses were all hanging out together."

They were also working together as a new management group, although none of them was new to the company. "You simply cannot attract new people into a company that looks like it is going down the tubes," quips Gish. "We had to look internally and size up our own people who we felt could either do the job or grow into it. This meant that a lot of people who under normal circumstances may not have been given the opportunity to show their stuff, in fact were. To our benefit, it created a highly motivating environment."

However, the new management and board of directors didn't have time to reflect on the motivation inherent in their new responsibilities. Their immediate task was to convince their lenders that none of them was associated with the creation of Turbo's problems. "The main thing we were trying to do was to convince our lenders of our integrity," explains McClinton. "We presented a plan that we believed would solve the initial financial problems. We used this plan to establish our credibility as the people who were now running Turbo and could make the company into what we knew it could become."

The first part of the plan was to bring the debt down to a workable level. The key step was to get rid of the cash-draining assets. In August 1982, the Royal Bank did a restructuring with Challenger, which allowed the Royal to put more money into the drilling company to keep it alive. At this point Challenger and its management separated from Turbo, although Turbo remained Challenger's main creditor for the $200 million it had invested in the company. Other immediate divestments included the blending and packaging operation, many of the real estate holdings, some retail outlets, and the chemicals division.

With the debt reduction strategy underway, the next step was to consolidate the remaining decentralized divisions into one corporate entity. The change in corporate leadership, combined with the divestment strategy, had brought about the departure of all but one of the corporate officers – Bruce Millar, the current vice president of marketing. In his role as president, Gish centralized the business planning and budgeting processes as well as the financial and administrative functions of accounting, personnel, and information systems. "Norm took a company that had a whole bunch of diverse directions and profit centers and pulled them together into a centralized organization," explains Don Murray, manager of refining operations. "This involved a fair amount of bureaucracy, which was new to Turbo. It was a very interesting exercise since each division was used to doing its own thing without worrying a hell of a lot about what the rest of the company was doing. I'm not sure everybody was comfortable with Norm dismantling the barriers, but he was relatively successful."

To break down the divisional walls, Gish formed a management committee with his vice presidents, all of whom were new to their positions, aside from Millar. To replace the decentralized, divisional mindset with an informed corporate-wide philosophy, the committee's weekly management meetings concentrated on cross-divisional issues. The board meetings also served the same purpose, but with higher stakes. "The board meetings were certainly educational," recalls Paul Core. "What they really taught us, was that we could no longer sit on the fence. Each member had to make a commitment. We each had to decide if we were going to be a part of this company or not." This was a particularly significant decision for Core, who had not felt any obligation to Turbo up to this point. His job had been to get the refinery up and running. With this task complete, he had planned to move on to other challenges.

It was Norm Gish's style that appealed to Core as well as to the rest of the management team. Gish's mastery of diplomacy and conciliation made him the right man at the right time in Turbo's history. Gish believed that Turbo's employees were as important as the lenders. Both groups had to have confidence in what the company could do. Gish explains, "My management philosophy is based on the premise that once you have given employees, at all levels, a sense that there is strong leadership with clear objectives and a significant opportunity to succeed, they really respond. It was therefore very important for us to set out the company's direction for everyone. We tried to do this through our statements of business philosophy and the subsequent meetings we held to openly review and discuss these beliefs. I also sent out frequent, frank memos, called Employee Updates, telling them what was going on, where we stood, and what was going wrong."

Gish kept his finger on the pulse of the company through his constant personal contact with employees. He was able to maintain the difficult balance between staying on top of the day-to-day issues, while allowing the vice presidents to run their own divisions. Not only did he know the majority of the head office and refinery staff by name, but he took every opportunity to listen and discuss the fears and concerns of anyone who needed his attention. This was certainly a new leadership style for Turbo. "Norm is a very classy guy," attests Gerry Sioui. "When I first met him, he was an outdoorsy type – corduroy suits, knit ties – a straight arrow among a group of pretty raunchy guys. Going to Ottawa and Toronto on a business trip with Norm was just wild. Norm was in bed by 9 p.m., so he could be up by 5 a.m. to jog. The rest of us, on the other hand, would be going to bed at 5 a.m. – the same time he was getting up."

"We were responding to a continual series of crises, which meant we just had to keep running at full speed. Staying in excellent physical shape was critical to me," confirms Gish. "I have always maintained a rigorous early morning fitness program. This meant that by the time I hit Turbo at 7:30 a.m., I was flying." Gish had to be enthusiastic, or at least appear to be, to lead the company through its roller coaster journey. "Restructuring offers an interesting study in psychology," he explains, "because it is very difficult to maintain morale and enthusiasm among both the management and employees. The whole process takes a tremendous toll on employees, particularly the senior management, because they are at it seven days a week, 24 hours a day. Tough times bring out the best and the worst in people. There were a lot of different periods where it came close to being the end for us. I and the other senior managers had to keep a stiff upper lip and remain optimistic. That wasn't easy. You almost had to stand in front of the mirror every morning and pump yourself up."

This was particularly important for Gish because everyone could read him like an open book. "I knew that the employees could read me," says Gish. "I had to always be very optimistic and confident that we were going to succeed so that they could feel confident. It was a real test of personal leadership, which was very rewarding and also extremely tiring."

Paul Core confirms the success of Gish's strategy: "There were no secrets in the company at all. This meant that there were no closed door sessions that we in the management team were not involved in. We knew everything that was going on, whether it was ultra-confidential or not; good or bad." And yet the real hook for Core was the same as it was for all Turbo employees: "Once you understand where the company is going, along with the role and accountability you are expected to fulfill, then you feel involved—a part of it. This makes you ready to give your total commitment. In the end, it's the same as going to the movies—you can't leave the movie until the last reel has been run."

The Hunk of Steel That Saved the Company

Turbo's management team realized that the show couldn't go on unless it concentrated on its one cash-generating operation—the marketing of transportation fuels—and the supply of these fuels. In 1980 Turbo's supplier, Gulf Canada Ltd., refused to meet the company's increasing product demand. Brawn had become extremely worried about being squeezed out of the supply he needed to support Turbo's retail expansion. Gerry Sioui gives Brawn's response: "His answer was to go out and build a refinery." In January 1980, planning started on the refinery under the management of Frank King, vice president manufacturing. In the midst of construction, at the same time that the projected $160-million budget for the refinery was about to run out, Turbo fell apart.

The CIBC was faced with another difficult decision. Should it invest additional funds or liquidate? Robert McClinton puts the decision in context: "If they chose to liquidate, they would receive 30 bucks a ton for molten steel. On the other hand, because of the innovative modular design, they didn't know if the refinery was even going to run once it was completed."

"The industry didn't really support the whole concept of modular design," explains Paul Core, maintenance manager at the time. "The majors didn't really believe that it could be built, let alone be operational." Added to this concern was the 1980 fire that had wiped out a major part of the Edmonton lubrication plant. Turbo's reputation had been significantly damaged by this incident.

While the construction continued, the CIBC conducted a number of yield, operational, and management analyses, while it pursued the option of selling off parts of the refinery or securing joint venture partners. The bank began to develop a strong confidence in the refining and construction experts Turbo had recruited from all over North America. Finally, the CIBC decided to risk investing the full amount. "The refinery in the end is what helped save the company," says Gish. "They decided to give it a chance and put in approximately $60 million to finish it."

These challenges brought with them a special type of motivation. Core explains, "If you really want to motivate people, just tell them they can't do whatever they think they can." Don Murray, the refinery operations manager, adds, "We were just a little smaller than some of the other players, that was all. We never perceived ourselves limping along as a second-class company. What was important was that we believed we could compete against anybody."

The construction team met the challenge. The refinery, built in a record 18 months, was in operation on October 1, 1982. It had the shortest construction time frame of any North American refinery, with the exception of the wartime effort in Sarnia, Ontario. The cost of Turbo's 30 000 barrel per day refinery, including the financing costs, was $230 million. The 55 barrel per day Shell refinery in Fort Saskatchewan, Alberta, built at about the same time, cost over a billion dollars, including its petrochemical plant. In spite of the fact that the technologies were different, Turbo was proud of its efforts, considering the economies of scale.

The tightly woven group of handpicked refinery personnel had made a commitment to one another to build a top notch refinery. "The fundamental presumption we made was that we had to have a credible and viable operation if we were to maintain the business and our jobs, regardless of the corporate name that was on the sign," says Don Murray. "Through the first few years, when we were trying to establish a track record, we lived and died on credibility. If we lost this, our security would be gone." The belief that their jobs would be secured, despite the employer, removed a considerable amount of stress from these employees. The refinery's critical contribution to keeping the company alive, however, was not lost on the refinery team. "The best thing we could do for Turbo was to process the amount of oil the company needed to sell in a high-quality, cost-effective manner," continues Murray. "Anything we were doing in that direction was consistent with Turbo becoming a success again."

The newness and challenge of the construction had attracted a very diverse and young group of professionals, along with a key number of "old hands." Chaos was the name of the game. Job descriptions were unheard of as were desks, chairs, and organization. Murray, who had left a secure job with the staid operation of Esso, describes his introduction to Turbo as "culture shock." While the fast-moving pace brought with it the energy needed to put the refinery onstream, its sink or swim approach created frustration. Those that needed direction were swallowed up by the activity, as were the individuals who had ideas and no one to listen to them.

It was the unheralded heroes, who channeled the ambition and drive of the excited, inexperienced team members, along with the seasoned professionals, who deserve a large part of the credit. Together they had to cut new paths in product specifications, processing, blending, and the early policies associated with these. The synergy and buzz of activity sheltered the refinery from the brutal realities being faced by the rest of the organization. The refinery management chose to buffer their staff from the more tumultuous events that were going on in the corporate office. "We kept people informed about significant events or information that was going to be in the public domain," Don Murray explains. "We tried as much as possible to scrub the frightening news and inform our employees before they heard about it in the newspaper. Face-to-face meetings and posted press releases helped, but it was tough covering all the angles with a shift operation. Maintaining confidentiality as it related to insider information also restricted us. All in all, this was an area where we could have done better."

Keeping the Lid On

Sheltering employees from one crisis to another was a very weighty task, especially since Turbo came to the brink time and time again throughout its difficult three and a half years of financial restructuring. A sense of humor was not only a luxury, but a necessity. One such incident involved the controlled limit the CIBC had installed on Turbo's cheque-cashing practices. Any cheque that exceeded the company's line of credit would not be honored. In mid-1983 Turbo wrote a large federal tax cheque (which was critical due to the personal liabilities of the board of directors) that put the company over its limit. The CIBC account manager phoned Don Heron, Turbo's treasurer, and told him, "We're not going to put this cheque through, so I suggest you put a stop payment on it."

"Fine," replied Heron, "but if you guys bounce one more cheque on us, we are going to take our business elsewhere." Heron then hung up.

Half an hour later, the account manager's boss phoned McClinton.

"What the hell are you guys doing over there? You should have seen this guy's face when he stormed into my office to tell me what had happened. His biggest fear was that he had missed the memo saying that Turbo was a good customer again."

Aside from the occasional day or so limit extension, Turbo rigorously maintained its cash in-cash out agreement with the

CIBC. With its new lean and financially responsible mindset, the company was able to cover all of its operating expenses with its sales revenue. As each month passed, Turbo's integrity and credibility gained momentum. Decisions on the suspended loan repayments and interest charges, however, had to wait until the Merland controversy was resolved.

In early 1983, the Merland minority shareholders set up an ad hoc committee using the OSC as a referee. The former OSC chairman, Henry Morse, had been replaced by Peter Dey, a less confrontational player. By then the facts had changed, since it was obvious that Turbo was in severe financial difficulty. The OSC realized it had an obligation to protect Turbo shareholders as well as the Merland minority shareholders. The deal that was finally struck involved the sale of Bankeno Mines Ltd. The first $133 million would go to the CIBC as they had the security in the shares. The next $56 million would go to the Merland minority. In essence, Merland shareholders would keep their shares and get a pro rata share up to $56 million. All of this was based on the premise that Bankeno would sell for $189 million. It was a risk that the Merland minority were willing to take, mainly because they had developed confidence in Norm Gish during the negotiations. They believed that Turbo would work hard at getting them the best price. This spirit of conciliation was a far cry from the dissension that had spurred on the fight in mid-1981.

In the end, this was a crucial yet futile paper exercise; Bankeno was finally purchased in September 1984 by North Canadian Oils Ltd., a Hees corporation, for $125 million. With the company sold to new owners, Brawn resigned from his position as Bankeno's CEO to pursue his career with OEMV Oil and Gas Ltd., the Austrian national oil company.

Throughout 1983, as the deal was being negotiated with the Merland minority, the Schedule 'B' banks and trust companies were in the midst of suing the CIBC and furiously jockeying among themselves for their "right of claim" to be repaid by Turbo. They felt that the CIBC was not entitled to the security it was holding on Turbo shares. Canada Trust, in particular, wasn't about to lose its claim without a fight.

"The Canada Trust people were frustrated that the CIBC would not deal with them on an equal footing," McClinton explains. "They had refused to be bound by the September '83 agreement made with the Merland minority. On November 11, 1983, Canada Trust registered a Writ of Execution and sent the sheriff and a bailiff over to our offices to get their hands on some Turbo assets. They decided to go after our Challenger shares, which weren't worth anything, but were unencumbered. The sheriff and bailiff hauled us out of our management meeting and showed us the writ. I immediately phoned our bankruptcy lawyer, John McNiven."

"What should we do?" McClinton asked.

"You cooperate totally with the sheriff is what you do," McNiven replied.

"Where are the shares?" asked one of the management team.

"We've got them in our vault downstairs," McClinton replied.

"No, they are not there," countered David James, the corporate secretary.

"Bloody hell. I remember bringing them back from the bank," McClinton claimed.

"The bank list says they are over at the bank," James responded.

"Dan Heron, the treasurer, left for the CIBC with the sheriff," McClinton continues. This sent the CIBC off madly to find their top brass, who in turn tried to get a hold of their lawyer. Meanwhile, the sheriff was hopping. She had been steamed ever since Norm had mistakenly introduced himself to the male bailiff, thinking that he was the sheriff. Finally the sheriff said, 'Look, if you don't go and open that safety deposit box right now, I'm going to charge you with obstruction of justice. So let's move it.' The next thing that happened was that we got this panic phone call from Dan, who was sitting in the vault with the sheriff and the bailiff and an empty safety deposit box—empty except for a paper clip and a dead fly. 'I think I'm going to jail,' Dan told me over the phone. After I had explained to the sheriff that the shares were probably in our vault, she and the bailiff accompanied Dan back to our office and found them. At that moment, you have never seen a more relieved guy than Dan Heron," concludes McClinton.

After the sheriff left with the Challenger shares, McClinton contacted all their lenders who, like Canada Trust, had consent judgments. Each lender in turn filed their Writs of Execution, forcing the assets to be held on behalf of all the creditors. While Canada Trust had been stonewalled, the incident triggered a weekend emergency meeting of the senior CIBC and Turbo managers. "The bank was of course concerned that they would have to appoint a Receiver to protect itself from actions like the one Canada Trust had just taken, or any other lender jockeying," says McClinton. "We spent three days trying to convince the bank that such a move would be a mistake." The threat of receivership was indeed frightening to Turbo, because it would mean the disappearance of supply and trade credit, as well as putting the service station leases at risk. With the subsequent loss of customers, Turbo would no longer be able to fight for its survival. By the end of the meeting, CIBC had agreed to suspend the receivership decision, with the hope that the worst was over.

The worst, however, was not over. This time it was the Royal Bank that took a kick at the cat. Although Challenger had been taken over by the Royal's management in 1982, Turbo still maintained a $200-million credit in the company. By 1984, the Royal was no longer willing to wait until the Turbo financial restructuring was complete to transact the sale of Challenger. "They wanted us out," recalls McClinton, "so we said fine, here's our price. The Royal came back a couple of days later to our boardroom and presented us with the price they were willing to pay. We refused to accept the offer."

"No deal. This is our final offer. Take it or leave it," responded the Royal's representative.

"Fine. Here are the keys. Call in the Receiver," McClinton angrily replied. He threw his keys attached to Turbo's #1 key ring onto the middle of the table and left Turbo's boardroom with Norm Gish. The Royal entourage had to find their own way out. "As in any poker game, it was a tense moment. Once you've played your ace, you can't take it back," says McClinton.

Two weeks passed in silence. Finally, one of the Royal's senior managers called Gish. "All right," he said, "let's stop this silliness and make a deal." In September 1984, the Royal purchased Challenger International Services Ltd. with cash, Challenger's non-drilling assets, and $50 million in the form of forgiven debt owed to the bank by Turbo.

With the sale of Bankeno, Challenger, and the Ontario service stations, Turbo was able to turn to its strong suits. By the end of 1984, the refinery had increased its throughput to 78.6%, a 31% increase over its startup capacity. The 1984 revenues were $589 million, up $85 million over the previous year. Such achievements were to a large extent the result of the 35% increase in sales volume brought about by the supply and distribution division. Aside from fulfilling their responsibilities of crude oil supply and product exchanges, this group had developed an important export market in northern Montana through Flying Jay Inc.

Out of Intensive Care

Turbo was now in the position to restructure its debt. "It wasn't difficult once we had something to base the restructuring on," says McClinton. "Turbo wasn't pro forma, it wasn't a dream or high tech bullshit. It was a solid operating company with a good reputation in the marketplace, increasing marketshare, and a refinery that was doing better every month. Now there was something to refinance."

Over the preceding months, countless plans and proposals had been developed and shared between Turbo and its lenders. Each problem and its resolution brought with it a greater understanding of what was possible and what wasn't. The flexibility shown by the lenders, in particular the CIBC, was a testament to the massive learning curve experienced by all parties. "The lenders started off rejecting any foreign ideas, such as converting debt to equity," explains Gish. "In the end, they had come to accept them as the only way to keep Turbo alive. A lot of people underestimated the elasticity of both the lenders and our management to go through such a major trauma and survive. The key is that you have to solve one problem at a time and then go back and solve another. You just keep working away at it and pretty soon your mountain turns into a molehill you can move."

Turbo presented the CIBC with a five-year business plan, outlining the goals the company would be pursuing and its history to date that confirmed the feasibility of these targets. The immediate steps were laid out along with the financing that would be required. It was critical for Turbo to convince the CIBC to restart the capital program to fund the expansion of the marketing chain. Unless cash flow was increased, the chances of the CIBC being repaid within a reasonable period of time were minimal.

On July 5, 1985, the business plan and financial restructuring were approved. Simply put, the total debt was reduced by $420 million through a complex set of share transactions that converted debt to equity. The remaining debt of $317 million was refinanced by extending the repayment terms over ten years and giving Turbo an interest-free holiday until 1988, or until such time as Turbo generated sufficient cash flow from its operations to service the debt.

Turbo was at last back in business. The company's renewal now made it possible for Gish to rebuild the board with outside directors. Not waiting for July, he had attempted to attract individuals with a strong social stature and marketing experience from British Columbia, Saskatchewan, and Alberta. Bob Brodie fit Gish's criteria to a tee. A self-made millionaire, Brodie and his brothers had started Merit Oil Co. Ltd. with one gas station in 1959. By 1980, their 56 gas stations, under the brand names of Merit, Pay-N-Save, and Beaver, had captured 7% of the B.C. retail gasoline market. In 1981, having sold Merit Oil and its stations to Petro-Canada, Brodie went on to develop a group of real estate investment and development companies—Cardiff Estates Ltd., Norgal Investments Ltd., and Townsite Apartments Ltd.

Although Brodie was a perfect fit for Turbo, Turbo was not attractive to Brodie. He had turned down Turbo once before when Bob Brawn had invited him to merge Merit Oil with Turbo. Brodie's refusal had been a smart decision. He wasn't about to fall into a trap now. "In May '85, Norm called me in Vancouver to ask me if I would be interested in being a director of Turbo," recalls Brodie. "I said, 'No, I am not getting mixed up in that mess.' Norm proceeded to tell me about the restructuring, so I agreed to discuss it with him once the restructuring was finalized. True to his word, he phoned back and in late July, I was at my first official board meeting.

"In November '85, Norm called me again," continues Brodie. "This time it was to tell me that he'd been offered the position of CEO of North Canadian Oils Ltd., the company that had purchased Bankeno Mines Ltd. He wanted me to head up a subcommittee on behalf of the board to find a new president. I agreed to help him out." Norm Gish had actually been approached by North Canadian Oils in mid-1985; however, he had put off his departure from Turbo until the restructuring was fully in place and a board established to prepare the company for its second restructuring. Gish explains, "It had been impossible to get the lenders to bite the whole bullet the first time around. Even though we had completed the first phase, Turbo was by no means out of the woods. It wasn't going to collapse, but it was going to be a matter of grinding along, working on behalf of the lenders to pay down the debt. Until the second restructuring was complete, Turbo couldn't offer excitement and growth to any of the management."

Gish was indeed tired. He knew he was not the individual for this next phase. "Could I do it again?" Gish asks. "No. People say that it must have been a fabulous experience. In some ways, that's true, but most of it is a myth. I learned a great deal, but it was baptism by fire. Certainly I proved my credentials, but it was a tough way to do it."

While Gish was relieved, his departure created a feeling of loss among the employees of Turbo, particularly the members of the senior management team. "We were like a group of guys that had been in a concentration camp for five years together. We felt like we had a restricted club that had gone through so much together and now the head honcho was leaving. It was never going to be the same again," recalls Gerry Sioui.

Life was never going to be the same for Bob Brodie either, once he accepted the challenge of finding Turbo's new president. Gish had promised North Canadian Oils that he would move into his new position by January 1986. Because it was already November, Gish asked Brodie if he would accept a nomination at the December board meeting to act as Turbo's interim chairman and CEO while the search was conducted. Brodie accepted the nomination but viewed the position as only temporary. "The situation intrigued me," recalls Brodie. "I fully thought we were going to hire somebody."

After Brodie accepted the director's position, he had bought 55 000 shares to make his involvement "interesting." On his acceptance of the interim leadership position, he purchased another million shares. He started his new job on January 6, 1986, exactly five years after he had sold Merit Oil to Petro-Canada.

As director, shareholder, and interim CEO, Brodie had a vested interest in finding a topnotch recruit for his job. Turbo, however, did not offer an attractive career opportunity for the type of individual the company needed. "If an executive is doing well, why wouldn't he stay where he is?" Brodie rhetorically asks. "Everyone knows that the farther up you get in a company, the closer you are to the door. With Turbo, there has always been a good chance that it will be sold and then you'd be the first guy out of the door. Becoming Turbo's CEO could then be a number one prescription for destroying your career."

At the end of February, the search was called off, and Bob Brodie committed himself to the positions of CEO, president and chairman of Turbo, knowing full well that the CIBC would sell the company at the drop of a hat. He further raised his involvement by purchasing an additional million shares. "It's no fun if you don't have a piece of the action," says this born and bred entrepreneur. "If you don't, it's just a job. Since I didn't need or want a job, my involvement had to be fun. That's what makes business interesting." Sacrificing his personal life and real estate ventures, Brodie began commuting between Vancouver and Calgary on a weekly basis.

The Marketing Thrust

Bob Brodie had big shoes to fill. The overt warmth and

charismatic style of Norm Gish did not come naturally to the new president. While Gish had enjoyed physically getting out among the employees, the more reserved and private Brodie preferred to manage from behind the scenes. But he did capitalize on the dedicated team of high-performing professionals Gish had developed. The leverage he chose was strategic direction and accountability. "I like to push accountability as far down into the organization as I can," says Brodie. "A tremendous amount of power is unleashed when people understand what we are trying to do collectively and have the ability and autonomy to do what is necessary."

Brodie also brought to Turbo an innate understanding of the downstream business. His forte was, and still is, marketing. This was a perfect fit given the two-fold mandate Brodie saw in front of him in '86. Although the most critical issue was reducing the debt, it was essential to maintain a credible and productive operation to make the second restructuring possible. Therefore his second mandate was to add sufficient service stations to the retail chain to bring the refinery's production up to full capacity on a continual basis.

In 1986 alone, Turbo added 27 stations to its network of 245, enabling the refinery to produce at full capacity for nearly half the year and top levels for the remaining months. This expansion was based on a marketing business plan – something new to Turbo. "When I joined Turbo in '86, it was very entrepreneurial, customer-focused and informal, possibly to the point of being disorganized," recalls Greg Thompson, retail marketing manager. Thompson discovered that the marketing strategy was in each manager's head and not everyone shared the same picture. Planning, it appeared, had not been a hot topic, at least as it concerned strategically locating service stations throughout the four western provinces, with the right type of dealers. However, the autonomous entrepreneurial spirit that had built Turbo was still alive and well in the marketing division. The good news was that their efforts were all going in the same direction – outstanding customer service, Turbo's trademark.

The bad news, Thompson discovered, was the inconsistent policies and programs in the various regions. Regional managers had been given full autonomy to run their own show and had interpreted this as license to do whatever they wanted. Added to this, they saw their goal as regional rather than corporate success. As such, direction from head office was all too often seen as interference. Thompson explains: "The company's decentralized structure had previously promoted full initiative and action at the field level within the regions. It was almost as if they had their own little Turbos." The lack of "big picture thinking" became evident when the retail outlet network blueprint showed gaps and overlaps on outlet locations. Once the marketing business plan was developed, Thompson set about filling the gaps in the retail network and replacing the dealers and marketing managers who had difficulty with the more strategic, involved management style.

Bruce Millar, vice president of marketing, and Greg Thompson understand the entrepreneurial spirit that builds an outstanding marketing organization. They realize the fine line between having their direction and guidelines interpreted as motivational support or as handcuffs. This is a significant challenge given the self-directed type of people who are attracted to the marketing function. For these reasons, they created a marketing organization structure that delegates full accountability to the lowest possible level. The territory manager is responsible for everything that goes on in his assignment—from building service stations to hiring and training dealers. This wide range of responsibilities is made possible by a formal two-way goal-setting process along with its substantially lower territory manager to dealer ratio (one to eight compared to one to 30). The same philosophy applies to the regional managers, who are responsible for coordinating the efforts of five to six territories. "As we create territories and territory managers, they have to have a boss that has the time to spend with them to develop them and their area," says Thompson.

Turbo's marketing management have also realized that a feeling of ownership is essential for dealers and territory managers. For this reason, they hire their territory managers before their expansion strategies are implemented to enable the new managers to be involved in planning, constructing, and recruiting for their stations. "So when he stands up on the opening weekend, he does so with pride and ownership. He can say 'I found it, I built it, and I put the guy in,' " says Thompson.

Everyone hired by the marketing operation must meet the same criteria, no matter what the position. These characteristics include self-confidence, being a self-starter, having a team orientation, flexibility, and trustworthiness. As Thompson explains, "If we were to put in place hundreds of controls, we wouldn't be effective. Our attitude is, 'I'm not going to write you a memo or an eight-page report. You know what you should be doing.' If I spent my time second-guessing my guys, then I wouldn't have the time to be out there developing new programs with them."

Likewise, if the dealers and territory managers spent their time politicking with the corporate office, they wouldn't have the time to devote to the individual that pays the bills—the customer. Turbo's philosophy is simple: everything is done for the customer. "Full service at self-service prices" is the credo that drives dealers to make an unenjoyable experience enjoyable. "The first thing I discovered was that Turbo's commitment to service and value is a way of life rather than a bunch of words," says Thompson. "I mean these dealers hadn't simply read Tom Peters. It isn't a fad for them. They believe in service through and through."

One of the practices Turbo uses to support its philosophy has to do with "your friendly neighborhood gas station." Dealers are expected not only to live in the community they service, but also to be a part of at least one community association. As the local neighborhood gas station dealer, they are required to know at least half of their customers by name. Their customer orientation is also reflected in their advertising and promotion policy. Turbo's customers have told them that expensive television advertising doesn't sell gasoline. What does is community involvement. Thompson explains, "When a company puts out advertising like the Petro-Canada commercial that has this beautiful rig in the middle of the ocean, with a car filling up with gasoline, or the Esso ad that has a 747 pulling into a gas station, has it asked itself the question 'Has its commercial made an existing customer happy, or attracted a new customer?' Customers know that this advertising is expensive, which in turn they pay for at the pump. When we bring in a new territory manager or dealer, we tell them that promotion in their market is through themselves, the community associations, the Scouts, the Guides, the hockey or softball clubs, and the like."

Turbo has learned that customer loyalty is earned not bought. "When a neighborhood facility has burned down or a community hall requires an extension," continues Thompson, "we don't just write a cheque. Our attitude is that we can throw money at programs, or we can give our time, our effort, and our bodies. So we offer to head up their fundraising or coordinate the planning. We don't insist that our people carry out these types of activities; we attract dealers and managers who personally enjoy and encourage community participation." In keeping with their philosophy, regional managers are expected to carry out a strong "corporate citizen" role, which requires them to be actively involved in their local Chamber of Commerce, the Petroleum Association Boards that deal with such issues as the environment, and government regulatory agencies.

It's the customer Turbo is thinking about when it builds its service stations for one-third the price of its competition. Their marketing and customer service programs are not purchased from Toronto or San Francisco consultants; instead, they are designed by their own dealers and managers. There is no such thing as a customer service department, because every dealer is the focal point of customer complaints and concerns. Instead of complaints, Turbo stations get bouquets in the form of satisfied customer letters.

Turbo's new marketing business plan coupled with their traditional customer service philosophy paid off immediately. Record sales volumes, record cash flow, and earnings up 222% to $15 million made 1986 a banner year. Their marketing thrust has also been helped by the collapse of crude oil prices. This was not a stable drop in prices. The world's swaying perceptions of OPEC's ability to control the worldwide glut induced considerable market volatility and price swings. When it appeared OPEC would reduce production to handle the glut of crude oil, prices firmed. Conversely, when it appeared that OPEC would maintain production, prices fell. The hardest hit by the collapse in crude prices were the upstream operations which saw their profits wiped out. The large oil companies had to achieve their profits through their downstream operations by increasing refining and marketing margins. Many consumers felt the impact in the form of severe gas wars. The underlying cause of gas wars is an excess of refinery capacity. In Canada this excess was reduced by 520 000 barrels per day by 1986 due to the closure of ten refineries since 1980. Although the declining demand for refined products appeared to stabilize in 1986, the excess amount of refined product in Turbo's principal marketing area, the four western provinces, found the company fighting for their margins at the pump.

Despite the volatile market, Turbo made enough money to end its interest-free holiday. Not only did the company have to pay $13 million in 1986, it had also cut itself off from the benefit for the remainder of the debt restructuring period. Ironically, Turbo had made too much money!

The War at the Pump

The following year, 1987, was a year of contradictions. While enormous progress was made in the company's operations, Turbo registered a disappointing $3.2-million loss. The additional 27 retail outlets and 86% capacity production of the refinery were unable to substantially affect the margins. The squeezed margins resulted from the increasing price of crude throughout the year and additional fuel taxes. Competition at the pumps was fierce. The succession of price wars was joined by promotional wars featuring every imaginable kind of giveaway, including discounts, rebates, and coupons. Although the company registered a loss, it was forced to pay interest of $10.5 million. By the end of 1987, Turbo had reduced its debt by $86.5 million, leaving the CIBC still holding the weighty balance of $230.5 million. Both the CIBC and Turbo's management realized that immediate action was necessary. "What we had was a thoroughbred racehorse with a 400-pound jockey on its back," comments Brodie.

Since Brodie's arrival, a long and difficult exploration process had been underway. The bank needed to investigate all the possible options that would realize a return on its 47.7% share ownership. It was obvious that Turbo required more equity capital if it was going to expand and thereby increase its ability to repay the debt. "You can imagine that the bank wasn't too interested in putting in more capital. They wanted more money out, not in," says Brodie. "One can hardly blame them, since we'd been a financial disaster." At the end of '87, Turbo retained RBC Dominion Securities Inc. to help them with financial and investment advice in relation to the sale of CIBC's holdings. "While CIBC has been extremely supportive of Turbo, we have all recognized that CIBC would prefer to attend to its own business of banking and ultimately would like to sell its Turbo holdings," Brodie wrote in Turbo's 1987 Annual Report.

After serious consideration, the CIBC reached the conclusion that it would have to make Turbo more palatable to the market in terms of debt load before it could attract the investment community, and in turn, get its money out. In May 1988, a second financial restructuring was completed. The CIBC tore up 86½ million common shares. As Bob Brodie describes "a bit of a haircut on their debt," the bank forgave $2.00 of debt for every one of these shares, totaling $180 million. Since investors would be unlikely to purchase common shares with the CIBC holding $50 million in preferred shares, the bank converted $1.50 per share. The resulting 33 million in common shares brought their ownership down from 47.7% to 17.6%. With the issuance of difficulty term-preferred shares, the CIBC and its co-lenders (six banks, two trust companies, the federal and Alberta governments, and the European debenture holders) agreed to bring the debt down to $170 million at 8% interest. The federal and provincial governments pitched in by allowing their debt of $20 million to be interest-free and amortized over ten years with a balloon payment at the end of five years.

Now Turbo was ready to secure new investors. The individual they called on was Eric Sprott, the owner of Toronto-based Sprott Securities Ltd. Sprott had made a proposal to Turbo in 1986 when its strong earning results showed investment potential. In late '86, when the refining market was turning around, the CIBC had financed Li Ka-shing's takeover of Husky Oil Ltd. At that point some consideration had been given to merging Husky and Turbo. The result was that Sprott's proposal was put on hold. Husky appeared unlikely to make a bid in 1987, due to Turbo's financial deterioration. It was Brodie's message in the '87 annual report that sparked Sprott to renew the contact. "Nineteen eighty-seven was a disaster from a financial point of view," recalls Sprott. "But when I read Bob Brodie's closing comments that said, 'Boy, doesn't the future look bright,' I thought, how can a guy come up with a comment like that having just completed the kind of year he had? As his comments rang in my head I thought, 'This guy has a vision and we better figure out what the hell it is and stay with it if it is a good one.' "

Sprott approached the CIBC to discuss Turbo at the end of May 1988. "I just happened to call Peter Ferrara at the CIBC and asked him if I should be talking to him. He suggested that he think about it. Then a week later he phoned and said, 'Look, I have Bob Brodie and Robert McClinton in my office. Why don't you come over?' I had no idea what he wanted." What Ferrara and Brodie were looking for was new equity financing through a share offering. Sprott's significant track record greatly appealed to them. "In my judgment, he was the only one who could do it. He runs a financial boutique, as it were. A big company would lose too much of the investment message by the time the boss had told his assistant, and then the sales force, and so on. By then the moment would be gone. We needed a top guy to make the deal between us and the investor," explains Brodie. Two days after the meeting, Sprott accepted the challenge. "It looked in my mind as a win situation for everyone—the bank, Turbo, and the investors," recalls Sprott.

Brodie confirms the investment attraction: "If you look over your shoulder, you wouldn't touch it with a ten-foot pole. But if you look and see what is happening all over North America, you can see that refineries are closing and the great glut of oil is ending. Refining and marketing operations have been showing profits they have never seen before. It's been happening in the States, Ontario, and Quebec. Next it will be the prairie provinces. After that it's simple arithmetic. If our markets increase by one cent a liter, that puts $16 million on our bottom line, or 8½ cents a share. So the investor says, 'Gee if I buy one of these shares for approximately 50 cents, and margins increase just one cent a liter, then investment will double.' And this is happening all over North America, so it's bound to happen here." Brodie is not talking hype. On the downstream, Exxon Domestic went from a $50-million loss for the first nine months of 1987 to a $414-million profit in the first nine months of 1988.

Institutional investors confirmed Brodie's and Sprott's optimistic view. Between July and October 1988, Sprott sold 80 million Turbo shares (45% of the company), at 55 cents per share bringing $40 million of new equity financing into Turbo and $4 million into Sprott Securities. Inter-City Gas (ICG) subscribed for 18.2 million shares, making them Turbo's second biggest shareholder after the CIBC at 9.6%. (The Inter-City shares have subsequently been sold in the stock market.)

The oversubscription, compared with the intended 30 million share offering, indicates the amount of confidence investors had in Turbo's future, or as Robert McClinton explains it, "This is Turbo coming back into a market that it left in disarray in 1982. What took three and a half years for the first restructuring, took 90 days to complete the second time around." Turbo is now poised, ready to take advantage of the stabilizing retail and wholesale markets. The biggest worry Eric Sprott sees ahead is the acquisition of Turbo at a low price.

But was this a turnaround based on fancy financial negotiations alone? Brodie, Sprott, the investors, and Turbo's management are adamant that this is not the case. "The underlying strength of the whole financial restructuring was that if we had not been able to demonstrate the enormous progress we were making in the market, no one would have been interested," attests Brodie. In 1988, earnings increased to $12.9 million compared to the previous year's loss of $3.2 million, and cash flow rose from $13.4 million to $27.7 million, both of which were based on a combination of increased sales volumes, lower interest expense, and solid strategic planning.

Strategic planning, however, is a bone of contention for many of the "old timers," who saw Turbo through its peaks and valleys. In their minds it was flexibility and responsiveness that took Turbo through those rough days. For them, strategic planning seems to have taken the "fun" out of the oil business. "You don't know today what is going to happen tomorrow. A strategic plan, no matter how good it is, can't cast you in stone. And unfortunately, this is what happens," surmises Gerry Siuoi. "I just get concerned that there are people here that don't want to change because they are happy with the plan, and I just don't think you can be. I think you've got to be ready to go a different way." These sentiments reflect the frustrations of the generation of managers that were attracted to Turbo's chaotic excitement and freedom. Although accountability is alive and well throughout Turbo, specifically in the refinery where they have moved to shifts without supervisors, it's a shared accountability based on a strategic direction. While expensive tools such as the integrated strategic information system are seen by the new, up-and-coming management as criticial to Turbo's success, they are often viewed as corporate constraints by the older management. Whereas middle management relish the opportunity for cross-divisional decision-making and job rotation; senior managers see these initiatives as infringements on their divisional autonomy.

"When we first started our management meetings and then our strategic planning," Brodie recalls, "fur flew. The vice presidents were interested in protecting their own turf." It appears that divisional autonomy is one of the remnants from the Brawn era that still pervades the executive floor. The strategic planning process is designed to be the champion of integrating the major business functions. While tenacity proved to be the winning ticket during the long road of the turn-around, it may prove to be a stumbling block to the company-wide integration.

Bob Brodie, in his quiet determined way, is spearheading

the professional integrated teamwork that will allow Turbo to reach its ten-year goal of being a fully integrated oil and gas company—the same dream that Bob Brawn and Ken Travis believed in. In May 1989, Brawn's sentiments are: "I think the Turbo story has yet to be completed. Turbo made a lot of people, it broke a lot of people—not just financially but physically. We were the builders. Unless you take the risk, you never accomplish anything. It's much easier to calculate your mistakes after the fact. The proof will be in the pudding if Turbo is a final entity or not. It was in the '70s, it is today, and I think it will return in the '90s. If you have an entity to work with, it's not because it appeared magically out of the blue. It's because somebody worked awfully hard to build it and re-structure it."

Three different eras; three unique presidents. Maybe, in their own way they could subscribe to the words on Gerry Sioui's wall, but with a couple of changes:

Every morning in western Canada, Turbo wakes up,
It knows it must run faster than the biggest major,
or it will not survive.

Every morning a major wakes up,
It knows it must run faster than Turbo,
or it will lose its marketshare.

It doesn't matter whether you are Turbo or a major,
When the sun comes up, you had better be running.

Snapshot of Turbo Resources

Crisis (mid-1982):

Turbo's aggressive expansion strategy collapses, incurring $923 million in long-term debt. Its takeover bid of Merland Exploration Ltd. backfires. Turbo is unable to raise the necessary funds to meet the required followup offer to Merland minority shareholders. By 1983 year end, Turbo's consolidated loss is $278 million.

Turnaround Strategy

- Install a rigorous economic restraint program
- Put in place new leadership
- Divest unprofitable divisions and cash-draining assets
- Form a management committee to deal with corporate-wide issues
- Implement a two-way communication strategy to disseminate new business philosophy and ongoing updates of issues
- Complete new refinery
- Sell Bankeno Mines Ltd., including Merland Exploration Ltd., shares to North Canadian Oils Ltd.
- First financial restructuring reduces outstanding debt to $317 million, financed over a ten-year period
- Initiate strategic planning process
- Put in place aggressive retail outlet expansion strategy throughout western Canada
- Second financial restructuring reduces outstanding debt to $170 million
- Share-offering of $80 million is oversubscribed

Result: Turbo's dramatically reduced debt load, highly productive refinery (operating at 98.1% capacity), and aggressive retail operation have enabled the company to significantly strengthen its profit picture and positioning in the marketplace.

Conclusion

Ten organizations, ten different stories, ten unique situations, and yet there are a number of common threads that link all of them. With the wisdom of hindsight, it's easy to say that many of these factors seem obvious. However, it's not always easy to predict which ones will be more important in any one given situation. What can be said is that the following were factors common to these ten turnarounds, listed in chronological order:

Common Factors

- The first, and probably most obvious factor is a change in top management. External factors key to maintaining financial stability force the existing management to admit the necessity for change. The managerial group seen to be responsible for creating the problem lacks the credibility required to initiate and implement the solution. In every case, new blood has to be brought in to orchestrate the transformation. The transitional period can vary from immediate to as long as a one-year period.

In most cases, the former management leaves the organization, although in a few rare instances there are attempts to merge both old and new management. But in every instance, when members of the old guard remain, they are forced to change and adapt to the new management style.

The turnaround process does not only require new, more competent leadership, but in another sense it also creates the leadership required. Good leaders become even better through the learning process imposed by the transformation.

• The new executive has to redefine the organization's business focus. In some cases, a new mission is developed early in the process, while in others it evolves more slowly. The timing usually depends on external factors such as changes in economic trends, government regulations or consumer buying habits. These factors have to be researched, and their impact on the organization must be clearly understood before establishing a new focus. The greater the shift in focus, the longer it is likely to take to achieve the new mission.

• Financial restructuring and reorganization takes place. The closure of unprofitable divisions and product lines is a visible symbol of the organization's commitment to reduce its debt-load. This belt-tightening sends a strong message to the organization's financial backers and shareholders, ultimately encouraging them to back innovative financial solutions to the remaining problems. Reorganization of corporate structures also acts as a visible reminder of the new approach the organization is taking to its business on a day-to-day basis.

• Significant downsizing is almost inevitable, with the majority of dismissals coming from the top ranks and from non-productive divisions.

• The core of the work force stays with the organization, although it too must change. The attitudes of the employees must be turned around if the organization is to be successfully transformed. This is a complex and long-term undertaking, which involves turning a loser's attitude into a winner's frame of mind. Programs such as strategic planning sessions, budgeting, performance appraisals, and incentive programs are all used to communicate the new orientation and rebuild the work force's confidence. The most meaningful technique, however, is for members of management to present themselves as role models for the change in culture, demonstrating their commitment to the new way of doing things.

• The transition involves a change in corporate culture. Culture, in this context, is defined as the underlying philosophy that guides the way work is done within the organization. These ten organizations all made significant changes to their respective cultures. And interestingly enough, they all concluded that the cultural shift would occur spontaneously, provided the right type of leadership and strategic direction was put in place.

• In the initial stages when changes are occurring on many fronts, there is confusion, anxiety levels go up, and productivity goes down.

• In each case, communication is the key to a successful turnaround. The importance and value of all forms of communication are underestimated in initial stages.

• The lack of clear precedents and experience force everyone into an ongoing learning process. This creates a greater tolerance for risk-taking and mistakes.

• Hard work characterizes the successful turnaround – 18-hour work days, seven days a week, are the rule, rather than the exception. Once the initial turnaround has been achieved, and some measure of financial stability achieved, the pace slackens to a more normal work schedule.

The Other Face of Turnarounds

Almost as important as the common factors is an examination of what was missing from these examples.

• The common factor that links all these turnaround cases is their singular lack of a clear and comprehensive change strategy. Armed with such a change strategy, all these organizations could have reacted much more swiftly and effectively to deal with the complex business and human relations issues generated by the turnaround turmoil.

• Although most executives paid lip service to the concept, real team-work was scarce. There was too much reliance on the skills of the architect of the change, and not enough on building a solid team to shoulder the responsibilities more evenly. Too great a reliance on one individual creates the risk of a relapse. The change strategy should be communicated to all and involve every level of management.

• The majority of the senior managers who survived a turnaround experience agree that they all underestimated the cost in terms of pain, stress, and human trauma.

• Unfortunately, the turnaround architect usually has little choice about dismissals, if he is to achieve a successful transformation. So the real casualties of a turnaround are the countless numbers of dismissed workers, many of whom bear little responsibility for the organization's poor performance. All too often they suffer as a result of the incompetence of their managers.

• In the initial stages of the turnaround, old, ineffective work habits tend to be discarded, and more innovative approaches attempted. As the turnaround begins to take effect, a tendency to slip back into the old habits recurs, with the inevitable result of a decrease in productivity.

• The majority of these turnaround organizations undervalued the role of training in effecting the necessary transformation. Enunciation of a clear vision and values is not enough to ensure company-wide change. More clearly defined training programs, aimed specifically at triggering attitude change would be more effective, and would shorten the period of anxiety and confusion among employees.

• Although in general terms, the architects of change portrayed in these ten case studies were eventually successful, not every strategy they tried flourished.

• The impact on the workers who shoulder the responsibility of leading the turnaround should not be underestimated either. Week after week, month after month, of long hours, overwork, and enormous stress take their toll on these individuals and on their families. The behind-the-scenes supporters are every bit as important as those on the firing line.

Guiding Principles

Some organizations manage to weather the turnaround more quickly and less traumatically than others. A major reason for this difference centers on the chief executive officer's understanding of the core principles necessary to guide the organization through the process. These principles are not to be found in business school courses or textbooks. They are the sum of hardearned experience, combined with commonsense, intuition, and a healthy dose of luck.

The principles that shaped these turnaround stories are grouped into three major categories: business strategies, leadership, and communications.

Business Strategies

• Stay focused on the one or two key initiatives needed for success. Getting the budgeting process back on track was the first priority in almost every case. Putting the emphasis on financial controls clearly spelt out what was really important. Each company then identified a second key initiative for action: NatSea selected product quality; while Manufacturers emphasized customer service; Hospital for Sick Children chose team-building; Fruehauf concentrated on growth through acquisitions.

• Immediate implementation of new strategies helps to cut down anxiety. A time for grieving must also be built into the overall plan. Before employees can embrace the new, they have to be allowed to mourn the passing of the old organization.

Realizing that the merger with Dominion Life was creating a lot of unnecessary stress, Manufacturers accelerated the existing timetable, hoping to speed up the integration process. Although this attempt to move beyond the crisis did relieve some of the pressure, it backfired, by not allowing sufficient time for people to grieve over the loss of their old organization.

• Strategic planning becomes increasingly important in diversified organizations, as well as in those embarking on a significant change in direction. It often takes several years before people become comfortable with the process. In the case of Toronto's Hospital for Sick Children, it took two years before David Martin was ready to tackle the strategic planning process. Priority was given to the more immediate issues of budget control, administrative restructuring, and team-building. In spite of the limited control the hospital exercises over its annual government budget allocation, the executive team still believes in the importance of long-term planning. Although they cannot forecast with any certainty what their budget allocation will be five years hence, they remain convinced that they must plan for the competitive future they foresee in health care.

Once financial security has been re-established, planning must shift from short to long term. In 1986, NatSea turned its attention to a five-year investment plan that focused on a two-pronged strategy: capital expansion for its most profitable product – fresh fish – and international acquisitions. This strategy was designed to minimize the impact of possible future reductions in Canadian fish quotas. When these quota reductions actually occurred in 1989, their long-term plan had been designed to take this factor into account.

• Making use of innovative work structures forces employees to abandon old and unproductive work habits. They become tangible symbols of the change process. Early in Royal Trust's restructuring, all titles, positions, bonuses, and perks were eliminated. Three teams of senior employees reorganized all jobs around a sales results orientation.

Eliminating a whole tier of refinery supervisors underscored the importance of change at Turbo Resources. In fact, these former supervisors went back to work on a variety of special projects. This change also had the effect of extending decision-making down the line.

• Setting high expectations and holding people accountable go hand in hand. When Royal Trust first introduced its objective-setting process, few employees took it seriously. When employees filled out their objectives, many were rejected on the basis of, "If it's not measurable, it's not an objective." They later learned the importance of this exercise when it became clear that they would be appraised on the achievement of their objectives, rather than on competence alone.

• In many instances, giving the new management the right to earn a share in the profits creates commitment and accountability. As a result of Royal Trust's incentive program, the senior management group currently own more than $65 million in company shares.

• No one answer exists to solve all the problems. It's necessary to keep juggling many balls in the air at once, so even if one falls, it's not enough to bring down the organization. In the early stages of the Federal turnaround, Jack Fraser pursued a variety of different solutions to the many problems facing him: cost-cutting, divestitures, downsizing, closing of unprofitable divisions. Not all of those strategies were equally successful, but enough of them worked to create a strong foundation for the emerging new company.

Relying on a single expansion strategy very nearly proved fatal for Canadian Pizza Crust. Although the decision to open a U.S. plant looked promising initially, it quickly became a drain on the Canadian operation's very limited resources. The company would have gone into receivership without Aurora Deluca-Weinlein's quick action in closing the American plant.

• The extent and timing of the crisis are critical to its success. By the time Bob Brawn took action to try and arrest Turbo Resources' downturn, it was almost too late. Radical surgery was required just to save the company. Being forced to divest itself of potentially profitable divisions retarded its growth and limited the extent of the recovery.

Leadership

• In the initial stages of a turnaround, it is essential to centralize decision-making. As results improve, it becomes important to once again loosen the decision-making process and decentralize control. Gordon Cummings's first major initiative was to rejuvenate NatSea's moribund operating committee. Starting with the budgeting process, all decision-making was channeled through this committee, resulting in marathon ten- to twelve-hour weekly sessions. Cummings released responsibility for operating decisions once the senior management group demonstrated accountability. The operating committee then reverted to a policy-making body.

Jack Fraser shouldered all key decision-making in the early days of pulling Federal Industries back from the brink. But as soon as he had managed to put the company back on a level financial footing, he started to hire new managers and began handing over increasing amounts of responsibility. In fact, once the company grew increasingly large and diversified, in a move he termed "the toughest decision I ever had to make," Fraser removed himself almost completely from the operational side. The only way to ensure that growth would continue was to devote himself to strategic and long-range planning.

• No one individual accomplishes a turnaround on his or her own. A network of supporters, both inside and outside the organization, provide much needed backup. The clearest example is provided by the volunteers who made it possible to bring in Georg Tintner to revive Symphony Nova Scotia.

Manufacturers sent an SOS back to corporate headquarters when they needed help in straightening out outstanding insurance claims during the merger. Large numbers of the company's Toronto employees volunteered many weekends to sort out the backlog.

Both the financial, as well as the moral support supplied by the Brascan network, backing Michael Cornelissen's initiatives at Royal Trust were vital to the success of that turnaround.

• Turnarounds require different leadership styles at different points in the turnaround cycle. In some cases, a change of leader is required to complete the turnaround cycle successfully.

Norm Gish felt that he was not the right leader to take Turbo through its second restructuring. Not only was he tired, but the operations and marketing thrusts required the type of entrepreneurial skills that only a marketer such as Bob Brodie could bring to the organization.

The different skills of Ed Van Doorn and Andy Tarrant were required at different stages in the Fruehauf turnaround. When the more volatile Van Doorn lost patience with the slow pace of negotiations before the financial arrangements were completed to allow the managers to buy Trailmobile from its U.S. parent, Andy Tarrant persevered with quiet determination until all the details were worked out. But when the more cautious Tarrant was pessimistic about the chances of the buyout succeeding, the more ebullient Van Doorn bolstered his belief in the concept.

Communications Principles

• Communicate, communicate, communicate! When you think you've done enough, then go back and start communicating all over again. The majority of executives leading a turnaround badly underestimate their employees' ability to absorb the messages they are sending out. This frequently occurs out of management's mistaken belief that it must have all the answers before it goes to its employees. In fact, during a turnaround, every employee, from top to bottom, is faced with more questions than answers. In addition, the change process acts like a moving target—as soon as one goal is achieved, another pops up in its place. In the majority of these examples, it was only when employee anxiety levels reached peak levels, to the extent that they seriously interfered with business efficiency, that management was forced to pay attention to the issue of effective communication.

When Jack Fraser took over Federal Industries, he made a conscious decision to try and communicate right from the start. He armed himself with a flip chart, on which his management principles were printed, and as he traveled from division to division, he grabbed every opportunity to discuss them. This was his way of communicating how he intended to run the company.

At Manufacturers Life, it was only when employee morale plummeted and productivity slumped that management realized there was a lack of communication during the merger process. The company started paying attention to employee information needs by introducing communication trouble-shooters, focus groups, and producing interactive news-letters. Once these were put in place, morale improved.

Once Michael Cornelissen and the senior executive group at Royal Trust had formulated their "Vision 1990" document, they took to the road to sell their new corporate vision. Realizing that employees are every bit as important as shareholders, Royal Trust publishes "Reflections," the employee annual report, and follows up with regional annual meetings designed exclusively for employees.

• Bottom-up dialogue is vital. Sending the message from the top-down is simply not enough. It's all too easy to under-estimate the workers' understanding of what's going on in the organization. To really change grassroots attitudes, the executive has to grasp what employees at the basic level really feel and believe. The clever turnaround expert attempts to put his finger on the pulse of the organization by becoming in effect a "corporate spy." One senior executive who specializes in turnarounds, says he gets his best information by going under-ground. He puts on his jeans and spends a few days on the factory floor, finding out what's really going on before deciding what strategy to use to turn the company around.

Turbo's Norm Gish used a different but equally valid approach. By being open and direct even in the toughest moments of the turnaround, he was able to probe below the surface, to unearth the genuine causes of the employees' anger, so that these could be addressed in widely circulated employee update memos.

• The new direction is reduced into a simple rallying cry that everyone can understand and embrace. This requires a process of simplification. After a two-day strategy session, Royal Trust emerged with a wordy and complicated mission statement, which included the key elements of their new strategy. Over a matter of months, they distilled it into an effective rallying cry —"Make a million people wealthier every day."

The turnaround process is a traumatic, uncomfortable, exhilarating, and stimulating experience all rolled into one. And in some cases, it can even last as long as several years. Although very few successful survivors of a turnaround would be willing to embark on a second such experience, most readily agree that it was a fascinating journey which they wouldn't have missed for the world. And probably the single most useful lesson learned from the experience echos the old proverb: "An ounce of prevention is worth a pound of cure."

Index